Studies in Ethics
Outstanding Dissertations

edited by
Robert Nozick
Pellegrino University Professor
at Harvard University

Other Books in This Series:

Ethics and Epistemology in Sextus Empiricus
Tad Brennan

The Bounds of Choice
Unchosen Virtues, Unchosen Commitments
Talbot Brewer

Deliberation About the Good
Justifying What We Value
Valerie Tiberius

Moral Self-Regard
Duties to Oneself in Kant's Moral Theory
Lara Denis

Thinking in Moral Terms
Sigrún Savardóttir

John Stuart Mill's Deliberative Landscape
An Essay in Moral Psychology
Candace A. Vogler

The Metaphysics of the Moral Law
Kants Deduction of Freedom
Carol W. Voeller

Friendship and Agent-Relative Morality
Troy A. Jollimore

Learning and Coordination
Inductive Deliberation, Equilibrium and Convention
Peter Vanderschraff

Consensualism in Principle
On the Foundations of Non-Consequentialist Moral Reasoning

Rahul Kumar

NEW YORK AND LONDON

Published in 2001 by Routledge
711 Third Avenue, New York, NY 10017, USA
2 Park Square, Milton Park, Abingdon, Oxfordshire OX14 4RN

First issued in paperback 2016

Routledge is an imprint of the Taylor & Francis Group, an informa business

Copyright © 2001 by Rahul Kumar

All rights reserved. No part of this book may be reprinted or reproduced or utilized in any form or by any electronic, mechanical, or other means, now known or hereafter invented, including photocopying and recording, or in any information storage or retrieval system, without written permission from the publishers.

Library of Congress Cataloging-in-Publication Data

Kumar, Rahul, 1967–
    Consensualism in principle / Rahul Kumar.
      p. cm. – (Studies in ethics)
    Includes bibliographical references (p.) and indexes.
    ISBN 0-8153-3983-6 (alk. paper)
      1. Ethics. 2. Consensus (Social sciences) I. Title. II. Studies in ethics (New York, N.Y.)

BJ1012 .K77 2001
171'.7–dc21   00-067371

ISBN 13: 978-1-138-97154-7 (pbk)
ISBN 13: 978-0-8153-3983-0 (hbk)

Table of Contents

Acknowledgments	vii
Preface	ix
Introduction	1
Chapter I Unanimity and Impartiality	5
Chapter II Relevant Reasons in Moral Argument	43
Chapter III Consensualism and Non-Consequentialism	77
Chapter IV Unanimity and Aggregation	117
Appendix Reasonableness in Consensualism	149
Bibliography	155
Subject Index	161
Name Index	165

Acknowledgments

My greatest debt in preparing this study is to my supervisor, Derek Parfit. His insightful, detailed, and patient criticisms of various drafts of this material, combined with helpful and encouraging suggestions, have helped to shape and vastly improve it at every stage over the past three years. I suspect that only those who have had the privilege of working with him will appreciate how much I owe to his excellence as a teacher and as a critic.

Tim Scanlon's paper "Contractualism and Utilitarianism" inspired this study, from which, together with his other papers, I have learned and continue to learn a great deal. I am also grateful to him for many helpful e-mail discussions during the winter of 1994, which helped clarify for me many of the issues discussed in chapter four.

Joseph Raz and Bernard Williams supervised my work on this topic for my B.Phil. thesis, and I am grateful to them both. Raz, in particular, brought many important questions to my attention during that time which influenced the direction of my D.Phil. research, and to which I continue to seek satisfactory answers.

I am grateful to the Association of Commonwealth Universities, the Social Sciences and Humanities Research Council of Canada, and Balliol College for funding throughout my D.Phil. research. I also thank the department of philosophy at Harvard University for their hospitality during the 1993-94 academic year.

Finally, I should like to acknowledge my indebtedness to many friends from Oxford, and most of all, to my parents. Without their encouragement and support, I know I would never have been able to see this project through to the end.

Preface

The manuscript upon which this monograph is based was originally submitted to the University of Oxford, England, in August of 1995, in fulfillment of the requirements for the degree of Doctor in Philosophy.[1] At the time, there was little existing literature on the subject of Scanlonian contractualism, and the only major statement of the theory by Scanlon was the original sketch of the account he offers in 'Contractualism and Utilitarianism' (Scanlon 1982). In late 1998, Scanlon published *What We Owe To Each Other*, a book length presentation and defense of his contractualist account of moral reasoning about matters of duty and obligation. The publication of Scanlon's long awaited opus has generated a great deal of discussion of contractualism in recent philosophical literature, and interest in the theory promises to continue to grow unabated for some time to come.

The relationship between Scanlonian contractualism as he now understands it, as he originally presented the theory, and consensualism (which is an interpretative development of contractualism as Scanlon first sketched it) is a complex one. A detailed discussion of all the relevant issues is more than I can pursue here. However, some comment is called for, and in what follows I will review what I take to be a few of the most important points of both convergence and difference between the account I discuss here and Scanlonian contractualism as it is presented in *What We Owe to Each Other*.

The decision to label the view I discuss here 'Consensualism' rather than 'Contractualism' had two central motivations. The first was that the name 'contractualism' seemed to suggest that the account must have some affinity with contractarian (i.e. Hobbesian) accounts of moral

---

[1] I am particularly grateful to David Wolach for his assistance in preparing the manuscript for publication in its present form.

reasoning, which take as their intended audience those who initially do not take themselves to have an interest in complying with moral standards, and tries to show how it is that compliance with moral standards better advances an individual's non-moral interests than non-compliance with such standards.

Contractualism is in no way concerned with presenting non-moral reasons, to those who do not recognize moral standards to be authoritative guides to proper reasoning and conduct, as to why it is in their interest to adopt such standards as authoritative. It is a characterization of moral reasoning that is firmly in the tradition of taking as its intended audience those who already recognize morality to be authoritative for them in their practical deliberations. Its aim is to illuminate the basis of this authority, and to abstractly characterize the form of reasoning that one is committed to if one recognizes moral standards as authoritative for one's deliberations. That such an account will, at best, bolster the commitment to the importance of complying with moral standards of the already committed, rather than persuading anyone to commit, is not a concern on this kind of view, as explicating morality's authority and characterizing the contours of moral reasoning in non-moral is not something to which it aspires. As the view has no interesting relation to contractarian tradition, a change in the name of the theory, one that would avoid invoking such associations, presented itself as a sensible way of pre-empting various kinds of spurious criticisms of the account.

Second, consensualism is committed to what I here call the 'personal reasons restriction'. The incorporation of the restriction as one of its defining features, I argue, is essential to the general plausibility of the account, although nothing in contractualism, as Scanlon originally presents it, explicitly commits Scanlon to such a restriction as a defining feature of the account. Both Parfit and Brink have, in fact, argued that the theory is more plausible without such a restriction. In light of this deep source of disagreement, consensualism clearly presents itself as both a reconstruction and interpretation of Scanlonian contractualism, rather than a direct explication of it. It therefore becomes necessary to distinguish my reconstruction of the theory from contractualism as Scanlon first sketches it.

In his more recent statement of the contractualist account, Scanlon does explicitly incorporate into it something like the personal reason restriction. To that extent, consensualism is much closer to contractualism, as Scanlon currently understands it, than it is to the earlier statement of the contractualist position. Why he does incorporate the restriction into the recent statement of view is not, however, there explained in detail. In chapter one, I argue for the importance of the incorporation of the restriction as part of the theory, on the grounds that without the personal reasons restriction as part of the theory, contractualism relinquishes a commitment that is essential to its being a distinctive account of moral reasoning.

The second chapter of this monograph takes up the question of moral salience in consensualist moral reasoning. Specifically, it discusses the relationship between the consensualist characterization of moral reasoning and the kinds of considerations that are, arguably, relevant for reasoning about the validity of specific principle. The aim of the discussion is to show how reasoning, on consensualist terms, about the relevance of a kind of consideration proceeds, and argues that the form of reasoning defended is better able to do justice to our commonsense intuitions about what, and why, certain considerations are morally relevant, while others are not.[2]

This is a topic that is not at all addressed in *What We Owe to Each Other*. Though the account presented in chapter two requires further development to be wholly satisfactory, it is, I believe, the start of a plausible account of the process of coming to see a kind of consideration as morally salient that fills an important laçuna in contractualist theory in its current stage of development.

The final two chapters of the monograph discuss in detail the question of whether or not consensualism is able to plausibly illumine the rationales for certain deep features of common sense moral reasoning, focusing on the much discussed question of how to understand the importance of deontic constraints and options, plausible rationales for which have proven to be difficult to develop in consequentialist terms. This discussion is one that I take to be complementary to Scanlon's discussion of substantive moral reasoning on contractualist terms, as it exploits points over which contractualism and consensualism are in agreement, to defend the framework as one that is able to yield illuminating rationales for commonsense options and constraints. Such a defense is an important part of validating contractualism's claim to be a plausible non-consequentialist moral theory.[3]

---

[2] It is worth noting that the discussion of moral salience relies heavily on the idea that there is a normative ideal of the person that has an important role to play in shaping the consensualist characterization of moral reasoning. In neither of his major discussions of contractualism does Scanlon mention a normative ideal of the person as playing a role in contractualism as he understands it, which suggests that the inclusion of such an ideal in the elaboration of consensualism is a point at which the consensualist account is significantly different from Scanlonian contractualism. Whether that is really so is debatable: Scanlon's discussion of the value of a person (Scanlon 1998, 103–107) can, arguably, be read as playing the same role in the contractualist account of moral reasoning that the normative ideal of a person plays in the consensualist account.

[3] A better, more recent version of this discussion can be found in my "Defending the Moral Moderate: Contractualism and Commonsense", *Philosophy and Public Affairs* Fall 1999 28(4) 261–91.

Scanlon's current statement of contractualism does address the question of whether judgments that appear to appeal to aggregative considerations (i.e. judgments that one ought to save the greater number) can be made sense of in contractualist terms, pursuing an issue that is mentioned, but not discussed, in the original statement of the contractualist position. The discussion of the issue here largely parallels Scanlon's approach—both discussions draw heavily on the pioneering work in this area by Frances Kamm—though it differs in the details of the argument.[4]

Scanlon's discussion, however, is limited to cases where the central concern is fairness e.g. is it fair to the one to save the many rather than her? There are cases, however, in which, intuitively, an appeal to the large number who stand to benefit or saved from harm can count as valid grounds for justifiably overriding the legitimate claim of another not to be treated in a certain way. Scanlon does not investigate cases of this kind, though showing how contractualism can account for them is an important part of the defense of contractualism's claim to be a plausible characterization of common sense moral reasoning. The discussion of aggregation in chapter four sketches the rudiments of a promising approach to such cases, though it requires further development before its plausibility can be properly assessed.

University of Pennsylvania,
October 2000

---

[4] See Michael Otsuka's "Scanlon and the claims of the many versus the one" *Analysis* July 2000, and my "Contractualism on saving the many" *Analysis* (forthcoming). Otsuka, I believe, correctly isolates a significant problem in Scanlon's discussion of the duty to save the many rather than one; I offer a revised version of the argument in contractualist terms, one that respects contractualism's justificatory strictures.

Introduction

Every philosophy undergraduate is taught that consequentialist moral theories are unable to provide a compelling rationale for many of our intuitive convictions concerning the content of morality.[1] Amongst moral theorists, however, consequentialism continues to be widely acknowledged as an attractive and plausible account of the foundations of moral reasoning. There are many reasons for this, as consequentialism is certainly not a theory without its virtues. Part of the explanation for its continuing popularity, though, has nothing directly to do with its merits, but is due to the lack of a clear and convincing non-consequentialist account of the sources of morality and moral reasoning, one that is able to provide a compelling rationale for those features of common-sense morality that consequentialist moral theories are unable to account for in an intuitively plausible way. The failure of non-consequentialists to provide such a rationale leaves many receptive to the consequentialist suggestion that the aspects of common-sense morality she cannot account for on her view really do lack a foundation in reason. Rawls, it appears, was right to warn that,

> The criticism of teleological theories cannot fruitfully proceed piecemeal. We must attempt to construct another kind of view which has the same virtues and clarity and system but which yields a more discriminating interpretation of our moral sensibilities (Rawls 1971,587).

---

[1] By *consequentialist* moral theories, I have in mind that family of normative theories which subscribe to the meta-ethical thesis that the aim of morality is to promote well-being (which I will refer to as consequentialism).

Scanlon's contractualism is an important formulation of just such a view.[2] At the heart of it is the thought that what a plausible alternative to consequentialism as an account of the foundations of morality must do is reject the idea that the subject matter, or aim, of morality is the promotion of well-being. Any non-consequentialist theory that does not do so will soon find itself enmeshed in the familiar puzzle of how it can ever be morally justifiable to choose that which promotes well-being less well than something which, at no extra cost to oneself, would better promote well-being.

The rejection of the promotion of well-being as the subject matter of morality manifests itself in contractualism in at least two important ways. First, appeals to the aggregate value of outcomes have no foundational role to play on this account of moral reasoning.[3] Second, according to the consequentialist, moral justification is, ultimately, always a matter of considering how well what is being justified contributes to the promotion of well-being. Contractualism firmly rejects this explanatory asymmetry between the promotion of well-being and other moral notions, which the consequentialist claims is a deep feature of moral reasoning.

Scanlon, I believe, is right to think that contractualism presents a more plausible characterization than consequentialism of the framework of reasoning in which our common sense moral ideas about duty and obligation operate. This study presents part of the case for that claim, through a discussion of how a suitably developed version of contractualism is able to offer a unified account of reasoning about duty and obligation in which the rationale for various 'deontological' features of common sense morality, which have long resisted explication in consequentialist terms, can be made clear.

I have called the version of contractualism that is developed in this study *consensualism*.[4] All versions of contractualism have a common core, which is the characterization of what an act being wrong consists in, that states,

> An act is wrong if its performance under the circumstances would be disallowed by any system of rules for the general regulation of

---

[2] The details of Scanlon's contractualism have thus far only been sketched in a handful of very important papers, particularly his "Contractualism and Utilitarianism" (Scanlon 1982).

[3] The importance of rejecting appeals to outcomes as having a foundational role to play in a non-consequentialist account of moral reasoning is also emphasized by Philippa Foot. See her discussion of this point in her 'Utilitarianism and the Virtues'. In *Consequentialism and its Critics* Samuel Scheffler. Oxford, OUP. 1988 224-242.

[4] Derek Parfit suggested this name to me, for which I am very grateful. One general reason that I have chosen to adopt this name for the theory is that it helps distance this view from neo-Hobbesian contractarianism, with which it bears, at best, a superficial resemblance.

behavior which no one could reasonably reject as a basis for informed, unforced general agreement.

What they disagree on is the question of what the best substantive characterization is of the process of intersubjective moral argument, in which parties to the contractualist hypothetical consensus work out which principles no one can reasonably reject. For example, different versions disagree on the questions of what sorts of considerations can be appealed to in moral argument as valid grounds for wanting to reasonably reject a proposed principle.[5] Consensualism adheres, I believe, to the central features of Scanlon's account of contractualist moral argument, particularly those that sharply distinguish the theory from consequentialism, e.g., the rejection of aggregation. Certain features of the view as presented by Scanlon in "Contractualism and Utilitarianism" have, however, been abandoned, and others have been added that do not have a role to play in the theory as he presents it.[6] In particular, consensualism emphasizes the importance of a specific *normative ideal of the person* for understanding the foundations, in moral reasoning, of the deontological features of common sense morality. Other substantive disagreements with, and reasons for departing from, Scanlon's stated view have been noted in footnotes throughout this study.

The discussion of consensualism is presented in four chapters. Chapter one discusses the competing conceptions of the requirement of impartiality in moral reasoning which account for many of the important differences and disagreements between consensualism and consequentialism. The aim here is to argue that the differences in how the two theories characterize impartial deliberation about questions of duty and obligation can be accounted for by basic disagreements over how best to understand the role and importance of duties and obligations in our practical lives.

Chapter two is devoted to examining the implications of the consensualist account of moral reasoning for our understanding of both what general categories of considerations are relevant for the assessment of substantive principles of duty and obligation, and why these general categories of consideration matter. The discussion here is presented in two principal sections. The first presents an account of how it is possible for parties to the hypothetical consensus, who disagree

---

[5] See, in particular, Scanlon (1982) 122-23 and the discussion of Scanlon's view in Parfit (forthcoming). Brink (1993) and Nagel (1991) both present different interpretations of contractualism; each argues that his version better accords with the important insights of Scanlon (1982) than the version of contractualism that Scanlon presents in the original paper.
[6] Though I am critical of the presentation of contractualist moral argument in Scanlon (1982), my own presentation of it, in consensualism, is very indebted to the model of moral argument over principles presented in Scanlon (1990).

sharply in their beliefs about value, to argue about the validity of, and reach a consensus on, principles for the general regulation of behavior that no one can reasonably reject. The second section argues that consensualism is able to offer a plausible rationale for the moral relevance of many of the considerations that do not concern (directly or indirectly) the promotion of well-being, but are intuitively relevant for purposes of moral justification. The inability of consequentialism to account for the relevance of these kinds of considerations is a large part of the explanation of why the consequentialist cannot provide a compelling explanation of the importance of many of the deontological features of common sense morality.

Chapters three and four are devoted to arguing for consensualism's non-consequentialist credentials. Chapter three further elaborates certain aspects of the consensualist account of moral reasoning, particularly the role of legitimate expectations and of principles (or rules) in the theory. The resources of consensualism are then used to show how plausible rationales for specific options *and* constraints can be developed in the consensualist framework of moral argument.

Chapter four addresses the question of aggregation. It is considered a strength of consequentialist accounts of moral reasoning that they are able to offer an explanation of our intuition that, in some circumstances, the number of people involved in a situation who may be harmed or benefited as a result of the course of action we choose, is a relevant consideration in determining how we are morally required to act. For instance, we intuitively believe that, in some circumstances, when faced with a choice between saving the one or saving the many, we should save the many. We also believe that harming a person in a way that is normally prohibited may be permissible when a great number of lives are at stake. Accounting for these intuitions, without following the consequentialist strategy of appealing to the aggregate value of outcomes, has long been a stumbling block for non-consequentialist accounts of moral reasoning. This chapter develops consensualist rationales of both the duty, under certain circumstances, to help the greater number, and the permissibility, under certain circumstances, of harming another in order to prevent greater harms from befalling each of a great many others. These accounts are important because they explain how consensualism can offer the non-consequentialist rationales for why the numbers at stake are sometimes relevant in moral reasoning and justification, rationales which *do not* involve appealing to the aggregate value of outcomes.

Chapter One
Unanimity and Impartiality

§I

(a) Any form of rational deliberation, or inquiry, is constituted by certain practical norms which must be respected if the arguments for conclusions, reached through deliberation or inquiry, are to be even *prima facie* valid. This is as true of scientific inquiry as it is in specifically moral deliberation, where what is considered are questions of how one is required to conduct oneself in one's relations with others. The norms governing impartial moral deliberation, as in other areas of inquiry, set standards for both what sorts of considerations may or may not be taken into account in deliberation, as well as how different relevant considerations are to be taken account of, or combined, to reach practical conclusions.

What the appropriate norms are for governing impartial moral deliberation is a matter of contention between different moral theories. Any theory that is to count as a theory of *impartial* moral deliberation will, of course, assert that a norm of 'formal impartiality' must be respected. But compliance with this norm only demands that all the constituents of the moral domain must be taken into account, and taken into account in the same way, if one's deliberations are to be truly impartial. What forms of life are included in the moral domain, and how exactly these constituents are to be taken into account, are but two of the issues over which substantive characterizations of moral reasoning disagree. These disagreements cannot be resolved by appealing to a norm of formal impartiality, but are a matter of detailed philosophical argument.

There are different levels of abstraction at which this argument can be conducted. One may, for instance, appeal to intuitions about the normative consequences of different characterizations of impartiality. This method, which I will call *case implication critique*, has considerable force. But it lacks the resources to meet the challenge posed by its critics: that in rejecting any theory that does not fit our pre-theoretical intuitions, all we end up with is a theory that offers a clear articulation of the basis of the dogmas of common sense morality. This is not to say that we can't appeal to intuitions in making judgments about the plausibility of different moral theories. All that is being claimed is that we can't simply rely on our intuitions about the acceptability of the normative consequences of a theory as the basis of an indictment of that theory. For one of the things we need to be open to in arguments about the best characterization of impartiality is that the intuitively most plausible characterization may have quite radical revisionist implications for common sense morality.

To be intuitively plausible, a characterization cannot have normative implications that are completely counter-intuitive. But its plausibility may rest principally on the intuitive plausibility of the specific commitments that account for the differences between it and other characterizations of impartiality which are not judged to be quite as plausible. These commitments concern, amongst other things, what the best normative characterization of those included within the moral domain is supposed to be, a normative characterization of society, particular views about the purpose of morality in human life, claims about the "point of view" from which moral judgments are made, and an account of moral motivation (perhaps better thought of as an account of the kinds of consideration(s) or values that move those who care about morality to care about morality in the way that they do, giving it a special importance in structuring their deliberations).[1,2] The plausibility of the commitments a theory of impartial deliberation makes on these

---

[1] I express the point about motivation in this more complicated form to take into account 'motive utilitarians'. The point still holds, even for this type of utilitarian, that the ultimate reason agents have for structuring their deliberations as the theory dictates is that what they are ultimately concerned with is the promotion of human well-being.

[2] Note that the conception of the person that is relevant here is *normative*, not factual or metaphysical; its appeal rests on a normative judgment that a morality which views persons in this way has an appeal that moral systems built on the basis of different normative conceptions of the person lack. David Brink has usefully distinguished claims about what personal identity consists in from the idea of a normative conception of the person by distinguishing between *conceptions* and *ideals* of the person. Conceptions of the person provide accounts of diachronic and synchronic personal identity or survival. Ideals of the person concern those features of persons that are thought to be of importance *for moral purposes* (or perhaps more clearly, for purposes of moral justification and deliberation). What the relation between the two might be is an issue that I remain agnostic on. See Brink 1989, 313.

issues constitute part of the argument for the plausibility of that theory.[3]

This should be no surprise. For it is a reasonable demand to make of any theory that it go some way towards helping us make sense of the importance we attach to the demands of morality in our practical lives. Showing how morality's demands are connected with valuable and appealing ideals of the person and society is a critical part of this process of demystification. As Strawson puts the point, "our practices do not merely exploit our natures, *they express them*" (Strawson, 80; italics added)[4]

A theory's specific commitments may also be used as part of an argument for the plausibility of that theory in a way not yet considered. Aside from being plausible in themselves, a theory's commitments may allow it to account for various features of morality that we intuitively believe a convincing characterization of moral deliberation should be able to account for, but that other theories, with different specific commitments, cannot account for. One of the strengths of the consensualist characterization of impartiality, as will be shown, is that it is able to do precisely this in building its case against utilitarianism.

(b) Consensualism offers a distinctive conception of impartial moral deliberation:

> An act is wrong if its performance under the circumstances would be disallowed by any system of rules for the general regulation of behavior which no one could reasonably reject as a basis for informed, unforced general agreement (Scanlon 1982,110)

Moral deliberation, on this view, is best characterized by the paradigm of a hypothetical consensus, in which all of those within the moral domain gather together and seek a consensus on principles, for the general regulation of behavior, that no *one* can reasonably reject. These principles are to form part of the basis of each of person's practical deliberations, principles "which each us could be expected to employ as a basis for deliberation and to accept as a basis for criticism" (Scanlon

---

[3] Rawls, for instance, in his "original position" interpretation of impartiality, claims that part of the argument for accepting his two principles of justice rests on the appeal of the original position device as a conception of impartiality. This conception represents the "moral point of view" as the point of view from which parties to a hypothetical consensus, not knowing who they are, choose principles for the regulation of the basic structure of society, which each of them, in their daily lives with full knowledge of their identities, have a reasonable assurance of being able to comply with. Further, this conception incorporates, according to Rawls, an intuitively appealing normative ideal of the person, as a free and rational being, and of society as an ongoing co-operative enterprise, bound together as a community by the principles of justice. The intuitive appeal of these ideals , and the way they are combined in the original position conception of impartiality, constitute part of the argument for Rawls's two principles of justice. See Rawls, *A Theory of Justice*, sec. 40 "The Kantian Interpretation".
[4] Peter Strawson, "Freedom and Resentment" in Gary Watson ed., *Free Will* (OUP:1982) 51-80.

1988b,166). The validity of any principle depends on its being justified by reasons which it would be unreasonable for *anyone*, assessing the principle from *her own point of view*, to reject as constituting a sound justification of that principle. Unreasonable, that is, *provided* her assessment of the principle is conducted in light of the goal, common to all parties to the hypothetical consensus, of being able to justify her actions to others by appeal to principles that others, similarly motivated, would be unreasonable in rejecting.[5]

As a characterization of impartiality, consensualism has a great deal of plausibility. Its announced ambition, however, goes beyond being just another plausible characterization of impartiality, as it is presented as a successful alternative to utilitarianism (or meta-ethical utilitarianism), one that is able to sap the sources of its strength (Scanlon 1982,103).[6] It isn't clear, though, what the reasons might be for believing consensualism to offer a better characterization of impartial moral deliberation than utilitarianism. In particular, two problems need to be addressed. First, it isn't clear why the consensualist claim that what is sought in moral deliberation is *unanimity* should be thought to be more plausible than the utilitarian's claim that what is relevant is the promotion of well-being. Second, why would someone concerned to conduct herself, in her relations with others, in the way morality requires her to conduct herself, be moved to be guided in her conduct by principles for the general regulation of behavior that no one can reasonably reject?

---

[5] By the term 'her own point of view', I have in mind quite an ordinary, common sense notion, of a person's point of view, as it consists of those beliefs, values, principles, commitments, etc. which structure how a persons sees the world. Part of what is important about this idea is just how ordinary it is. The idea of "seeing", it should be emphasized, refers particularly to a person's *normative* appreciation of the world; what she sees as valuable or worthwhile, or admirable, or beautiful, and generally what reasons she sees herself to have for doing certain things and forming certain beliefs.

[6] It is important to distinguish here between meta-ethical utilitarianism, which claims that what morality is about is the promotion of well-being, and direct and indirect utilitarianism. Meta-ethical utilitarianism will, throughout the thesis, be referred to as utilitarianism. Direct and indirect utilitarianism are normative theories, specifying what the objects of utilitarian evaluation are supposed to be. They need not be based on a utilitarian meta-ethic. A direct utilitarian will claim that anything that can plausibly be chosen—acts, rules for the general of behavior, dispositions etc.—should be evaluated in terms of how well that choice will promote well-being, which for the direct utilitarian is always the objective standard of rightness. An indirect utilitarian, such as a rule-utilitarian, will claim that only rules should be evaluated in terms of how well they promote well-being. Acts are to be assessed in terms of compliance with the requirements of the rule, where the rule is the only standard of what is right.

In all chapters, except for points in chapter 3, I refer to utilitarianism and direct/indirect forms of utilitarianism, not consequentialism. This is because I take as consensualism's principle interlocutor only that subset of consequentialist theories which specify the goal to be promoted solely in terms of well-being (leaving aside questions of how best to characterize well-being). This is meant to exclude consideration of forms of consequentialism such as the one Sen defends, in which rights are included in the goal to be promoted, but are thought *not* to derive their importance from human interests. This is a proposal I do not consider in this thesis. See Amartya Sen, "Rights and Agency", in Scheffler ed. *Consequentialism and its Critics op cit.* 187-223.

To clarify what the puzzle is here, compare a utilitarian account of the correct procedure for evaluating the moral validity of a principle for the general regulation of behavior, with what a consensualist would claim. What the utilitarian claims is that, in evaluating the moral justifiability of this principle, what we should appeal to is the consequences of its general acceptance, in the world as we know it, for the promotion of aggregate well-being. We should do so because, according to the utilitarian conception of impartiality, the aim of morality is to promote well-being. In moral reasoning, our concern is to work out how our institutions should be structured, and how we should live our lives, if we are to advance this goal.

There are different routes by which one may be led to view this way of understanding moral justification as plausible. One way is characteristic of direct and act-utilitarian theories, which hold that the standard of rightness is the promotion of well-being.[7] Such views are most plausible if one is led to believe that the promotion of well-being is the aim of morality by two thoughts: first, when we are morally moved to help a person who is suffering, it is just the fact of their suffering, or that *suffering is going on*, that appears to move us to try and end it, or at least reduce it. Second, because no one counts more than anyone else in moral deliberation, no one's suffering has a greater or lesser claim on us than anyone else's just because of who they are. This thought, which might be characterized as the pressure of reason making us extend our concern for the suffering of others, lends support to the idea that what we should aim at, in moral deliberation, is the determination of what must be done to minimize suffering.[8] Most direct and act utilitarian theories speak of the promotion of well-being, as the range of interests that are thought to be the valid bases of moral claims includes much more than just suffering. But the intuitions at work that make these views plausible are the same as those that motivate the negative utili-

---

7   The term 'standard of rightness' is clearly discussed in David Brink. "Utilitarian Morality and the Personal Point of View." *Journal of Philosophy* 83 (1986): 417-38.

8   It isn't clear what the best way is to characterize the impulse behind utilitarianism. One might say that what moves a person is the thought that another *person* is suffering, or one might say that it is the thought that some suffering is going on, which effectively eliminates the person as intermediary. That is, if utilitarianism is viewed as a theory concerned with suffering, it would be inaccurate to describe utilitarianism as a theory particularly concerned with persons, except as a class of beings who have the appropriate physiology to be *loci* of suffering (i.e. if plants are found to be capable of suffering, they will count just as much as a human being). If one accepts this second version of utilitarianism, then the second thought in the text is irrelevant. If what one is moved by is the fact of suffering, one does not need the claim about the moral equality of persons to get one to extend one's concern about suffering to other *loci* of suffering. I've adopted the first version, to emphasize more clearly the intuitive connection between utilitarianism and the very vague idea of the recognition of the moral equality of persons as a constraint on impartial moral deliberation. Which version is best is an issue I do not, in this discussion, want to take a stand on. For a helpful discussion of this issue, see Will Kymlicka. "Rawls on Teleology and Deontology." *Philosophy and Public Affairs* 17 (3 1988): 173-190.

tarian view of morality as being concerned with the minimization of suffering.

One reason that act and direct utilitarians tend to dismiss rule-utilitarian views, which claim that the justified rules, and not the promotion of well-being, constitute the standard of right conduct, has to do with the fact that they reach the view that the promotion of well-being is the aim of morality in this way. Rule-utilitarians have tended to reach this conclusion by quite a different route, the best example of this being Mill's discussion of the connection between our common sense notions of duty and obligation (what Mill labels considerations of 'justice') and the general good (the doctrine that Utility is the criterion of right and wrong).[9] Mill's starting point for reflection is not with anything like suffering, but with the special importance we attach, in common sense morality, to notions of duty and obligation. His phenomenological description of what he has in mind by duty makes it reasonably clear that what he has in mind is just that sphere of morality that consensualism is concerned with, where the notion of accountability to one another plays such an important role (cf. *Utilitarianism* V, para. 14). Considering the basis of the authority of this sphere of morality, what he refers to as the special strength of feeling that surrounds it, Mill concludes that its importance can only be accounted for in terms of general utility (though it is important for his view that the relevant aspects of utility concern vital interests).

Mill's view, then, is that moral justification of common sense moral principles must ultimately end in an appeal to how those rules promote well-being. This differs from the direct and act-utilitarian views, which make the additional claim that moral motivation attaches directly to a concern with the promotion of well-being. It is the tension between these two views that explains why the direct and act-utilitarian have difficulty with the idea that, if well-being is what morally matters, one should be guided by general rules, when doing other than what the rule prescribes would better promote well-being.

For purposes of this discussion, what matters is that the utilitarian is able to provide a plausible account of the source of morality (a concern with the well-being of others), one which implies the utilitarian characterization of impartial moral deliberation. Of the two different routes to reaching the conclusion that the promotion of well-being is what ultimately morally matters, the Millian (rule-utilitarian) route is

---

[9] The relevant text is *Utilitarianism* V, para. 16-24. Here I will assume a controversial interpretation of Mill, which claims that by 'criteria' of right and wrong, Mill does not have in mind what is now known as a 'standard of rightness'. Rather, I believe that his view is better read as claiming that the general good should be the basis of *selecting* those principles which are to constitute the principles of right, which themselves form the only standard of right and wrong. Defending this view is an exegetical matter that cannot be pursued here. Lyons (1994) provides a helpful discussion of this matter.

the more important for this discussion, as that theory, amongst the family of utilitarian views, has the greatest structural resemblance to consensualism.

In contrast to utilitarian views, consensualism tells us, in evaluating the principle, to consider whether or not that principle, as a basis for the general regulation of a certain kind of behavior, is one that no one could reasonably reject. That is, the reasons that are supposed to justify the principle as valid must constitute a justification for that principle from the point of view of any person within the moral domain, assuming she is motivated to be able to justify herself *to* others on grounds they cannot reasonably reject. Notice that this form of moral deliberation invokes a special kind of unanimity. For what is sought, in justifying a principle, are reasons for the justification of that principle that *all* can agree on, each from her own point of view, rather than reasons that *most* can agree on. Unanimity is more than something that valid justifications aim for, but is a constitutive condition for a principle's validity.

What is supposed to make this conception of impartiality a superior one to that offered by the utilitarian? One feature that Scanlon mentions is that it is non-aggregative (Scanlon 1982,123). But this is not an argument in favour of consensualism, as what needs to be explained is why we should believe that the best characterization of impartiality will be non-aggregative. Our intuitions about cases where aggregating well-being gives wildly counter-intuitive results may, after all, be unsound. What is required here is a consensualist account of the source of morality, one that will suggest an explanation for why it is that *moral* deliberation is appropriately characterized as a search for principles, for the general regulation of behavior, that no one can reasonably reject as the basis for unforced, informed, general agreement.

§II

(a) The place to look for such an account is in the consensualist account of moral motivation, which states that the parties to the consensualist hypothetical consensus are motivated to be able to justify themselves to others on the basis of principles for the general regulation of behavior that no one could reasonably reject (given the desire to find principles that others similarly concerned with mutual justification could not reasonably reject) (cf. Scanlon 1982,116-17). Here the notion of wanting to be able to justify one's actions to another is central, as it is importantly different from the looser idea of being concerned to act in a way that is morally justifiable, where the justification is one that anyone, provided they take up the right point of view, has access to. Utilitarian justifications are, for example, compatible with the looser idea, but at least not obviously compatible with the notion of justifying oneself to another.

Nagel offers a helpful characterization of what the difference between the looser and the more specific notions consists in:

> [utilitarian justifications] are really justifications to the world at large, which the victim, as a reasonable man, would be expected to appreciate...[but this] ignores the possibility that to treat someone horribly puts you in a special relation *to him*, which may have to be defended in terms of other features of your relation *to him*....If the justification for what one did to another person had to be such that it could be offered to him specifically, rather than just to the world at large, that would be a significant source of restraint (Nagel 1979,68; text in brackets added; italics added).[10]

In desiring to be able to justify oneself to another, what one is concerned about is that one's behavior in relation to another be such as to express an attitude of respect for, and towards, that person.[11] One knows that one is justified in believing that one's actions express such an attitude towards another by considering the kinds of reasons one would cite in explaining one's actions to another, where the "other" could be a person who believes that, in acting as one did, one failed to take her sufficiently into account, or some third party, who takes offense at your having acted as you did because in acting that way you failed to take someone else into account in a way you should have.[12] What is important is that those reasons be reasons that it would be unreasonable for another, from her point of view, not to accept as jus-

---

[10] See Thomas Nagel. "War and Massacre." In *Mortal Questions*, 53-74. Cambridge: Cambridge University Press, 1979.

[11] It would be a mistake to place too much emphasis here on the notion of an "action". Depending on the context, doing nothing can result in the right kind of relation obtaining between oneself and others for others to demand that you justify yourself to them. See, on this question, Phillipa Foot's "The Problem of Abortion and the Doctrine of Double Effect", in her *Virtues and Vices*.

[12] The idea that justifications should justify one's actions both to those who stand in some kind of direct relation to one's action, as well as those who stand in some indirect relation to one's action and are demanding that one account for oneself *on behalf of* those who stand in a direct relation to one's action, is crucial for explaining why Scanlon speaks of wanting to be able to justify oneself to "others". The idea is not that one wants to be able to justify oneself to groups; rather, the thought is that there are different standpoints from which other individuals can legitimately demand that one account for oneself, and one wants to be able to justify oneself *to* whomever legitimately demands a justification. It isn't clear just how complex the notion of a third party legitimately demanding that one account for oneself might be. One thought that might help clarify the idea is this: if I shoot you, then not only are you in a position to demand justification from me, because of the relation that is established between us when I point my gun at you, but others are as well, insofar as in pointing a gun at you, in the absence of a valid justification, I am disregarding a (normative) property of you, which is characteristic of all persons, that I ought to take as sufficient grounds for not treating you this way. It is as if, in showing contempt for the reasons there are for not shooting you, I am showing contempt for others as well. For the same reasons there are not to shoot you are reasons I have for not shooting them.

tifying the action as one that is appropriate, where the notion of an action being appropriate implies, at least, that one has not failed to respect the other as a person in so acting.[13]

The idea that, if one is to be able to morally justify one's actions, those actions must be *justifiable* to others, plays no fundamental role in the utilitarian conception of impartiality. In that theory, a person knows her conduct to be morally justified if she has been guided in her conduct by those considerations that she ought to follow if she is to best promote aggregate well-being. She can even say that her actions are justifiable to others. But note the difference between this claim in a utilitarian theory and the importance of being able to justify oneself *to* others in consensualism: she takes her actions to be justifiable to others because she has acted for the best from a point of view that takes each person's well-being into account. In taking each person's well-being into account, she has given each of them the kind of consideration they are owed out of respect for their moral equality as persons. In consensualism, what one fundamentally owes each person is that one's actions be justifiable to them; this *may* require acting for the best from a point of view that gives each person's well-being equal weight. Whether it does or not, the requirement that one act this way will be derivative from the basic requirement of being able to justify one's actions to others.

What motivates this disagreement over the kind of consideration each person is owed is a basic disagreement about what the property of persons (or all those within the moral domain) is in virtue of which they morally matter; it is a disagreement, at root, about the appropriate normative ideal of the person.[14] The utilitarian believes that what matters is a person's capacity to suffer; it is this capacity that justifies a person's claim to have the importance of her suffering being minimized (or the enhancement of her well-being) be taken into account, on an equal

---

13 Nagel offers a penetrating gloss on the idea of justification to a person along these lines, claiming that such justifications require that "whatever one does to another person intentionally must be aimed at him as a subject, with the intention that he receive it as a subject. It should manifest an attitude to *him* rather than just *to the situation*, and he should be able to recognize it and identify himself as its object" (Nagel 1979,66). My objection to the way Nagel puts this point is that it puts too much weight on the notion of what one does *intentionally*; a person may place herself in a relation to another *unintentionally*, yet the relation may still be one which makes it appropriate for the other to demand that the person account for herself *to the other.*

14 My remarks in this section are, in various ways, much indebted to excellent discussions of the importance of the normative conception of the person in moral theory by Samuel Scheffler and Norman Daniels. See Norman Daniels. "Moral Theory and the Plasticity of Persons." *The Monist* 62 (1979): 265-87;Samuel Scheffler. "Moral Scepticism and Ideals of the Person." *The Monist* 62 (1979): 288-303; and Samuel Scheffler. "Ethics, Personal Identity, and Ideals of the Person." *Canadian Journal of Philosophy* 12 (2 1982): 229-246.

footing with the legitimate claims of all others who share this capacity, in any process of impartial moral deliberation.

Central to the conception of impartiality to which the thought that valid justifications must be justifications that can be offered *to* anyone (who is also interested in being able to impartially justifying her actions to others) belongs is an ideal of the person which emphasizes the importance to the person of her having a *rational will*; it is in virtue of having a rational will that a person is able to organize how she lives her life in complex and imaginative ways, guided by her substantive beliefs about value.

What is of fundamental importance to a person with a rational will is not her capacity to suffer (or her well-being), but being able to direct her life in the pursuit of valuable ends through the exercise of her own rational will. This normative ideal of herself leads her to attach pre-eminent importance to having as much of her life as possible be, from her point of view, under her own control, something she is responsible for. What she wants to be minimized is not her suffering, but the extent to which things *just happen* to her. Being motivated to be able to justify oneself to another is to be motivated to conduct oneself in a way that is respectful of others as persons who see themselves in this way.[15,16]

The connection is this: showing one's actions to be justifiable *to* others, on the basis of principles that no one could reasonably reject, is like reminding another that she was consulted before hand on what the appropriate course of action would be, the chosen course of action being one that she could not reasonably refuse to authorize (assuming she is motivated to be able to justify her actions to others on grounds that no one could reasonably reject). A person has reason, then, to view the way others treat her, and the consequences of the actions of others for her, when justifiable *to* her, as *not* just things that *happen* to her, but as a result of what she herself has authorized. The importance the person attaches to being able to view her life as under her own control, the course of which she is responsible for, is therefore respected when an act is shown to be one that is justifiable to her.

---

[15] Notice that the consensualist emphasis on the person as rationally self-directed provides a plausible explanation as to why Scanlon believes that a product of the consensualist hypothetical consensus will be principles concerning moral responsibility. He certainly believes that such principles will form part of the basis for the general regulation of behavior that is agreed to, but does not explain why this is so (cf. *The Significance of Choice*). The explanation that emerges here is that respecting a person as one who directs her own life according to her own choices requires holding a person responsible for her choices. For respecting a person's choices and holding her responsible for those choices are flip sides of the same coin, that of viewing the person as the author of her own life. Principles that no one could reasonably reject concerning responsibility are required for specifying how we should treat others if we are to treat them as self-directed, responsible agents.

[16] Throughout the thesis, this normative ideal of the person, central to consensualist moral argument, will be referred to as a person's *status*.

(b) The consensualist account of moral motivation suggests that consensualism embodies a normative ideal of the person that is distinct from that of utilitarianism. This suggests that the debate between utilitarianism and consensualism may turn on the question of which ideal of the person is judged more plausible. The debate need not, however, be conducted in these terms. For there is certainly a case to be made for the claim that the utilitarian, in emphasizing the importance of the person as sufferer, is unable to offer an adequate explanation of certain kinds of moral judgment that we make, particularly judgments of an act being *wrong*.

Consensualism and utilitarianism both offer accounts of this notion. Consensualism claims that,

> An act is wrong if its performance under the circumstances would be disallowed by any system of rules for the general regulation of behavior which no one could reasonably reject as a basis for informed, unforced general agreement.

Utilitarianism claims that an act is wrong if it is other than what it would have been best to do, where "the best thing to do" is evaluated in terms of the utilitarian goal of the promotion of well-being, the pursuit of which is understood to be each person's principal moral duty (which isn't to deny that there may be other duties; they are just derivative from the principal duty). What the utilitarian sense of wrong leaves out, though, is the idea of an act being wrong because, in acting that way, we judge that one has *wronged* another (as distinct from *harming them*, or *failing to benefit them*). It is this thought, that an act is wrong because someone has, or would be, wronged by such an act, that is central to the consensualist account of the property of an act being wrong.[17]

Why does the notion of a person being wronged have no natural home in utilitarianism? The answer can be traced to a theme that is central to the utilitarian characterization of impartiality, that morality is concerned with the *promotion* of whatever values are thought to be morally relevant. On this view, the aim of morality is to promote well-being. The notion of a person being *wronged*, and the "deontic" notions, such as rights, whose violation is a way of being wronged, resist explication in utilitarian terms because they are not judgments

---

17 The idea that an act is wrong *because* a person has been wronged is an idea that is central to many of the non-consequentialist features of morality. Failure to notice this point, I believe, is the basic flaw in many consequentialist attempts to make sense of many of the traditionally "deontic" aspects of morality, such as rights. See, for instance, Philip Pettit's excellent discussion of consequentialism and rights in his paper, "The Consequentialist Can Recognize Rights." Philosophical Quarterly (38 1988): 42-53. The flaw in Pettit's otherwise compelling discussion is his failure to notice that a consequentialist will not be able to capture the idea that if one violates someone's right, one has *wronged* the right holder.

about the promotion of anything.[18,19] Rather, they are judgments concerned with how one has *related*, or ought to *relate*, to another. In judging that a person has been wronged, one judges that the person has not been accorded the treatment, or consideration, that she is *owed* in virtue of being a person. Wronging someone consists, not in a failure to best promote a value, but the failure to appropriately *recognize* another in one's deliberations.[20]

The utilitarian characterization of the property of an act being wrong also suffers from a further difficulty. Wrong acts are intuitively associated with failures of duty; this is what distinguishes them from acts that are bad, but not wrong. The utilitarian accepts this, insofar as she believes that all of morality consists of just one supreme duty, to act in the way that best promotes well-being. One acts wrongly if one acts in a way other than that which best promotes this goal. Consensualism is a product of a competing view of how to divide up the moral domain. On this view, duty and obligation represent a distinct sphere of morality, but not the only one.[21] It is perfectly reasonable to speak of an act that is morally good to do, but is not morally required, yet is not supererogatory. For instance, at a conference I recently attended, a well known, and very busy philosopher, after talking to me for a while about my research, volunteered to read and comment on a paper I was work-

---

[18] Though see the end of §II for a qualification to this claim.

[19] Notice that utilitarian theories that are *distribution sensitive*, and hence are not fully aggregative, don't escape this claim. Such theories still view values as 'to be promoted', as parts of valuable states of affairs. They just present a different theory of how states of affairs are to be ranked. But as they still share a utilitarianism account of impartiality, they are still unable to locate the wrongness of a wrong act in the right place, and so cannot account for the idea of a person being *wronged*. This, I believe, is the central difficulty with David Brink's reading of Scanlon's contractualism, presented in his David Brink. "The separateness of persons, distributive norms, and moral theory." In *Value, Welfare and Morality*, ed. R.G. Frey and Christopher Morris. 252-289. Cambridge: CUP, 1993. There, Brink believes that Scanlon's view should lead him to adopt a form of complaint minimization, not the unanimity standard of justification. He is led to this view, however, by assuming that Scanlon's principle concern is to rectify the distributional insensitivity of standard consequentialist accounts of moral reasoning. This isn't completely wrong; it is just that Brink misses the Scanlonian diagnosis of *why* consequentialism has, traditionally, been distributionally insensitive.

[20] As Kant puts the point, the morality of duty and obligation concerns the *form* of the relation between individual wills insofar as they are free, specifying how individuals should relate to one another if the actions of one are to be reconcilable with the freedom of another, where "reconciliation" requires that the action be one that the other could consent to without undermining her own freedom (see Kant, *The Metaphysics of Morals*, Doctrine of Right, *Ak.* 230). For more modern statements of the general point behind the promoting/relating distinction, see Thomas Nagel. "War and Massacre." In *Mortal Questions*, 53-74. Cambridge: Cambridge University Press, 1979., sec. V esp. 67-68; and Christine M. Korsgaard. "The Reasons We Can Share: An Attack On The Distinction Between Agent-Relative and Agent-Neutral Values." *Social Philosophy and Policy* 10 (1 1993): 24-51.

[21] Here I will somewhat arbitrarily distinguish between duties and obligations by characterizing obligations as duties which we voluntarily acquire by our choices, or the goals we choose to adopt. I assume, for purposes of this discussion, that nothing important hinges on how best to draw the distinction.

ing on, but having a hard time with. There was nothing which involved a great sacrifice in this, which is what one associates with supererogation; but it was certainly a morally worthy act, insofar as his comments are bound to be tremendously helpful. But he didn't *have* to volunteer to read my paper and comment on it; he was just being nice.

On the consensualist view, the importance of the sphere of morality concerned with duty and obligation is that principles of duty and obligation set standards for the minimum in treatment or consideration that we owe one another, and which we can legitimately expect of one another, in virtue of the status we each have as persons.[22] Compliance with these standards is required in order to maintain relations of mutual respect with others. Hart suggests two features of this sphere of morality that distinguish it: first, an impartial judgment that an act is morally required is, on this view, not to be accounted for by the value of the consequences of the act, but by the normative character of the relationship in which one stands to another, or others (e.g., what is required of one because one stands in a relationship to another as a teacher).[23] Second, failure, or threatened failure, to comply with the requirements of this sphere of morality is justified grounds for the application of social sanctions to those who fail to live up to the standards that the principles of this sphere of morality lead others to expect them to live up to. The principal sanction relevant for understanding morality is *blame*, and the associated responses that one aims for in blaming someone, are *guilt* and *shame*.[24,25]

---

22   Mill captures the idea that duty and obligation specifies a minimum level of consideration that is necessary if we are to claim to have taken the status of another as a person seriously, where he refers to importance of duty and obligation as "the claim we have on our fellow creatures to join in making safe for us the very groundwork of our existence" (Mill 1993,56; Utilitarianism V, para. 24).

23   Hart discusses the idea that there are different spheres of morality in several important papers. See H.L.A. Hart's discussion of this issue in "Are There Any Natural Rights", repr. in Waldron ed., Theories of Rights, "Legal and Moral Obligation", in A.I. Melden, Essays in Moral Philosophy, and "Legal Rights" in his Essays on Bentham (Oxford:1982).

24   The connection between social sanctions and the morality of duty and obligation is not unique to Hart; something very close to it is expressed by Kant, in the Metaphysics of Morals, and is also elegantly stated by Mill, in Utilitarianism: V:

> There are other things...which we wish that people should do, which we like or admire them for doing, perhaps dislike or despise them for not doing, but yet admit that they are not bound to do; it is not a case of moral obligation; we do not blame them, that is, we do not think that they are proper objects of punishment...I think there is no doubt that this distinction lies at the bottom of the notions of right and wrong (Mill 1993,para. 14).

"Punishment", for Mill, appears to encompass legal punishment, the disapprobation of one's peers, and the reproaches of a person's own conscience (Mill 1993,para. 14).

25   As Hart points out, moral sanctions are usually associated, not with the use of force, but with appeals to standards of behavior that the person herself has internalized:

> The typical moral pressure takes the form not of an appeal to fear of harmful consequences or to the futility of refusing to do what in the end one will be forced to do but to the delinquent's presumed respect for the rules he has broken (Hart 1958,103).

Why is it that, on the consensualist account, principles of duty and obligation are uniquely related to maintaining relations of mutual respect with one another, in a way that other spheres of morality are not? Understanding this point requires a further look at the importance of the distinction between *promoting* value and being concerned with how we *relate* to one another. On the utilitarian view, our duties direct us in how to conduct ourselves if we are to promote well-being; it dictates how we are to behave *with respect to* others, in order to bring about, or better promote, this goal. On the consensualist view, the aim of the morality of duty and obligation, unlike other spheres of morality, is to give recognition to the significance of the fact that persons, unlike other animals, have a rational will. Its principles set out standards of conduct, compliance with which is *owed to* other persons in recognition of the moral importance of their having (or, the *status* they have in virtue of having) a rational will (whose moral significance was previously discussed).[26] Taken as a system, these principles establish a framework for interaction between persons, in which a person can reasonably pursue her interest in living a rationally self-directed good life, in a way that is not inconsistent with *respecting* the interest that others, as persons, also have in living such a life.

Notice that these principles secure a framework for persons to live together on a basis of mutual respect by instructing persons on how to conduct themselves in a way that is not inconsistent with each person having a reasonable possibility for leading a rationally self-directed good life. This is not to deny that each person, by doing more than their duty or fulfilling their obligations, could do more to bring it about that people lead rationally self-directed good lives. Nor is it to deny that different principles may make it more likely that more people *do* lead rationally self-directed good lives. But the aim of the principles is to direct conduct in a way that no one, in the pursuit of one's goals, ends up *disregarding* the interest of another in being able to pursue her own goals, not to bring it about that as many as possible lead rationally self-directed lives.

---

26   Scanlon offers a clear account of what it is to have a rational will, which he refers to as the capacity for critically reflective, rational self-governance:

> critically reflective' because it involves the ability to reflect and pass judgment upon one's actions and *the thought processes leading up to them*; 'rational' in the broad sense of involving sensitivity to reasons and the ability to weigh them; 'self-governance' because it is a process which makes a difference to how one acts...The critical reflection of a person who has this capacity will have a kind of coherence over time. Conclusions reached at one time will be seen as relevant to critical reflection at later times unless specifically overruled. In addition, the results of this reflection will normally make a difference both in how the person acts given a certain perception of a situation *and in the features of situations which he or she is on the alert for and tends to notice* (Scanlon 1988a,174; italics added).

(c) This approach to understanding the significance of the morality of duty and obligation claims that only those with rational wills can be wronged. By implication, we owe no duties, and cannot obligate ourselves to animals, who lack a rational will.[27] Nor can we make sense of owing duties, or being obligated, to those humans whose capacities are so limited that we cannot attribute to them a rational will, i.e., infants and the severely mentally underdeveloped.[28] Here, the consensualist understanding of the importance of duty and obligation places it squarely at odds with utilitarianism in a very practical way, for the utilitarian will certainly insist that there is no conceptual confusion involved in sometimes condemning the treatment of animals and sub-rational human beings as wrong.

What is the significance of this point? Does it argue in favour of a utilitarian conception of reasoning about duty and obligation? First, consider the case of animals. There is much that can be said about the ill treatment of animals, without invoking notions of rights and duties. One might, for instance, indict factory farming simply on the grounds that it is gratuitously cruel. Why isn't this enough? Some may object that this doesn't give the person who is treating the animal cruelly enough of a reason to desist. But why think that a person who does not respond to a charge of behaving cruelly will respond to a charge of behaving wrongly? Or, to put the point another way, why think that a person should care less about accusations of behaving in a gratuitously cruel manner than she does about behaving wrongly? Something needs to be said about this if not being able to claim that we owe duties to animals is to be counted as a genuine loss.

This argument can be challenged on the following grounds: there seems to be an intuitive connection between an act being cruel and an

---

[27] Scanlon (1982) does not accept this conclusion, suggesting (obliquely) that some notion of trusteeship could be used to account for our obligations to animals (Scanlon 1982,113). More importantly, he stresses, as a necessary condition for another being standing in a moral relation to us, that its good be sufficiently similar to our own to provide a basis for some system of comparability (Scanlon 1982,113-14). On the view presented here, moral relations of the kind consensualism is concerned with concern the relations between rational beings; trusteeship does not enter into the picture. One reason for thinking this is the case is that it isn't clear why it would be important to be able to justify oneself to rather than justify oneself *with respect to* non-rational beings.

[28] On this point, see Peter Carruthers. *The Animals Issue*. Cambridge: CUP, 1992. His discussion contains a valuable treatment of why a Rawlsian contractualist theory will not extend the framework of rights, duties, and obligations to animals, and why, by the same reasoning, it will leave out of this framework humans who have not yet realized their potential for rational self-governance, or may simply lack such a potential for biological reasons. I disagree, though, with his attempt to dissolve the counter-intuitive implications of this point, by claiming that we have a general duty of beneficence, which encompasses caring for the mentally underdeveloped , animals, and infants.

act being wrong, such that when we say an act is cruel, we are also saying it is *wrong*. Consensualism can grant this point, by pointing out that it is only concerned with understanding that class of wrong acts that are wrong because another (or others) has (have) been *wronged* by that act; wrongs, in other words, that are a result of a failure to behave in a way that is consistent with what we *owe* others. Cruel acts, then, can be acknowledged as wrong, without also allowing the claim that in acting cruelly one is always wronging another.

The significance of this concession for consensualism's plausibility is difficult to assess. Nothing in consensualism commits it to the view that there is only one true meaning of wrong; it aims only to explicate the framework that guides (not dictates) one very important and central use of wrong, one for which other theories, particularly utilitarianism, have failed to provide an adequate analysis. Explicating the considerations that guide other uses of wrong will require developing frameworks specific to other uses. There is no reason to think that they can be usefully explicated in consensualist terms. However, because consensualism aims to illumine the framework that guides a use of morally wrong (and other moral notions associated with duty and obligation) that we associate with having a special stringency, or a kind of 'bindingness' that we associate with constraints imposed upon us by forces outside our control, it cannot allow that there could be other uses of wrong, used in a moral context, that have this feature.[29] The implications of this are clearest in practical cases, such as those concerning animal welfare, where this analysis will allow that factory farming can be wrong, but not in the sense that the factory farmer's behaviour places us in a relation to her that empowers us to hold her accountable for her treatment of the animals. This is not to deny that there may be a kind of bindingness, or necessity, associated with the standards in virtue of which factory farming is wrong; all that consensualism is committed to denying is that one can be held accountable by others for deviations from these standards, in the way we believe that a rational person can be held accountable for behavior that wrongs another (or other) rational persons. Many will find this counter-intuitive, but I believe that the degree to which it is counter-intuitive is a matter of substantive moral argument, and cannot be settled by an appeal to intuitions alone.

At the very least, pointing out that wrong may well have different meanings allows consensualism to offer what some judge to be a plausible response to the question of the status of animals in the theory: while we do not stand in the appropriate relation to animals to have

---

[29] The point here can be put in these terms: consensualism aims to understand morality in the narrow sense, concerning duty and obligation, not the broad sense (what Bernard Williams calls the ethical) associated with the art of living and doing well.

our treatment of them governed by the principles of duty and obligation that consensualism gives an account of, nothing in the theory precludes there being other moral standards in virtue of which it is wrong to treat them cruelly.

Sub-rational humans raise more difficult questions. While duties owed to infants may be explicable on the grounds that we owe them a certain degree of care as potential rational beings, the same cannot be said of the mentally underdeveloped, who will always be sub-rational.[30] Perhaps the most plausible stand to adopt here is one similar to that adopted on the issue of animals: there are moral standards in virtue of which it would be wrong not to take care of the sub-rational, but caring for them is not something we *owe* them. This will strike many as counter-intuitive; indeed, many will find the suggestion that our relations to the sub-rational are like our relations to animals to be morally abhorrent. The best that can be said here is that this is just an instance where the theory requires us to revise our beliefs.

Such a revision may be less threatening if we consider a consensualist explanation as to why we may believe ourselves to owe duties to the sub-rational that can be traced to the same source as the duties we normally take ourselves to owe to other people. According to consensualism, duties and obligations partially structure the various ways we might relate to another. For example, there are certain duties that are partially constitutive of friendship, which determine how one must treat another if one is to be a person's friend. The same holds true of how we ought to relate to family members, teachers, those we have commercial transactions with, and complete strangers.[31] Part of moral habituation involves coming to understand the principles that govern our relations to others, to the point that they structure our practical deliberations.

Now, the mentally sub-normal do not exist in isolation; they have parents, are members of families, and are, by birth, considered to be members of the wider human community. That they are identifiably human, and are born into a network of specific relations to others, leads us to believe that we owe them certain duties, which vary depending on our relation to them. Strictly speaking, this is a mistake, as the sub-rational will not meet the condition of having a capacity to rationally govern their own behavior that is necessary if they are to stand in the appropriate relations to others to have their relations with others

---

[30] The kind of case I am concerned with here is that of the severely mentally underdeveloped person, who lacks all rational self-control. The spectrum encompassed by the term 'mentally underdeveloped' is a wide one, the greater part of which is sufficiently rational to be able to make clear, in consensualist terms, why we have certain duties that govern our treatment of them, though not the full range of duties owed to those who are not mentally underdeveloped.
[31] This is discussed in more detail in chpt. 3, §I&II.

governed by the principles of duty and obligation that regulate relations between those who have the capacity for rational self-governance.

But this does not mean that it would be better if everyone stopped thinking of themselves as owing certain duties to the severely mentally underdeveloped. One reason for this is that it is clearly a morally very good thing that they are taken care of. Another is that being disposed to think of oneself as owing certain duties to another in virtue of the character of one's relation to her, without considering whether or not the other person fulfills the necessary conditions to have duties owed to her in virtue of her relations with others, is a sign of being properly habituated into the moral system. It is no doubt better if people don't try and make the very difficult judgments concerning another's cognitive capabilities that are necessary to decide that they are not sufficiently rational to have duties owed to them. If individuals were generally disposed to try and make such detailed discriminations, rather than just assuming that because another is human certain things must be owed to them, they would be more likely to misjudge the matter, and end up failing to give others the kind of consideration they are owed.

This may not be the best way to explain our intuitions about our relations to the severely mentally underdeveloped, but it is enough to show that arguments are available to defuse the threat to consensualism's plausibility that might arise from some of its counter-intuitive implications concerning the sub-rational.[32] And that is what consensualism requires to defend itself against the utilitarian, who will draw attention to these sorts of implications in support of her view against consensualism.

(d) The discussion so far has been directed at examining the differences between consensualism and utilitarianism. The utilitarian could object to this, on the grounds that, though some of the points made have force against *acts* as the focus of utilitarian evaluation, they do not have force against a utilitarian theory that focused on *rules*. As it will be understood here, rule-utilitarianism is the view that the rightness and wrongness of acts are determined by rules, where the validity of the rules rests on their being, from amongst the sets of rules that could be generally accepted, the set of rules whose general acceptance would best promote well-being.[33] Note that, as in the case of consensualism,

---

[32] Whether or not these counter-intuitive implications are deeply counter-intuitive is difficult to assess. I actually doubt whether many have clear intuitions about what we owe the severely mentally underdeveloped.

[33] Something like this form of rule-consequentialism is attributed to Mill by David Lyons; see his "Mill's Theory of Morality." In *Rights, Welfare, and Mill's Moral Theory*, 47-66. Oxford: Oxford University Press, 1994. This view is also developed in papers by Brandt; see R.B. Brandt. "Some Merits of One Form of Rule-Utilitarianism." In *Morality, Utilitarianism, and Rights*, 111-137. Cambridge: CUP, 1992. Also see Brad Hooker. "Rule-Consequentialism." *Mind* 99 (1990): 67-77.

right and wrong are determined by reference to valid rules; utilitarian considerations are brought to bear on the question of evaluating which set of rules it would be best to inculcate in persons, but they do not themselves constitute an independent standard of right and wrong.

It isn't clear why one would think that a rule-utilitarian normative theory avoids the difficulties raised for utilitarianism as an account of the morality of duty and obligation. Part of the reason for thinking that it might is that rule-utilitarianism allows one to be a meta-ethical utilitarian and a deontologist at the normative level. The problem identified for utilitarianism, however, is not that an indirect normative utilitarian theory cannot be developed that will explain the deontological structure of common sense morality, but that a utilitarian view cannot give an account of the moral significance of the deontological features of morality. Compliance with rules for the general regulation of behavior will not, on the rule-utilitarian view, be *owed* to others; rather, their authority will rest on the fact that they best promote well-being. The rules, then, may justify as valid a morality that contains rights, constraints, options, and other deontological features of common sense morality, but they cannot explain, in a sufficiently deep way, why it is that one is *wronging others* in failing to obey the prescriptions of the rules.

It is important that this claim about rule-utilitarian views be qualified by the clause 'in a sufficiently deep way'. For the rule-utilitarian can object that because the theory treats the deontological features of common sense morality, like rights, as valid, it can explain what it is for a person to be wronged in terms of another failing to respect a deontological prohibition. To this extent, the rule-utilitarian is right to object. But the criticism here is not that she cannot, in some sense, explain what it is for a person to be wronged. It is that her explanation is too superficial: for the explanation of why a failure to be guided by the rules is a moral failure will ultimately appeal to the promotion of well-being, not to the relation between oneself and the person (or persons) whom one has wronged. A rule-utilitarian normative theory simply cannot escape the problems identified for the utilitarian meta-ethic.

§III

(a) Being able to justify one's actions to another (who is also motivated to be able to justify herself to others on grounds that no one could reasonably reject), is necessary for determining that, in acting as one did, one has given the other person the kind of consideration that is owed to her, out of respect for her status as a person. If one has given the other the kind of consideration she is owed, she cannot claim that one has *wronged* her in acting as one did.

Consensualism agrees that a concern that one's actions be justifiable to others lies at the heart of morality, claiming that

> the basic motive behind morality is the desire to be able to justify one's actions to others on grounds that they have reason to accept *if they are also concerned with mutual justification* (Scanlon 1993,196; italics added).

It claims more, however, than a straight forward reading of this quote would suggest, as it says that, in considering the impartial justifiability of one's conduct, one should consider whether or not that action would be disallowed by a system of rules for the general regulation of behavior, that no one could reasonably reject, as the basis for *unforced*, *informed*, general agreement. The appropriate question isn't just whether or not the action can be justified to *a particular person*, provided she is appropriately motivated; it is whether the act can be justified to anyone by reference to rules for the general regulation of behavior, which are justifiable to anyone, at any time, provided they are appropriately motivated.

Why should those who are concerned with being able to justify themselves to others be concerned with rules whose validity requires unanimity, where the process of reaching unanimity on a rule excludes threats, the consideration of unequal bargaining positions, and misinformation or false (though perhaps reasonable) beliefs, as inadmissible grounds for believing that others have reason to agree to a particular principle? The question of the role of rules in the characterization of impartiality is complex, and will be discussed at length in chapter 3. Here I will consider the justification of the other constraints on the process of reaching a consensus, and what (if any) their relationship is to the interest parties to the consensus have in being able to justify their actions to one another.

(b) That false, though perhaps perfectly reasonable, beliefs have no role to play as the basis for an agreement on consensualist principles is clear.[34] Parties to the hypothetical consensus seek principles for the general regulation of behavior in the world as they know it, that *no one* could reasonably reject. Now, if any of the parties have false beliefs, it may be that they may not reject a proposed principle that they have reason to reasonably reject. But if there is in fact a reason to reject the principle, that is all that is required to make the principle invalid.

---

[34] This does not imply that the fact that a person has false, though reasonable, or perhaps unreasonable, beliefs should not be taken into account in moral argument e.g. recall the example of those who believe that fluoride is a deadly toxin. What is being excluded here are false beliefs being used as reasons that justify why a person cannot reasonably reject a principle, one which perhaps sets the standard for appropriate treatment of those who have false beliefs.

The reasons why a person has false beliefs make no difference to the fact that the principle would be invalid. A person may have a false belief that it is perfectly reasonable, given the state of knowledge at that time, for a person to have. It may even be that, at the time the validity of the proposed principle is being considered, no one could possibly know the truth (perhaps the necessary tools of inquiry don't exist yet, or important pieces of evidence have not been uncovered). These considerations are not relevant, except for explaining why it is that a principle that is in fact invalid may have been (and may still be) thought to be valid. For though the principles are for application to the world as we know it, the audience to whom justification is owed is not temporally restricted. So the 'one' who can reasonably reject the principle could well be someone in the future, at a time where the false belief has been uncovered, who is considering the question of what principles would be valid for the general regulation of behavior in the world as we know it.

Explaining the exclusion of coercion, threats, and facts about unequal bargaining positions is more complex. Intuitively, their exclusion seems to be motivated by the unfairness of citing these considerations as part of a moral justification. But this isn't enough for justification of the exclusion of these considerations, for the relevance of fairness does not follow analytically from the abstract requirements of impartiality. That considerations of fairness have a role to play in determining what factors are acceptable as part of a moral justification needs to be defended as part of a substantive conception of impartiality. It cannot be invoked without further justification of its relevance.

One way to begin considering why the above factors are excluded is to note that, once they are excluded, parties to the consensus are moved solely by the general aim of morality. That is, the only pressure that moves parties to the consensus is the desire that each person has to respect others in the way she conducts her own life, in light of the interest each party to the consensus has in pursuing a good life that is as rationally self-directed. Given their aim, the only considerations the parties to the hypothetical consensus have reason to give weight to in moral argument are considerations that relate, in some way, to the ability of persons to pursue a rationally self-directed good life.

Considerations of bargaining positions or threats will only carry force in the hypothetical consensus, then, if they are appealed to as considerations outside a person's control (arbitrary considerations), which need to be rectified in some way in order to restore her ability to rationally control her own life (as far as possible). For instance, they might count as considerations that would be relevant for the justification of principles that made contracts made under coercive circumstances illegitimate, or placed restrictions on what counts as a legitimate market transaction. Outside a context concerned with establishing principles to mitigate against them, such factors have no role to play in consensualist justification. For outside this context, one cannot claim that persons have reason to take these sorts of considerations seriously, as relevant reasons, in order to understand what is required to respect the interest of persons in rationally controlling the direction of their lives, though they may be relevant for those concerned to manipulate others.

Notice that fairness has not entered into the explanation for these constraints on the procedure by which consensus is to be reached. This is because fairness is most naturally thought of as a virtue of *distributive* procedures (such as lotteries, competitions, or procedures for the distribution of social resources): *very* roughly put, a person should not receive a lesser share of some good because of (or in cases of indivisible goods, her chance to acquire that good should not be reduced due to), factors completely outside her control. Reasoning about matters of duty and obligation do not generally concern distributive problems; rather, distributive contexts are a specific application of such reasoning. So it should be no surprise that fairness is not invoked in the justification of constraints on a general framework for reasoning about duty and obligation.

(c) One of the interesting features of consensualism, with which it has become widely identified, is that it is non-aggregative at the foundational level of justification; a justified principle is one that must be justifiable *to any* person, from her point of view (provided the person is interested in mutual justification), rather than one that is justifiable to as *many* points of view as possible.[35]

To help motivate the rationale for the requirement of unanimity, consider first the rationale for utilitarian aggregation. The utilitarian believes that the kind of consideration that each person is owed in impartial reasoning is that her well-being be taken into account in the same way as the well-being of everyone else: everyone is to count for one, and no more than one. Though the aim of morality is to promote well-being, the same choice will not best promote the well-being of each person, so some combinatorial principle is required, one that is consistent with the general aim of morality. That principle is one that says

---

[35] This does not rule out the idea that all justifications must take the form of showing how the act best promoted well-being. It does, however, change the nature of the argument that would have to be offered to make such a claim defensible. One would have to claim that (a) because, from their own point of view, what each person cares about is the promotion of well-being [a claim about the structure of individual practical deliberation], (b) justifications must take the form of showing how the act best promoted well-being, as this is the only kind of reason that, in the abstract, individuals recognize as having force, from their own point of view. The plausibility of this sort of justification, then, stands or falls upon a substantive claim about the nature of practical deliberation. Assessment of this claim, though I suspect it cannot be defended, is too large a question to be dealt with in this discussion.

choices are to be justified by aggregating well-being, where a choice is justified if it results in the best level of aggregate well-being from amongst the available choices.

Something along these lines can be said of consensualism. In the case of consensualism, though, it is each person's *point of view*, not each person's well-being, that must be taken into account. On the consensualist model of impartial justification, a person has been given the kind of consideration and shown the kind of respect, in impartial justification, that she is entitled to, if the reasons offered in justification for a choice are reasons that, from her own point of view, she has reason to accept, provided she is interested in mutual justification. Principles that are not justifiable *to* any (suitably motivated) point of view will fail to be totally impartial; hence the demand for unanimity in impartial justification.

It is very unlikely that any choice will be immediately acceptable from every point of view; negotiation and compromise are necessary if a choice is to be found that is acceptable to each person from her point of view. What makes this process of coming to agreement not *merely* ad hoc is that each party to the hypothetical consensus is said to assess the non-rejectability of a possible choice of principle in light of her aim, shared with others, of finding principles that will form the basis of a framework for interaction based on mutual respect for one another as persons (assuming the ideal of the person previously discussed).[36] In less abstract terms, this means that each person assesses proposed principles in light of (a) her judgment of what it would be like for her to have others governing their behavior by this principle (where this encompasses both their treatment of her and one another), (b) what it would be like for her to have to govern her behavior by this principle, and (c) whether or not this principle is one that could reasonably be appealed to in justifying oneself to another, as a principle that the other, from her point of view, has reason to accept.[37,38]

That the parties are seeking principles that are justified by reasons which constitute a justification for that principle from any point of

---

[36] Scanlon is careful to make this point: what each party to the agreement is concerned with is working out an agreement on terms for interaction based on mutual respect for one another. Agreement with those who do not assess, or are not interested in assessing, proposed principles in light of this aim is of no interest, as the kind of objections they bring to proposed principles, and the reasons for accepting a proposed principle that they are willing to accept, are not motivated by a concern that they be treated, and that they treat others, with respect for their status as persons (cf. Scanlon 1982,116).

[37] Once the fact that parties share a common aim is emphasized, the gap between acceptability and non-rejectability *within the constraints of the procedure of coming to agreement* might be put in doubt. The line of reasoning that makes non-rejectability, and not acceptability, the appropriate standard by which to assess principles is as follows: it might be that some parties to the hypothetical consensus have a particularly self-sacrificing disposition, such that they are willing to accept great burdens, that they would not have to bear under alternative principles, *"for the sake of what they see as the greater*

view explains an important feature of consensualist moral argument. This is the fact that the parties to the hypothetical consensus are sensitive to considerations of *symmetry*. This sensitivity leads to the exclusion of certain kinds of reasons from impartial justifications. For instance, rigid designators, such as proper names or addresses, will not be introduced into justifications. A person who introduced this sort of reason into moral argument would be attaching a special significance to herself because of who she is (or a special significance to someone else because of who they are), which she could not reasonably expect others, from their own point of view, to accept as a reason for choosing that principle. For others have no more (*prima facie*) reason to accept as a reason the fact that a principle favors someone with a particular

---

good of all" (Scanlon 1982,111). It is commendable of them to be willing to bear these burdens, but not unreasonable for them to refuse them. Since they could reasonably refuse to accept the proposed principle, the fact that they do accept the principle is not enough to establish its validity. To be valid, a principle must be one that no one could reasonably reject, not just one that everyone could reasonably accept.

This is a compelling argument, but I believe it can be challenged. What parties to the hypothetical consensus seek in considering the validity of a proposed principle are reasons for anyone, assessing this principle from her own point of view, to regulate her behavior according to this principle—provided she is motivated to be able to justify herself to others on grounds that show that she has taken the status of others as persons seriously. A valid principle, then, is one that anyone suitably motivated has reason to follow, in *virtue of being so motivated*.

The self-sacrificing person says she is willing to accept the proposed principle because she is concerned with the greater good of all, though she admits that she does not have reason to regulate her behavior according to the proposed principle just in virtue of her desire to be able to justify herself to others. But if this is the case, the principle cannot be valid, and her acceptance of it will not make it so. For valid moral principles must be binding on moral agents in virtue of what all moral agents *qua* moral agents have reason to care about, which in the case of consensualism is to be able to justify their actions to others on a basis of mutual respect (as Scanlon makes clear, the only pressure that moves the parties towards consensus is from this desire). But what the self-sacrificing person admits is that her commitment to interpersonal justification does not give her a reason to accept the proposed principle, and so it is not binding on her. The acceptability of a principle, then, will only validate a principle if it is accepted for the right reasons. This, I take it, is the thought that lies behind the original move from 'everyone could reasonably accept' to 'no one could reasonably reject'. The 'no one could reasonably reject' formulation is still preferable, I believe, as it is less likely to suggest that consent has a foundational role to play in consensualist justification.

38   The attribution to the parties to the agreement of a specific interest in reaching agreement provides a response to McKerlie's question: why should we seek principles that are most acceptable to the person for whom they are most unacceptable (the demand for unanimity), rather than principles that *as few* people as possible would find unacceptable? See Denis McKerlie. "Egalitarianism and the Separateness of Persons." *Canadian Journal of Philosophy* (1988): 219-220. The appropriate reply is that each person assesses the acceptability of a principle to them in light of how well it allows her to justify herself to others: a principle that is better for you than any other may not be acceptable to you if this principle is worse for someone else, who you want to be able to justify yourself to by reference to this principle, than another principle which is worse for you, better for her, but still results in your preferring your position under this alternative principle to her (improved) position under this principle.

name, or who live at a particular address, over any other name and address.

Similarly, in evaluating principles, a person may judge one option (W) preferable to another (U), yet her interest in interpersonal justification, and thus symmetry, will lead her to agree to U over W if it is the case that U has consequences for another that makes U more unacceptable to that other than W is for her (assuming that W is significantly more acceptable for the other). What is motivating the person here is the thought that she cannot justify to the other her refusal to accept U rather than W, at least not without attaching special significance to herself because of who she is.

The consensualist demand for a kind of unanimity in justification can be understood, therefore, as an interpretation of the more abstract requirement that everyone be taken into account, in the same way, in impartial justification. In this case, taking a person into account requires taking that person's point of view into account, as a point of view from which it is reasonable to judge the justification adequate, if it is to be valid.

§IV

(a) The consensualist account of moral motivation has played a central role in the discussion up to this point. It is, moreover, of central importance to the consensualist account of impartiality, and its intuitive plausibility no doubt accounts for much of consensualism's appeal. But nothing has so far been said to further our understanding of why one might judge it to be an intuitively plausible account of motivation. This is a significant lacuna, for a better understanding of consensualism's account of motivation promises to significantly advance our understanding of the theory as a whole, and in particular, its claim to provide an appealing alternative to utilitarianism.

One way of thinking about the question that needs to be pressed here is to consider what value, or cluster of values, the desire to be able to justify oneself to others on grounds that no one can reasonably reject (provided they are suitably motivated) is a response to.[39] Assuming this

---

[39] Many take Scanlon's remarks about how widespread the desire to justify oneself to others on grounds that one takes to be acceptable is to be a remark about a general psychological propensity amongst human beings (cf. Scanlon 1982,117). This may be the correct way to understand the desire to justify oneself to others on grounds that one takes to be *acceptable*, but it is not the right way to understand the more specific desire, central to consensualism, of wanting to be able to be able to justify oneself (and one's institutions) to others on grounds that no one can reasonably reject. This desire is morally loaded; it presupposes a normative conception of the person to whom justifications are to be addressed, and a specific view about the value or importance of being able to justify oneself to others, a view, one might say, concerning the source of morality's *authority*. The difference is important for appreciating why it is that the desire to

desire is not, to use Nagel's helpful term, an 'unmotivated desire' (Nagel 1970,29), there must be some answer to this question, and the relevant value (or values) must be of suitable importance to rationalize the importance that consensualism gives this desire in structuring our practical deliberations. Inquiring about the sorts of value(s) that inform the consensualist account of motivation will, hopefully, illumine its appeal as an account of moral motivation.

For purposes of discussion, it is worth considering two possible approaches that might be used to shed light on the question of why one would want to be able to justify one's actions to others, on grounds no one could reasonably reject. These I will label the *self-oriented* and the *pure beneficence* approaches. These approaches lie at different ends of a continuum of possibilities. What makes the consensualist account of motivation appealing, as will be argued, is that it represents a way of understanding moral concern that lies between these two extremes.

What the self-oriented approach claims is that a person is moved to take the interests of others, as equals, into account in her practical deliberations by the necessity of doing so if she is to preserve a certain self-conception or self-understanding. The value, then, that a desire to be able to justify oneself to others is a response to is the value of being able to understand *oneself* in a certain way (e.g. as free, or rational, or impersonally valuable). This sort of approach is often suggested in the writings of Kantian influenced thinkers. For instance, it is suggested by certain remarks of Thomas Nagel's, in his *The Possibility of Altruism*.[40]

Nagel's argument is aimed at understanding the foundations of the kind of judgment that underlies moral attitudes, such as resentment or indignation, towards another's treatment of oneself, or one person's treatment of another.[41] Attitudes such as resentment, Nagel claims, are grounded in the thought that some aspect of your situation gave the other reasons to relate to you in a different way than she has, reasons that were clearly available to her, and which it was wrong of her not to act on (Nagel 1970,83). Asking of another, "how would you like it if I did that you?" is, in Nagel's account, an invitation to that person to

---

be able to justify oneself to others on grounds that one takes to be acceptable could be attributed to those who trace the authority of morality to the will of God, while the desire to justify oneself to others on grounds that no one could reasonably reject could not. It is this more specific desire that is important for understanding consensualist moral argument.

40   Nagel's argument is exceptionally complicated. What I will present as his view, admittedly, may not be the best reconstruction of its view. As the purpose of presenting it is principally as an example of the self-oriented approach, I have not considered points of exegesis that would argue for a different reading of Nagel.

41   I take the fact that Nagel is concerned with attitudes of resentment, indignation, guilt etc. as a reason for understanding Nagel to be interested in judgments that are of the form "certain aspects of my situation provide reasons for another that she is *morally required* to act on", rather than judgments to the affect that "certain aspects of my situation are the source of reasons for others to act in certain ways, which they may or may not choose to act upon without incurring blame".

reassess her treatment of others in light of these reasons. The claim that certain aspects of your situation give another reasons to relate to you in certain way rests on your attribution to the other of a certain *normative self-conception*. For it is a central tenet of Nagel's argument that the *source* of our acceptance of certain facts as reasons for us is to be found in the normative ideal of the person that we accept, if we accept those facts as reasons (Nagel 1970,88;98;14). As he expresses the point, "altruistic reasons rely on a distinct conception that every person has of himself, a conception displayed in his acceptance of the relevant type of reason" (Nagel 1970,98). My belief, then, that certain aspects of my plight give you reasons for action does not rest on the claim that my interests should give you reasons because they are *my interests*, but on the claim that acknowledgment of these facts as reasons for you is required by the very normative self-conception that structures *your* practical deliberations.[42]

The self-conception that Nagel sees as crucial to understanding moral judgments is not clearly stated. The key idea, for present purposes, appears to be this: persons see themselves as valuable not just *for* themselves, but *in* themselves. In taking her life to have a certain value, a person does not believe that the fact that she values her life *confers* value upon it; rather, as she sees it, in valuing her life, she is only valuing what it is appropriate to value. The fact that her life is *her life* is not her (or even a) reason for thinking it valuable. This, as Nagel puts it, is to accord one's life an *impersonal* value.

The thesis that one's life has impersonal value is vague, but Nagel provides a very specific interpretation of this idea: to take one's life to be impersonally valuable is to believe that one's goals and projects provide one with reasons for action because these goals and projects are valuable.[43] This is a *very* strong claim, insofar as Nagel believes that no subjective factors enter into the explanation of why one pursues the goals one does; it is just the fact that these goals *are valuable*, and nothing else, other than facts about her position relative to opportunities to promote or pursue these goals, that explains why she promotes these and not other goals (Nagel 1971,122). As Nagel puts the point,

---

[42] The idea here is not so much that one should be concerned to give my interests weight because of who I am, but because I am another person. What the self-oriented approach claims is that that thought requires further explication, in terms of one's own self-conception, in order to understand why drawing attention to one's plight as a person should constitute a reason for another.

[43] Here, Nagel tends to run together the value of a person's ends with the value of a person; this is something consequentialists do intentionally, as their view is that to give a person the kind of consideration they are due is to take into account the value of their ends in the same way as one takes the value of one's own ends into account. This, I believe, accounts for the broadly consequentialist account of impartiality he has difficulty resisting in the final chapters of his book, dealing with the combinatorial problem. This is a point that will not be pursued in detail here.

> All the steps in practical reasoning from objective principles, down to the identification of appropriate courses of action, can be *impersonally represented*, with the sole omission being the personal premise. That is enough to avoid the practical analogue of solipsism, for the shift from impersonal to personal does not represent a change in one's judgments about the situation or about those acts which, *as it turns out*, one is in a position to perform (Nagel 1970,122; italics added).

Nagel's requirement is that for a reason to be a reason, not only must nothing unique, or idiosyncratic, to one's point of view at the time of acting (or at the time of deliberation) enter into the explanation of what makes a reason a reason for you, but that nothing at all about one's perspective, even something common to all persons, should enter into such an explanation. This, on his view, is the only way to avoid 'practical solipsism'. That is, the only way to understand how it is possible to say the same things about what one has reason to do from the personal point of view, and the impersonal point of view (the point of view of 'nowhere in particular', which is timeless) is if the reasons a person has to do certain things have *nothing at all* to do with a person's point of view.

Why should one worry about whether one is able to make the same judgments about one's reasons for action from a first or a third person perspective? Nagel's point is that what is threatened here is one's self-conception as impersonally valuable; if subjective factors enter into the grounds for one having a reason to do something, then a wholly impersonal account of one's reasons for acting can no longer be given. A shift in the point of view from which judgments of what one has reasons to do are made should not, according to Nagel, affect the object of judgment, which must be constant regardless of the point of view from which the judgment is made. 'Must', that is, if one has a self-conception of oneself as impersonally valuable.

When one person says to another, then, 'how would you like it if I did that you', what that person is doing is drawing the other's attention to the fact that some goal that she is pursuing in her own life is also a source of reasons for the other person, because that person is in a position to, in some way, contribute to the promotion of this goal. This has nothing to do with the fact that this goal has a role to play *in her life*. Assuming she is not mistaken about the value of the goal, she can claim that it is a source of reasons for the other insofar as the other person *sees herself as being impersonally valuable*. What is fundamental to the claim that one person has a legitimate claim on another, then, is *not* the fact that they stand in a certain relationship to one another, and *not* the fact that one is, like the other, a *person*, but facts about the value of the goals of the person who is making the claim against the other person, facts she has reason to be responsive to in virtue of her normative self-conception.[44]

(c) The self-oriented approach, of which Nagel's argument (as reconstructed) is an example, tries to find reasons for a person to recognize the value of others in her deliberations in beliefs a person has about her own value (or her normative self-conception).

Contrast this with the *pure beneficence* approach, most clearly exemplified in theories that are foundationally utilitarian. What it claims is that one has reason to be moved by the plight of others *just because of the character of their plight*. Moral concern, on this view, is not a matter of self concern, or a concern for *any* persons *qua* persons at all, for that matter. One is simply moved by a desire to avoid what is bad, and promote what is good. In being moved by the suffering of others, for instance, the morally concerned person is said to be moved by the apprehension of the fact that suffering is a bad thing, which ought to be avoided. The locus of the suffering, whether it be my suffering, or someone else's suffering, or an animal's suffering, is irrelevant to the grounds for the judgment that the morally concerned person has reason to try and put an end to it (cf. Nagel 1986,161). On this view, appropriate moral concern involves no thought of oneself as oneself. To the extent that one thinks of oneself in one's moral deliberations, it is as a stranger, whose plight is a matter of moral concern (though no special concern) in virtue of being a living thing.

The concern to promote what is good, and avoid what is bad, need not be understood to be limited solely to a concern that suffering be minimized; a much richer account of the good may be introduced here.There are limits; accounts of 'the good' that have to do with anything other than the prosperity of living things will strike few as a plausible object of moral concern, as they understand it, and many will be inclined to draw the line at human well-being.[45]

Much (though not all) of the appeal of utilitarianism can be accounted for by its incorporation of the pure beneficence approach. Many who are attracted to utilitarianism do believe that to have true

---

[44] Nagel would claim that, though we are driven to assess our reasons for action from an impartial (in his view, impersonal) point of view in order to maintain a certain self-conception, but from this point of view we come to recognize the equal reality of others as *persons*. I agree with this move: Nagel goes further, however, committing himself to the view that one is driven to accept the *value* of the projects and activities of others as sources of reasons that constrain and direct one's deliberations, in the *same way* that the value of one's own goals and projects structure one's practical deliberations. It is this further move, about what is involved in giving adequate recognition to the equal reality of others, that is deeply controversial, and which Nagel must defend.

[45] Some, for example, will want to include plant life in the account of the good that is the appropriate object of moral concern, but few, I believe, would accept that rare rock formations count, unless something can be said about their contribution to welfare of living things.

moral concern is to be moved solely by the thought of how much good one could do; to be moved to do good for one's own sake is thought to be symptomatic of being moved by considerations which have nothing to do with morality (e.g. egoistic reasons). This leads many to an intuitive rejection of the self-oriented approach, believing that it offers the wrong kind of explanation of the basis of moral concern. The pure beneficence approach, though, has difficulty recognizing what the self-oriented approach clearly recognizes: that it is morally important that one not undervalue oneself. A person who is moved exclusively by a concern for the general good can end up neglecting herself, to her own detriment. This has led many to argue that, though something like pure beneficence approach is an important part of the explanation of morality's hold on us, a legitimate morality must not demand that a person make a martyr of herself; some scope must be given for morally appropriate self-concern.[46]

Notice that the thought here is not that it is inappropriate to always govern one's conduct in light of moral standards; nor is it that morality must accommodate natural human weakness, or make room for the 'selfish' or 'egoistic' side in each person. Rather, the thought is that it is *morally* inappropriate to neglect one's own life in the name of concern for the lives of others; moved by a desire to treat others with the kind of respect they are owed, one can all too easily fail to respect oneself.[47]

(d) Consensualism portrays moral concern as neither a matter of pure self-concern, nor a matter of pure concern with the general good. Moral concern, on this account of motivation, focuses on the character of the *relation* that will be established between oneself and another (or others), depending on how one conducts oneself. Roughly put, one might say that the consensualist agent is moved by considerations of duty and obligation by her concern for how her conduct will appear in the eyes of the other (or others); she seeks a course of conduct that will allow her to look other individuals squarely in the eye, without feeling that some kind of reproach on anyone's part would be justified. Such a

---

[46] A fuller discussion of this point, one that cannot be adequately undertaken here, would require examining discussions of the tension between the impartial (interpreted as impersonal) point of view, and the partial (or personal) point of view, in ethical reasoning. Part of the appeal of the consensualist framework of impartial deliberation is that it rejects the view that there is such a tension. This rejection is directly related to the consensualist account of moral motivation. For seminal discussions of the tension between impersonal and personal, see Thomas Nagel. *Equality and Partiality*. Oxford: OUP, 1991, particularly chpt. 4-8; and Samuel Scheffler. *The Rejection of Consequentialism*. 1 ed., Oxford: Oxford University Press, 1982. Some of these issues are discussed again, in more detail, in chpt. 3.

[47] An example of a kind of critique that draws attention to this phenomenon is the feminist critique of wives and mothers who endlessly sacrifice their own interests in the name of fulfilling their duty to promote the interests of their spouse and children.

relation between oneself and others is achieved by being secure in the thought that one has acted in a way that is justifiable *to* other persons, from their own points of view. This allows the consensualist agent to act with the knowledge that she has acted in a way that all others can acknowledge took the consequences of acting that way, for each of them, into account in an appropriate way. She can therefore look each of them squarely in the eye, as their dignity has been in no way undermined by her conduct.

On this view, as with the pure beneficence approach, moral concern leads one to directly take into account the implications of one's actions for both oneself and others. Unlike the pure beneficence approach, though, the explanation for doing so is that both sets of implications are relevant for assessing how the character of the relations between oneself and others, where the 'others' that are taken into account are only other rational agents. It is also central to this account that one recognizes a firm asymmetry between oneself and others in one's deliberations. Rather than thinking of oneself as a stranger to oneself, one thinks of oneself as an agent, who has control of what her own goals are, and her own life to lead, trying to work out what course of action would be appropriate in light of the goals of others with a similar interest in leading a self-directed good life, goals which present themselves to her as fixed points, outside her control, but which (potentially) are sources of reasons for her to conduct herself in certain ways and not others. The difficulty that the utilitarian characterization of impartial deliberation runs into, of attaching no significance to the personal point of view, does not arise for consensualism, for moral deliberation always takes place *from* the personal point of view. Each person adjusts her claims on others, and others adjust their claims on her, until a compromise on a system of interpersonal claims is reached that is acceptable from all points of view.

It is important to note here that parties to the hypothetical consensus do not think of themselves, or their lives, as more important than those of others. In preserving a firm asymmetry between themselves and others, each person is simply acknowledging that her life matters to her in a different way than the lives of others matter to them. Part of the difference is this: while she has an interest in rationally directing her own life, and has a certain degree of rational control over her life, she has no such interest in the lives of others. Though she does acknowledge that others have such an interest in their own lives, and this interest of others is a valid source of claims against her, as is her interest against others.

(e) Nothing that has so far been said explains why it is that the consensualist account of moral concern is not, in fact, wholly self-oriented. It may be that a concern to stand in certain kinds of relations with others, relations characterized by mutual respect, arises solely out of a concern to be able to see oneself in a certain favorable light. Consensualism denies this. What is fundamental to the consensualist approach to moral concern is, as Scanlon says, "the desire for reasonable agreement, not the pursuit of mutual advantage" (Scanlon 1982,115 fn. 10); the value of this kind of agreement is not reducible to other values, but is, "in a more fundamental sense, *what morality is about*" (Scanlon 1982,128). The value secured by valid principles, will be here labelled the value of public mutual respect.

How best to characterize this value can be clarified by considering how a consensus on principles changes the normative situation. A consensus on principles allow each person to view herself, and others, as persons who can be *wronged*, rather than just harmed or disappointed.[48] Because the principles, in virtue of which each person is 'wrongable', are principles that each party to the hypothetical consensus accepts as the basis of her deliberations, and as a standard which can be appealed to in criticizing her actions, each person is able to form the legitimate expectation of being treated by others in a way that respects the importance she attaches to being able to live a self-directed good life, an expectation that others can reciprocally hold of her. This general expectation manifests itself in the various specific legitimate expectations that one may have about the conduct of others, in different kinds of situations, on the basis of the relevant principle.

Notice that principles play an important role here in securing the value of public mutual respect. The securing of this value requires that there be principles that set out the kind of consideration, in various kinds of relationships, which all can legitimately expect of one another, that persons *owe* one another just in virtue of their status as persons. This explains why the desire that characterizes moral motivation is what Freeman refers to as a "principle-dependent desire", in contrast to utilitarian views, where principles do not have a constitutive role to play in the achievement of its aims.[49]

Since valid principles are justifiable to each person from her own point of view, no one can claim that they do not have reason to comply with such a principle (unless they simply lack an interest in relating to others on terms of mutual respect). Principles, therefore, provide a basis for interpersonal accountability: anyone, in the face of an act which

---

[48] Nagel (1994) offers a vivid example of the difference here, considering the difference between two worlds, in each of which one is being tortured. In the first world, it is wrong to torture you, but in the second it is not wrong to torture you. Nagel, I believe, is right in claiming that though there is no difference in the amount one suffers, the fact that you are being *wronged* in the first world makes an important difference to how you understand what is being done to you.

[49] See Freeman, S. (1991). 'Contractualism, Moral Motivation, and Practical Reason'. *The Journal of Philosophy* 88(6): 281-301.

wrongs someone, due to a failure to comply with the relevant principle, can demand of the agent an explanation of why she did not respond appropriately to those considerations that should have, in light of the relevant principle, led her to act in a way other than she did. What counts as an appropriate explanation is, of course, determined by further principles that no one can reasonably reject. A failure to offer an adequate explanation is a legitimate ground for blaming that person for their behavior.

Notice, too, that the principles can only serve the role of being a basis for interpersonal justification, assessment, and criticism, because they are, in an important sense, *public*. This is so in two ways. First, the principles provide, much as the law does, a basis for individuals to anticipate what can be expected of them, what they can expect from others, and what they can expect if they unjustifiably fail to live up to what can be expected of them. This is important in consensualism, as a public basis for the formation of legitimate expectations allows individuals to better direct the course of their lives, and allows them to enter into many different kinds of valuable relationships with one another on a basis of mutual respect.[50]

Consensualist principles are also public in a second way, which better captures the importance of publicity in the theory, as it is a result of structural features of consensualist moral reasoning that distinguish it from utilitarian views. Because valid principles are those which are justifiable to anyone from her point of view, each person can be understood to have access to the reasons justifying the principle. Disagreements between parties can be resolved by reference to the shared principles, as their shared understanding of the rationale for the principles allows them to resolve their disagreement through further specification of the relevant principle(s).[51] Principles that no one can reasonably reject provide, therefore, a focus for moral argument between parties, which gains a particular importance where parties are deeply divided on questions of value.

Some forms of indirect utilitarianism, like rule-utilitarianism, may justify the adoption of principles that are public in the first way, without being public in the second. There are at least two reasons for this claim. First, one of the constraints that direct that the choice of principles in a rule-utilitarian theory is that the principles be teachable. Principles may be more teachable if the underlying rationale for these principles that is made public is much simpler than the true rationale for the principles. Second, suppression of the true rationale for the prin-

---

50 See chpt. 3, §1(c) for an extended discussion of this point.
51 This is particularly important for understanding how disagreements can be resolved between parties who disagree about fundamental questions of value. How such disagreements are resolved in the process of justifying principles is discussed in chpt. 2.

ciples may be necessary to secure their stability. If the true rationale for the principles were to be known, many might feel that they really have no reason to follow existing principles, if they are able to follow a more complex set of principles which would result in even more good being produced. Too many people deviating from the selected principles in the name of better conforming to the rationale of the principles would constitute a serious threat to the stability of a set of principles.

One way to avoid this kind of corrosion of adherence to a set of principles is to propagate a rationale for those principles that will make it unlikely that individuals will decide to deviate from in the name of better conforming to their rationale. This would still result in parties acting on the basis of the best principles, they simply wouldn't know *why* those principles were the best principles to act on. This results in a mystery, though, as to what happens in moral argument, where the rule either provides no guidance, or there is a disagreement about what one should do in light of the rule. For one cannot argue with another about the appropriateness of acting a certain way if she herself is unaware of the true reasons for believing that one is required to act that way.[52]

Taken together, the principles that emerge from consensualist moral argument form a public framework for interaction on the basis of mutual respect which is the kind of interaction Kant may have had in mind in speaking of a union of persons, or a 'kingdom of ends', that moral laws make possible.[53] It is because this form of interaction is itself valuable that the consensualist takes an agreement on principles to be 'what morality is all about'; in the absence of such principles, a world in which persons conduct themselves on terms of mutual respect would not be possible, and a valuable form of relating to others would be lost.[54]

---

[52] Consider, as an example of this kind of utilitarian theory, the version put forward by R.M. Hare. See R.M. Hare. "Ethical theory and utilitarianism." In *Utilitarianism and Beyond*, ed. B.A.O. Williams and A.K. Sen. 23-38. Cambridge: CUP, 1982.

[53] Carruthers (1992) explicitly claims Scanlonian contractualism to be an interpretation of Kant's Kingdom of Ends formulation of the categorical imperative. This is plausible, but is at best a suggestion in the absence of any analysis of the relevant sections of Kant's *Groundwork*.

[54] Frances Kamm and Warren Quinn attach a similar importance to the constitutive role of principles in creating conditions for the possibility of creating a community of persons based on mutual respect, though their idea is somewhat different. Their thought is that moral principles secure for each person a certain status, which she would not have in the absence of those principles. This 'status' can be thought of as the result of the property of being wrongable that each person has in virtue of the principles of duty and obligation. Hart also mentions this, claiming that principles specifying what we owe one another make each person into a 'little sovereign'. The importance of this status is said to lie in the value of having oneself recognized, by principles all have reason to comply with, as an independent being, who has an interest of pursuing a self-directed good life, in a way that is compatible with respecting the similar interest of others. While not denying that each person does have such a status in virtue of principles no one can reasonably reject,

This way of putting the last point, though, is inadequate, to the extent that it remains silent on the importance of the value of being able to relate to others on terms that no one can reasonably reject in a successful, or flourishing, human life. If this question is not addressed, consensualism will not be able to answer the question of why notions of duty and obligation are of such importance to us in our practical lives, which threatens its plausibility as a theory of duty and obligation. After all, it may be intrinsically valuable to be able to stand in relations to others in which your conduct is justifiable to them on grounds that no one can reasonably reject, but the loss of this value may not be a great loss in the lives of those who do care about it, nor a value that a person can be thought to have reasons to care about as a constitutive part of any successful life.[55]

The question here, it is important to note, is not the contractarian question of why it is that a person should, as a matter of self-interest, care about relating to others on terms of mutual respect. Rather, what is being asked is whether or not the value of being able to justify oneself to others on grounds no one could reasonably reject provides an adequate account of the importance—usually characterized by phrases like 'bindingness' or 'inescapability'—associated with duty and obligation by those who already take seriously their duties and obligations.[56]

This is a difficult question, to which I can only offer a sketchy reply.[57] As an analogy, consider the activity of studying philosophy. For the most part, this is a solitary activity, requiring many hours spent in private, reading, writing, and reflecting. Progress in developing interesting arguments that one feels confident constitute a genuine contribution to philosophical debate is often slow and intermittent. If one had to pursue this activity in isolation from others, it would be psychologically very difficult to resist sinking into complete apathy in the pursuit of philosophical understanding, as one's sense, or convictions about, the value of the pursuit began to wane, eroded by self-doubt and other dangers that accompany isolation.

---

consensualism attaches a special importance, not to how one is able to see oneself, but to the value of relating to others on terms of mutual respect. See H.L.A. Hart. "Legal Rights." In Essays on Bentham, 162-193. Oxford: Oxford University Press, 1982. esp. 182-86; F.M. Kamm. "Non-consequentialism, the Person an End-in-Itself, and the Significance of Status." Philosophy and Public Affairs 21 (4 1992): 354-389. esp. 385-89; Warren Quinn. "Actions, intentions, and consequences: The Doctrine of Doing and Allowing." In Morality and Action, ed. Phillipa Foot. 149-174. Cambridge: Cambridge University Press, 1993. esp. 167-74.

55   I am indebted here to Joseph Raz for pressing me on this difficult and important question.
56   Scanlon mentions these issues, but does not discuss them in his presentation of contractualism (Scanlon 1982,105).
57   What follows is in some ways, I believe, suggested by Rawls's remarks concerning the nature of a social union and human sociality. See Rawls's A Theory of Justice pg. 453-62 and 520-29.

Fortunately, philosophical inquiries are not pursued in a vacuum. One pursues one's interest in a community of others who share the same interest in philosophical understanding, allowing one to pursue one's own inquiries against a background that allows one to see one's own inquiries as part of a greater project that one is engaged in with others. This community consists not only of one's colleagues whom one sees on a day to day basis, or at conferences, but of those one engages with as interlocutors through their books and journal articles. In this way, the philosophical community is neither spatially nor temporally bounded. There is also teaching: training others to appreciate the value of philosophical inquiry, and observing the changes in their questions, writing, and thinking as their understanding improves is tremendously rewarding for all teachers, and strengthens one's sense of the value of pursuing philosophical inquiry.

What is important here is that it is crucial for a person who works in isolation from others much of the time to be able to see herself as engaged in an activity that others also value, and believe to be worth devoting so much of their lives to, if she is to psychologically sustain her conviction in the value of her own ongoing pursuits. Without such a conviction, she would not be able to go on. However, if she did not respect those who share with her a passion for a particular pursuit, believing that the fact that they value the same thing is evidence of its value, mere knowledge of the fact that they value (and have valued) the pursuit she values, and have also seen it as worthy of an investment of years of time and effort, would do nothing to sustain her in her conviction of the value of her own activity.

The importance of the value of being able to relate to others on the basis of terms spelled out by principles for the general regulation of behavior that no one can reasonably reject, can, I believe, be understood along these lines. On the consensualist account, the agreed on principles play a constitutive role in the different kinds of valuable relationship individuals may stand in to one another. Specifically, their role is that of establishing legitimate mutual expectations for the kind of treatment that those who stand in different forms of valuable relationship to one another may expect of one another, out of respect for one another's status as a person (a claim discussed in chpt 3, §I&II).

The importance of this system of reciprocal legitimate expectations for what one can expect from another in recognition of one's own worth as a person can be understood to secure, for each person, a context in which she can be secure in her sense of her own worth as she pursues her own life, independently of considering how successful she has been in achieving her goals, in a world where there is trenchant disagreement about fundamental questions of value.[58] One's own sense of self-worth is, on this view, a collective achievement. It requires both that one treat others as worthy of respect in virtue of their status as persons, and that others treat oneself as worthy of respect. The element of reciprocity is important here; a person cannot be affirmed in one's own sense of being valuable as a person by being treated by another as such (or least having the legitimate expectation of such treatment), unless one believes that the recognition by the other has significance. This can only be secured if one recognizes oneself as owing a certain degree of consideration to the other because of her status as a person. As in all things, the respect of peers one has no respect for is meaningless.

Standards which serve as the basis for interpersonal accountability also have a further significance for securing a person's sense of self-worth, insofar as knowing that she can be held accountable, or responsible, for her conduct by others re-enforces a person's understanding of herself as the author of her own life.

This explanation of the importance of being able to relate to others on the basis of terms that no one can reasonably reject is not meant to compete with the claim that relating to others on such a basis is intrinsically valuable. Rather, it is offered as a partial explanation of the importance of that value in practical life, which will hopefully help vindicate consensualism as an account of the morality of duty and obligation.

---

[58] It is important here that the relevant sense of self-worth is one that one has independently of one's accomplishments, or the value of one's particular goals. Though as Tom Hill's discussions point out, there is not a sharp line to be drawn between what is needed to secure one's sense of self-worth as a person and one's sense of self-worth because of one's accomplishments. See his two important papers on the topic of self-worth; "Self-Respect reconsidered." and "Servility and Self-Respect." In *Autonomy and Self-Respect*, 19-24 and 4-18. Cambridge: CUP, 1991.

Chapter Two
Relevant Reasons in Moral Argument

§I

(a) One of the traditional tasks of a philosophical theory about the nature of morality has been to articulate an abstract characterization of the formal structures of moral reasoning. In recent years, though, this ambition has come under vociferous attack. What drives these theories, it is claimed, is the ambition of developing complex algorithms for solving moral problems, which then can be applied, mechanistically, to particular situations to clarify questions about what morality requires in that situation, thereby freeing us from the bondage of reliance on common sense ethical intuitionism in working out moral requirements. The hope is that moral deliberation will becomes less a matter of marshalling various intuitions, and more a question of working out a theorem in rational choice theory.[1]

---

[1] Jean Hampton makes the important point that the question posed by a theory like consensualism, concerning "what principles no one could reasonably reject", should be understood not as a theorem of rational choice theory, but as "a model that contains ethical intuitions that are too complex and nuanced to successfully axiomatized, but which are present and alive to us in the right kinds of ways when we attempt to determine an answer to a moral quandary" by asking which principles for the general regulation of behavior no one couldreasonably reject as the basis for unforced, informed, general agreement. This, as she points out, makes the contractarian 'proof procedure' a messy, ill-defined business (by rational choice standards), "and so reliant on intuitions as to make it appear only a more sophisticated variant of traditional ethical intuitionism". Hampton's understanding of the role of the hypothetical consensus device in consensualism is, I believe, largely correct. Though it is questionable whether or not calling it a more sophisticated variant of traditional ethical intuitionism is really a *criticism* of the theory. See Jean Hampton. "Two Faces of Contractarian Thought." In *Contractarianism and Rational Choice*, ed. Peter Valletyne. 31-55. Cambridge: Cambridge University Press, 1991; and T.M. Scanlon. "The Aims and Authority of Moral Theory." *Oxford Journal of Legal Studies* 12 (1 1992): 1-23.

This ambition is thought not only to be mistaken, but pernicious. Amongst other failings that have been pointed out, it is said that such theories ignore the irreducible role of *judgment* in moral reasoning. The circumstances that confront us when we are to make judgments about what morality requires of us are too complex and varied to believe that all the relevant considerations that need to be taken into account in reaching a conclusion can be codified in a complex decision procedure that can be applied mechanistically. This insight alone is thought by many to render the exercise of theory construction futile.

It isn't clear that the critics of moral theory have a particularly strong case. Though some have drawn an analogy between moral reasoning and rational choice theory (notably Rawls in *A Theory of Justice* and David Gauthier in *Morals by Agreement*), it is certainly a caricature to portray all moral theories as attempts to develop elaborate moral decision procedures. A plausible characterization of moral reasoning need not deny the irreducible role of judgment in moral reasoning, while still claiming for itself a certain importance in influencing our views about the *kinds* of consideration that are *relevant* for moral deliberation. Moral theory can lead us to recognize new considerations as morally relevant for purposes of moral judgment, deepen our understanding of the interaction between morally relevant factors, and help us better understand why certain considerations are morally relevant at all (cf. Scheffler 1992,51).

The relationship between a moral theory and the general kinds of considerations that the theory identifies as morally relevant for moral judgment is best captured, I believe, by the thought that impartiality is as much required for the *identification* of considerations that need to be taken into account in judging whether an act is right or wrong, as it is in making substantive judgments of whether an act is morally justified. Because different moral theories offer competing substantive characterizations of impartiality, the considerations that a particular theory identifies as relevant for moral judgment may differ quite dramatically from those identified by a competing theory. And even when two theories don't differ in the general considerations they identify as morally relevant, they may well offer competing explanations of why these considerations matter for moral judgment.

In this discussion, I will examine the question of how morally relevant considerations are identified in consensualism. Consensualism claims that,

> An act is wrong if its performance under the circumstances would be disallowed by any system of rules for the general regulation of behavior which no one could reasonably reject as a basis for informed, unforced general agreement.

If one accepts the view that impartiality in moral deliberation goes all the way down, principles that no one can reasonably reject for the general regulation of behavior will need to be justified on the basis of considerations whose relevance for moral justification no one could reasonably reject. The question is, how is a certain consideration to be argued for, within the consensualist framework, as one that no one could reasonably reject? The response that is developed to this question has important implications for the kinds of considerations that are thought to be relevant for moral justification, some of which will be examined in the last part of this discussion.

(b) In order to help clarify what is distinctive about consensualism on this issue, it is worth considering the relationship between the utilitarian conception of impartiality, and the kinds of considerations that are identified as relevant on the basis of that conception.[2]

Like any substantive account of impartiality, the utilitarian account can be understood to be a plausible substantive interpretation of the very abstract and formal requirement that, in moral reasoning, what we *owe* each person in the moral domain, as a matter of entitlement, is equal concern and respect.[3] It makes two distinctive claims. First, in order to show concern and respect for a person, what we must take into account (and this is the only thing that need be considered about the individual) is the consequences of what is being evaluated for her *interests* (or well-being).[4] Second, it is claimed that, in order to show each individual the same degree of consideration, we should *add up* or *aggregate* individual interests, choosing that which will result in well-being being best promoted.

The justification of the first claim, that what we morally owe each person is to take her interests into account, is not often discussed. It is usually presumed by utilitarians that well-being just is, morally, *what matters*; facts about well-being constituting the very subject matter of moral judgments. There are various ways this claim might be justified, perhaps most plausibly on straight forward non-platonic intuitionist grounds. Such a justification would say nothing more than that, if one

---

[2] Some theories (such as rule utilitarianism) will distinguish between those considerations that are relevant for the justification of a moral system, and those considerations that a justified moral system directs one's attention to as one tries to guide one's life according to this code. In this section, it is the first kind of consideration that is being focused on.

[3] See Ronald Dworkin. "Justice and Rights." In *Taking Rights Seriously*, 150-183. London: Duckworth Press, 1978; Will Kymlicka, "Rawls on Teleology and Deontology", *Philosophy and Public Affairs*, Summer 1988 173-190 . The general topic of the utilitarian account of impartiality is discussed at length in chapter 1.

[4] It is this thought that I believe Scanlon has in mind in his discussion of *philosophical utilitarianism*, the thesis that the only fundamental moral facts are facts about the promotion of well-being (Scanlon 1982,108).

thinks about it, it is clear that what morally matters is that individuals not suffer, or that suffering be *minimized*, which in most utilitarian doctrines is stated as the more general and expansive aim of promoting well-being. The second claim, that individual interests are to be aggregated, is justified by the claim that no one individual's interests are morally more important than another individual's interests, and therefore individual interests should be aggregated.

The first claim, in particular, is important for understanding how morally relevant considerations are identified in utilitarianism. For what results is an asymmetry between well-being and other considerations: any consideration that the utilitarian conception of impartiality identifies as morally relevant is relevant because it either directly, or indirectly, concerns the promotion of well-being. For instance, if rights are important, the utilitarian will argue, it is because the recognition of rights are important for the better promotion of well-being.

(c) The consensualist conception of impartiality claims that an impartial justification is one that no one, considering the justification from *her own point of view*, can reasonably reject as valid, *provided* she is motivated to be able to justify her actions *to* others on the basis of reasons that others have reason not to reject if they are also concerned with relating to others on terms that no one could reasonably reject. As a conception of impartiality, it has important implications for both the kinds of reasons that can be cited as part of a valid moral justification, and the explanation of why those kinds of considerations are morally relevant.

For example, consensualism breaks down the asymmetry that exists in utilitarianism between well-being and other moral notions (Scanlon 1982,119). Facts about how best to promote well-being, rather than being a privileged starting point for moral argument, are thought to be just one of many valid starting points, whose validity are not themselves justified by facts about the promotion of well-being:

> Individual well-being will be morally significant, according to [consensualism], not because it is intrinsically valuable, or because promoting it is self-evidently a right-making characteristic, but simply because an individual could reasonably reject a form of argument that gave his well-being no weight (Scanlon 1982,119).[5]

In consensualism, there is one standard of validity, that of reasonable rejection, and it goes *all the way down*. It is invoked in the assessment

---

[5] Nagel, for one, appears to be amongst those who do think that at least some aspects of well-being are of a self-evidently right-making character. See Nagel 1986, chpt 9, sec. 3, for his discussion of this point.

of principles, as well as in the identification of relevant considerations for moral argument.

What needs to be clarified here is how the reasonable rejection standard of validity is used to identify relevant considerations. Arguments over the reasonable rejectability of *principles* involve (or so Scanlon suggests) at least the informal comparisons of benefits and burdens that will potentially accrue to individuals if a certain principle is accepted. But this presupposes an understanding of morally relevant benefits and burdens, and so is an inappropriate procedure for reaching a consensus on morally relevant reasons.

Recall that what consensualist impartiality requires, to establish impartial validity, is that reasons be offered that will justify the validity of what is being justified, which anyone, from her own point of view, would be unreasonable to deny constitute a valid justification. The question to be asked, then, is what considerations of this kind, satisfying this requirement, are relevant for purposes of moral argument over the general regulation of behavior?

Answering this question raises intriguing problems even if a background of value homogeneity is assumed. For even if everyone agrees on what sorts of pursuits and objects are valuable, they may disagree on the moral relevance of different values. It is reasonable to assume, however, a degree of *value pluralism*.[6] Individuals may, therefore, dis-

---

[6] By *value pluralism* I do not mean to suggest a skeptical thesis about values (e.g. that there are no truths concerning questions of value). Rather, what I have in mind is something along the following lines (which I take to be broadly Aristotelian): (a) there are many different ways of living a good life, each of which involves the incorporation of different values into one's life, and each of which is internally self-sufficient. [each is valid] (b) One cannot incorporate into one life all that is of value. For instance, if being a baker is part of a good life, and I choose this course, I will have to develop certain skills, certain physical abilities, and develop my general abilities in such a way become a good baker. This will result in certain other pursuits being closed to me; I cannot, for instance, become a concert violinist, because both activities are so demanding, and involve developing so many different aspects of myself in a certain direction, that they exclude one another. (c) in pursuing different kinds of lives, different individuals become sensitive to different ranges of values. For instance, in pursuing a life in academic philosophy, I have come to appreciate the value of slow, careful work, with lots of time to consider and re-consider points of detail. Someone who works as an investment banker, whose life demands quick decisions based on minimal information, may not see any value in the kind of work I pursue. Her lifestyle may have blinded her to its virtues, as my lifestyle may make it difficult for me to see what there is to value in her chosen pursuit.

Now, Scanlon claims that consensualist moral argument presumes that all the parties to the hypothetical consensus base their rejection of a principle on true beliefs about value. To that extent, consensualist moral argument abstracts from our present epistemic position (it is concerned with principles that are *objectively* reasonable or unreasonable to reject). It isn't clear, though, that this condition requires anything more than parties not be thought to hold beliefs about value they arrived at through engagement with activities about whose value they are mistaken. If this is so, and the previous claims about value pluralism are accepted, then parties to the hypothetical consensus will still have (potentially) irreconcilable points of view where questions of value are concerned, even when they are all thought to be pursuing truly valuable ways of life. For helpful discussions of value pluralism, see Thomas Hurka. *Perfectionism*. Oxford Ethics Series Oxford: Oxford University Press, 1993. ; and J.L. Ackrill. "Aristotle on Eudaimonia." In *Essays on Aristotle's Ethics*, ed. A.O. Rorty. 15-34. Berkeley: University of California Press, 1980.

agree not only on the relevance of different values for moral argument, but also in their very beliefs about what is valuable. This raises a different, and perhaps more fundamental, kind of problem than the problem of agreeing on the relevance, for moral argument, of certain values. For in order to argue over the relevance of certain kinds of considerations for moral argument, it is necessary that individuals agree, at some level, about questions of value. For instance, if two people disagree over the value of having a certain kind of choice, it is important that they agree that having a choice can sometimes be valuable. Or, say I want to convince a Marxist atheist that a principle that prohibits the public practice of my religious faith is objectionable. Pointing to the ways that the principle prohibits the practice of my faith, that I take to be grounds for reasonably rejecting the principle, will be to no avail, if the Marxist atheist believes that participation in organized religion ought to be discouraged, as it is a valueless, if not harmful, activity.

Value pluralism raises difficult questions about the possibility of parties to the hypothetical consensus being able to agree on principles for the general regulation of behavior. For if they cannot agree on questions of what is valuable, let alone whether or not these values are relevant for moral argument, it isn't clear how moral argument in a consensualist framework is to even begin. It is something like this thought that Dworkin may have in mind in claiming that the concept of reasonable rejection has too little content that is *independent* of individual conceptions of value to guide hypothetical persons, many of whom may have widely divergent, perhaps irreconcilable, views about value, to a consensus on what sorts of values are relevant for purposes of moral argument:[7]

> my views about what other people would be unreasonable to reject reflect my convictions about what lives are good or bad...if I think that it is obvious that a life without close communal ties is a waste, or that abortion is wicked, or that welfare is immoral because it saps self-reliance...then I will almost certainly think it unreasonable of others to reject the principle I embrace. I may not think them blameworthy for not agreeing with me; they may not have had the moral instruction I have had, or they may be too insensitive to see what I have seen. But I can hardly think that they gave good reason to disagree, that is, that their failure to agree is not unreasonable (Dworkin 1990,28; emphasis added).

---

[7] Here it is important to distinguish between *values* and *considerations*. Considerations I take to be ordinary facts, like "it is raining", or "that will make him happy", whose relevance in moral argument can be explained by the bearing that consideration has for promoting or respecting some value (like well-being, or inviolability) that is judged morally relevant. Disagreements about the relevance of considerations are different than disagreements about values, and it is the later kind of disagreement the discussion will now turn to.

There are at least two lines of criticism suggested by this passage, only one of which is of principle concern. The first, suggested by use of terms like "wicked", is that in assessing a principle, parties to the consensus may draw upon not only their convictions about value, but their *moral* convictions about right and wrong. Direct appeals to moral convictions must be disallowed, as far as consensualism is concerned, in considering whether or not a principle is one that no one could reasonably reject, if the whole procedure is not to be reduced to a treadmill. For the purpose of considering whether or not a principle is one that no one could reasonably reject is to uncover reasons for taking an act to be wrong; appealing to the wrongness of certain kinds of acts defeats the purpose of the exercise.[8]

It is the second line of criticism that is more worrisome. Its force can be captured by the following question: if two individuals disagree over the relevance of a value for moral argument, and neither of them has reason to think that she may be mistaken in her beliefs about value, what reasons do either of them have for compromising with one another over whether or not the disputed value will be given weight in moral argument? The fear here is that consensualism might not be able to offer any reasons for individuals to compromise, the absence of which places an insurmountable barrier in the path of the process of reaching agreement over what kinds of considerations are relevant for moral argument. If this is right, then it is a serious criticism of consensualism, for being able to agree on questions of value is (in consensualism) a necessary prerequisite for agreement on principles for the general regulation of behavior. If parties to the hypothetical consensus cannot agree on the importance of any values, or can agree only on the importance of very few values, then the consensualist framework will help us understand the basis of the validity of very few, or perhaps none, of the principles we intuitively take to be valid.

The criticism here is not that consensualism's explanatory power may not be great. Whether or not that is an important issue for consensualism turns on whether or not consensualism provides a suitable framework for developing illuminating rationales for at least our firmest convictions about what we owe one another as a matter of duty,

---

[8] Note that the problem here is with invoking moral considerations about the kind of act whose morality one is meant to be assessing in considering whether or not that act would be disallowed by principles no one could reasonably reject. This mistake is quite different from invoking, say, a fetus's right to life as a reason for rejecting a principle that permits abortion. There is nothing obviously wrong with invoking (what one believes to be) a valid moral principle (i.e. a principle that no one can reasonably reject) in defending, or arguing for, another valid moral principle. This seems to fit our intuitions about moral argument: often arguing about the appropriate principle for the regulation of one kind of behavior leads us to examine the validity of other principles, which are invoked to defend explicitly moral conclusions offered as reasons in arguing about the appropriate principle to regulate the kind of behavior under direct consideration.

and the issue should not be prejudged in the absence of actual attempts to develop consensualist accounts of the grounds of these convictions . For though it is an unreasonable demand to make of any moral theory that it provide the resources for explaining all moral principles that are thought to be valid, a plausible theory must be able to make sense of at least those intuitions about what our duties are over which there is little or no disagreement, if it is to merit the epithet of 'plausible'.

Dworkin's concern, rather, is that in the absence of any criteria for judging whether or not a disagreement between parties on a particular value is grounds for reasonably rejecting that value, it isn't clear how moral argument in a consensualist framework is to get started, let alone proceed. If no one happens to disagree with the relevance of a value, that value will carry weight in moral argument, but if there is disagreement on that value, it may be reasonably rejected. For consensualism appears to provide no reasons for the parties to try and overcome their disagreement in cases where the relevance of a certain value is disputed.

Further, the fact that parties disagree over the relevance of a value is not in itself a good reason for thinking that the value should carry no weight in moral argument, any more than the mere fact of agreement is sufficient to bestow moral relevance upon a value. But consensualism appears to provide no explanation of why disagreement on a value is not always reasonable grounds for reasonably rejecting that value as one that should be given weight in moral argument.

Some defenders of consensualism may be willing to accept this as their position: disagreements on a value are always grounds for reasonably rejecting that value as relevant to moral argument. This, though, would force consensualism to admit that, in the face of sufficiently widespread disagreements on questions of value, there may well be no valid moral principles. It is the intuitive unacceptability of this conclusion that motivates Dworkin's concerns about consensualism.[9]

What Dworkin overlooks in his criticisms of consensualism, though, is the central importance to the theory of the fact that all are motivated to be able to justify themselves to others on the basis of principles that no one, similarly motivated, could reasonably reject as the basis of unforced, informed, general agreement. As was discussed in chapter one, this desire can be understood to be motivated by the value of relating to others in a way that respects their normative status as persons.[10] Characteristic of all parties to the consensus, it can, I believe, provide both the appropriate pressure to lead parties to compromise

---

[9] Michael Smith, who also offers an analysis of morally relevant reasons as being those reasons that parties to a hypothetical consensus would converge upon, accepts the conclusion that on the basis of such an analysis, there may well be no valid moral principles. See Michael Smith. *The Moral Problem* (Blackwell's:1994), pg. 181.

with one another on disputed questions of value, and the needed criteria for identifying what must be true for an agreement on the relevance of a value to confer relevance on that value, resulting in an agreement on the relevance of certain values, *for purposes of moral argument,* as values whose relevance no one can reasonably reject.

The importance of this last proviso is this: in trying to persuade another party to the hypothetical consensus of the importance of taking into account in moral argument, a certain value that she does not, initially, take to be relevant for purposes of moral argument, what one tries to show is that anyone motivated to relate to others on terms that respect their status as persons has reason to give this value weight in her deliberations. What she must be persuaded of is that giving weight to this kind of consideration in one's deliberations, concerning the validity of principles for the general regulation of behavior, is both expressive of respect for, and is something that is owed to, others in virtue of their status as persons.

This form of argument is quite different from one of trying to argue that, though others may think they disagree with you about the relevance of a certain value for moral argument, if they think hard about it, they will see that they really do agree with you. Dworkin may well be right here: a desire to justify oneself to others is not a reason to alter one's convictions, especially when one has no reason to think that those convictions are mistaken. The desire to justify oneself to others on reasonable grounds may, however, rationalize giving weight to certain values in one's moral deliberations which one would not accept as reasons outside the context of considering principles for the general regulation of behavior.[11]

This thought requires further development if it is to be helpful in casting light on how it is that individuals who disagree in their views about value are to reach a consensus on what values are relevant for purposes of moral justification. Three proposals for how a consensus on relevant values is reached in consensualism, each of which incorporates this thought, are worth considering here. The first two, though they will be ultimately rejected, are helpful for clarifying some of the

---

10   By 'normative status of the person', I have in mind here the normative ideal of the person as one who has a fundamental interest in leading a rationally self-directed life in pursuit of valuable goals and engaged in valuable activities. The significance of this ideal is discussed in chpt. 1. Throughout this chapter, I will refer to it in terms of a person's 'normative status'.
11   The difficulty that consensualism encounters on this point is clearly related to one discussed by Thomas Nagel, in his "Moral Conflict and Political Legitimacy." In *Authority,* ed. Joseph Raz. 300-324. Oxford: Basil Blackwell's, 1990. Nagel's proposal is quite different, however, suggesting that the appropriate response to disagreement over the relevance of a value is that the value not be given weight in moral argument at all. To be fair to Nagel, he is in this piece discussing *political* morality, and it is unclear what special constraints he sees principled political argument introducing that would sharply differentiate it from ordinary moral argument.

difficulties that a plausible account should address. The third proposal, hopefully, resolves these difficulties in a plausible account of how relevant values come to be identified in the process of reasoning about what principles no one could reasonably reject.

§II

(a) One approach to tackling the problem that value pluralism presents for consensualism is for the parties to the hypothetical consensus to agree to circumvent their disagreements about value, by adopting a *restricted desire theory standard* (from now on, the "subjective standard") for the identification of legitimate objections to a proposed principle. This would commit parties to the consensus to the view that an individual has a reasonable *pro tanto* reason for rejecting a principle if acceptance of that principle would, in a world like the one we are familiar with, result in one of her desires remaining unfulfilled. The "restrictions" would exclude from consideration anti-social desires, such as racist or sexist desires, or perhaps desires whose fulfillment requires certain forms of harm befalling others.[12]

The subjective standard needs to be taken seriously, as it is one that all can agree to, despite differences in beliefs about value, as agreeing to it does not require that individuals agree on any substantive claims about value. For in agreeing to such a standard, individuals do not even have to agree with the claim that the number of one's desires that are fulfilled provides a plausible account of the sorts of things someone concerned to lead a good life may have reason to care about. They need only agree that, given widespread disagreement in substantive beliefs about value, and the importance of being able to reach a consensus on questions of value as a prerequisite for a consensus on principles, the subjective standard provides a suitable compromise position on a standard for the impartial identification of valid grounds for objecting to a principle. It is, in other words, a standard that is suitable for purposes of moral argument.

The appeal of the subjective standard rests, principally, on the thought that it is the best available compromise standard, given the fact of value pluralism. But is it an acceptable compromise standard? Any account of how parties are able to agree on questions of value, for purposes of moral argument, must satisfy two criteria. First, any values that are agreed to as relevant for moral argument must be endorsable from each individual's own point of view. Call this the requirement of *neutrality*. Second, the values identified as morally relevant must be such that each person can agree, from her point of view, that if others

---

[12] I assume, for the sake of argument, that these restrictions can be adequately motivated.

evaluate what reasons she might potentially have for rejecting a potential principle, by evaluating the consequences for her of that principle's general acceptance, in light of these values, she will have been shown the kind of consideration she is entitled to, given her status as a person. Call this the requirement of *relevance*.

The subjective standard meets the neutrality requirement by avoiding altogether substantive questions concerning value. But it fails the relevance requirement. Its failure is two-fold. First, it ends up counting, as legitimate *pro tanto* reasons for rejection, the frustration of desires that, even from the point of view of the agent whose desires they are, are not reasonable grounds for wanting to reject a principle. For instance, the subjective standard would count the frustration of my, at best whimsical, desire to own a laser printer as a reason for me to want to reject any principle which deprived me of the necessary resources to purchase one. And it would do so whether or not I myself see this as a legitimate ground for rejecting such a principle.

One could, of course, try and tinker with the subjective standard, in order to avoid the identification of the frustration of trivial desires as relevant reasons for the rejection of principles. But it isn't clear how this would be done without re-introducing substantive considerations of value, the appeal to which adoption of the restricted desire standard is supposed to circumvent.

Second, counting only frustrated desires as sources of valid claims results in many of the intuitively plausible reasons a person might have for objecting to a principle being ignored. For instance, a person might object to a principle because the allocation of powers which the general acceptance of this principle would result in arbitrarily concentrates certain forms of decision making authority in one person's hands. One does not have to *desire* that no one have this kind of authority to object to an allocation of powers that results in this state of affairs obtaining; but this, according to the subjective standard, is what must be the case if charges of unfairness are to be considered relevant in moral argument.

Even if we grant, for purposes of argument, that all charges of unfairness are based on a frustrated desire to be treated fairly, there is a further problem. What if a person is being treated unfairly, but the dominant ideology of the society the person finds herself in is such that no one cares about being treated unfairly? That she is being treated unfairly is no less of an assault on her status as a person just because she happens not to care, and parties to the hypothetical consensus would have every reason to want this unfairness to be recognized, by the system of valid principles for the general regulation of behavior in that society, as wrong. The subjective standard precludes this possibility, as the only possible grounds for a person being wronged is that one of her desires has been frustrated.[13] Despite its initial appeal, parties to the hypothetical consensus have every reason to reject the subjective standard.

(b) The core of the difficulty with the subjective standard is that it makes what reasons a person has for reasonably rejecting a principle too dependent on what that person might or might not happen to want. What is required is a standard that identifies, as potential bases for rejecting a principle, those things that a person has reason to want, or care about, given her status as a person, whether or not she does in fact care about them.[14] There is no way around having to make substantive claims about value, if the values identified as relevant for moral argument are to satisfy the requirements of relevance. Satisfying the requirement of neutrality, then, appears to pull in the opposite direction from what is required to satisfy the requirement of relevance.

One potential route to the resolution of this tension is to adopt what I will refer to as a *substantive basic preconditions* standard. This standard claims that, even though persons might have conflicting substantive views about what is valuable, there are some values whose importance all can uncontroversially agree to, as they are basic preconditions for the successful pursuit of a great many of the sorts of projects a person might pursue in her life. The elements of this list will consist of items such as "not experiencing chronic pain", "not being hungry", "health", "safety from attack", "shelter from the elements", etc. The list of what can be uncontroversially agreed upon will be influenced by prevailing social and natural conditions. The importance of these values for moral argument lies in the fact that, first, they are values that it is reasonable to expect anyone to acknowledge as morally important, from her own point of view, whether or not that person is concerned with being able to justify herself to others, and whether or not she herself values them.[15] That is, a person might not incorporate certain values on the basics list into her life, but not deny that their importance is largely uncontroversial. She may, for instance, see herself as living an unconventional, though successful and fulfilling, life, for which many of the values on the list are not necessary, while admitting

---

[13] Considerations such as this one usually drive the defender of some sort of desire theory of well-being to adopt an *informed* desire theory. This route is plagued by its own difficulties, but for reasons of space, I have put aside discussion of them.

[14] Which allows for the possibility that there may be, in some cases, reasons why the frustration of a persons desire gives her a legitimate basis for a complaint. On the general topic of the inescapability of value judgments in identifying the moral claims we have against one another and the state, see Scanlon 1975, 1991 & 1993.

[15] This need not be read as a statistical claim. One could come up with this list just by reflecting on the sorts of things it is plausible to take as necessary for pursuing any sort of worthwhile life in existing conditions.

that her way of living would suit very few. She need not deny, then, that the kinds of lives that suit most people do require, as necessary preconditions, the sorts of values on the basics list.

Second, because they play such a fundamental role as preconditions for most ways of leading a successful life, these values gain a significance for purposes of moral argument, as values whose relevance it would be unreasonable for anyone (suitably motivated) to deny. It is the 'pre-moral' consensus on these values that allows for a consensus on their relevance, allowing them to serve as an appropriately neutral and relevant basis for the identification of relevant considerations for or against a principle whose validity is being assessed in moral argument.

The basic preconditions view is superior in most respects to a subjective standard. Consisting of general categories of value whose relevance is not justified (solely) by what individuals happen to want, this standard overcomes the previous objections to a completely subjective standard for the identification of relevant reasons. And because the categories that constitute the basic preconditions standard are the object of pre-existing consensus, it is appropriately neutral.

But though the basic preconditions standard is the right direction to go in, it too is inadequate for purposes of consensualist moral argument. It identifies categories of relevant values, for purposes of moral argument, whose importance as preconditions for pursuing a successful and valuable life is uncontroversial. Many values one might cite as an intuitively plausible basis for reasonably rejecting a principle are not, however, so uncontroversial. *If* a person adheres to a particular religion, we will (within limits) think that whether or not she is able to freely practice her faith is a dimension of her life in which things can go better or worse for her which ought to be taken into account in moral argument. The importance of some kind of religious dimension in a successful life is anything but uncontroversial; it is certainly not a value that could plausibly claimed to be part of a pre-moral consensus on the sorts of values that are important for the pursuit of a successful life.[16] The same can be said of many other values that play an important role in lives of many, such as the value of having, and raising, children. The basic preconditions standard is just too minimal to do justice to the range of values we intuitively take to be potentially relevant for purposes of moral argument.

---

16 G.A. Cohen presses an argument along these lines against Scanlon's claim, in Scanlon 1975, that "religion or something like it has a central place in anyone's life". Cohen's argues that this claim does not stand up to scrutiny: it just is not true that there is something relevantly similar to religion that appears in every normal person's life (Cohen 1989,941). The reason for not including religion in the basic preconditions list is similar to this, and is one basis for thinking that the bases of morally relevant claims cannot be isolated by only considering what is important for 'every normal person's life'.

(c) The failure of the basic preconditions standard suggests another, more promising approach, which will be referred to as *the method of abstraction*.[17] Recall that the initial problem that consensualism faces is one of explaining how it is that the parties to the hypothetical consensus are able to agree on values that are relevant for moral argument, given the possibility of trenchant disagreement over questions of value. The substantive preconditions approach, though promising, failed because it was unable to account for many values which are thought to be relevant for purposes of moral argument, but do not have a role to play as preconditions for every (or most) worthwhile ways of life.

The method of abstraction tries to overcome this failing, while incorporating those values whose relevance can clearly be established on the substantive preconditions approach. Nagel captures the core of this approach with exceptional clarity:

> It is really a problem about the interpretation of the familiar role-reversal argument in ethics: "How would you like it if someone did that to you?". The answer that has to be dealt with is "How would I like it if someone did *what* to me?". There is often more than one way of describing a proposed course of action, and much depends on which description is regarded as relevant for the purpose of moral argument (Nagel 1987,309).[18]

What the method of abstraction draws attention to is the importance of how the relevant values, whose importance for moral argument is the object of disagreement, are characterized; "[p]eople can agree, for example, on the importance of having opportunities for self-expression even though they disagree sharply over the merits of particular speeches, plays, demonstrations etc." (Scanlon 1993,198). If disagreement over the relevance of a value for moral argument is, potentially, to be overcome, what is required is that the relevant value be characterized in a way that is sufficiently abstract and general that anyone would be unreasonable to deny the importance of that value *for purposes of moral argument*.

---

[17] Though he does not give it this label, Scanlon 1993 suggests this approach, as does Rawls, *A Theory of Justice*, §66, esp. 435-6.

[18] This approach is also clearly suggested in Nagel's penetrating discussion in Nagel (1987) §V. The direction he ultimately adopts to solve the problem of impartial identification of values in circumstances of pluralism is, however, very different than that suggested here. The explanation of this appears to be that Nagel underestimates the importance of the account of moral motivation as part of an adequate account of impartiality. However, as has been mentioned before, Nagel is discussing political morality, and it is unclear whether, and why, he might understand this fact to be significant for his discussion.

There are two important aspects of this approach that should be noted at the outset. First, the proviso that the values agreed to are *for purposes of moral argument* plays a central role here, as it draws attention to the fact that parties need a consensus on values to identify the salient ways in which a proposed principle for the general regulation of behavior *might* inhibit a person's pursuit of a self-directed good life. The consensus on values is, therefore, shaped to fit the demands of consensualist moral argument. Second, this method presupposes that the notion of a 'good' or 'flourishing' life has enough content that is *independent* of what people happen to want, to support objective judgments of the sorts of goods and activities that one might need, want, pursue or be engaged in, as part of a good life.[19]

In order to clarify the features of this approach, it is worth considering two sorts of cases. The first case is one in which abstraction is used to show why it is that certain aspects of a valued good or activity justify recognizing, under a description that highlights those aspects, the value of that good or activity in moral argument. In this sort of case, certain controversial values are recognized in moral argument, but in a way that (potentially) corresponds to no one's self-understanding of the importance of those values. In the second case, abstraction is used to bring out the fact that, in the case of controversial practices or activities, individuals agree on the value of pursuing certain goods, but disagree on the value of the controversial practices as means of realizing those goods. Once the source of the disagreement is isolated, an argument can be offered as to why no one can reasonably deny, as a valid *pro tanto* reason for rejection, not being able to pursue the value(s) in question, even if they disagree on the best way to pursue these value(s). The two cases bring out different aspects of how abstraction works in moral reasoning. Though no example is so pure that it exemplifies only the features of one kind of case, examples can be chosen that better exemplify the features of one kind of case, rather than the other.

As an example of the first kind, consider the plight of a person deeply committed to her religious faith, who wants to convince a Marxist-atheist that there are good reasons for her to reject a principle which would make it impossible for her to publicly practice her faith.[20] Appealing to the fact that general acceptance of the principle would not

---

[19] By 'objective', what I have in mind here is the sort of 'objectivity' that is secured by the idea that criteria are normative: what is good, bad, virtuous, or vicious is not solely *up to the individual*, but is to some extent fixed by criteria that are independent of the individual. The best examples of the kinds of arguments for this sort of claim, as I understand it, are to be found in Phillipa Foot's articles, "Moral Beliefs", "Goodness and Choice", and "Moral Arguments", all in her *Virtues and Vices*.

[20] In this situation, "good" reasons are reasons that anyone concerned with being able to justify their actions to others on grounds no one could reasonably reject would be unreasonable not to accept as compelling reasons for the rejection or acceptance of a principle.

allow her to worship the creator in the way He requires would have no force from the point of view of the Marxist-atheist, as he believes that it is clearly better if individuals are discouraged from participating in what he takes to be a worthless, if not positively harmful, activity. What the method of abstraction claims is that what is required here is that the religious person offer a more abstract characterization of the importance of her being able to practice her faith, one that makes the value she is appealing to one that it would be unreasonable for the atheist, *given his commitment to interpersonal justification*, to refuse to recognize as morally relevant.

For instance, one may appeal to the importance individuals legitimately attach to being able to shape their practical identities, through their own choices, by identifying with different kinds of respected communities in the society, without experiencing public disapprobation.[21] This is something that she can plausibly claim there is reason for anyone, given her status as a person, to value. Some might not, of course, value this freedom in their own lives; all that the claim requires, though, is that the freedom is one whose value it would be unreasonable for anyone (suitably motivated) to deny.[22] A principle which made public religious worship impossible would undermine the pursuit of this value for those who chose to identify with an organized faith, and thus provides a clear *pro tanto* ground for reasonably rejecting that principle.

Now, the religious person may claim that offering this kind of abstract characterization of the basis of her objection to the principle impeding the practice of her faith overcomes disagreement, not by resorting to higher levels of abstraction and generality, but by simply changing the basis of her complaint. Her reason for wanting to reject the principle is *not* that it prevents her from shaping her practical identity through identification with respected communities. Her reason is that it will prevent her from *worshipping God*.

This is an important point. But notice that claiming her reason for rejection to be that she will be prevented from worshipping God is not incompatible with the claim that one way of understanding the value of being *allowed* to worship publicly is that public worship is one way in which individuals form communities with which they identify. What the method of abstraction advocates is focusing on aspects of the activity

---

[21] For more on this approach to the moral importance of religion, see Joseph Raz, "Free Expression and Personal Identification", in his *Ethics in the Public Domain* (Oxford:OUP) 1994 131-154.

[22] An analogous case would be the kind of mistake a person would be making if they simply denied that Mozart's *Don Giovanni* has any merit, rather than just saying that they can see that there is much to be said in favour of it, though they are still left cold by it.

or good on which one is basing one's objection which make clear why a person, *given the status associated with a certain normative conception of the person*, might value that good or activity. For purposes of moral argument, one should choose a characterization of one's reasons for rejecting or accepting the principle that emphasizes these aspects.

This will result in a gap opening up between one's reason for wanting to reject a principle, as one sees it, and the reason one offers to others in moral argument for rejecting a principle. By focusing on only certain aspects of the good or activity, one leaves behind much of what makes it important in one's life. If the point of resorting to abstraction, in trying to establish the moral relevance of one's claims in moral argument, was to get individuals, who do not agree on questions of value, to come to understand why others value what they value, in the way that they value it, this would be a serious failing. But that is not what is sought: what is sought is a consensus on relevant values *for purposes of moral argument*. The religious person does not have to believe that the characterization of her reasons for wanting to reject a principle that the method of abstraction recommends, fully captures her reasons for wanting to reject the principle. All she needs to believe is that the characterization is one that is adequate to the task of providing others, who disagree with her on questions of value, reasons for accepting her claim to have plausible grounds for reasonably rejecting the principle in question.

Similarly, abstraction does not require that the Marxist-atheist *accept*, as a condition of accepting the religious person's grounds for rejecting the principle, that religious activity is a worthwhile pursuit. All that she is required to accept is that persons (with a certain status) have reason to value being able to shape their practical identity through group identification, and that religious worship is a way that individuals do this. Notice what this does not say: that the Marxist-atheist must *herself* value being able to shape her practical identity through group identification. It only claims that it would be unreasonable of her to deny that individuals, given their status, have reason to value the opportunity to shape their practical identity in this way.

This is not, of course, the only way that abstraction may be employed to argue for the moral significance of religion. Other plausible arguments are available, which do not necessarily offer competing explanations of its moral significance, but may instead reveal aspects of its significance not uncovered by other lines of argument. For example, the religious person may characterize the importance to her of religious worship in terms of the importance for a person of being able to live her life in light of what she takes to be important truths that have consequences for how she should live her life. In this case, the truth in question would be that God requires her to gather with others, in a place freely accessible to all, to worship Him.[23] The value for a person, given her status, of being able to guide her life in light of what she takes to be important truths that have implications for how her life should be lived, is a value whose moral relevance it would be unreasonable for the Marxist-atheist to deny. She need only reflect on the importance for her of being able to live her life in light of what she takes to be important truths, to understand the force of the way the religious person has characterized the importance of her being able to publicly practice her faith.

Notice that it is important to this defense that the truths in question must have important consequences for how one should live one's life. For example, certain North American indigenous peoples were known to believe that if their picture was taken, they would lose their immortal soul. One does not have to believe this to be true, or even believe in immortal souls, to accept that, in photographing a person who held this to be true, one would clearly be wronging her. It does not require much imagination to conceive of how she would see her life if she thought her immortal soul had been taken from her. Other controversial beliefs this same person has, though, may have few, if any, consequences for how she should live her life, and so will not have the same importance in moral argument. She may, for instance, believe that the earth is flat, but she is not therefore wronged by the display of globes in public places where she is bound to encounter them. This is because her belief in a flat earth is not one that informs, in any significant way, how she ought to live her life.[24]

Now, in the first two examples, parties to the hypothetical consensus agree to recognize, for purposes of moral argument, the importance of being able to practise one's religious faith. The understanding of religious faith they accept, one which will influence how the importance of religious faith can be used in arguing for specific principles, is, however, one that is at odds with their own individual self-understandings of the importance (or lack of it) of religious worship. Parties are led to give religion, so understood, weight in their moral deliberations because an agreement on values is a precondition for agreeing to principles that no one can reasonably reject, which is their ultimate aim in moral argument.

---

[23] This idea was suggested to me by Derek Parfit.
[24] One might be misled by this example into thinking that the belief in the flat earth, being a 'theoretical belief' has something to do with it not being significant for moral argument. But this is a mistake. For example, if a person believes that fluoride is a deadly poison, this would be a good reason, that carries weight in moral argument, for not putting fluoride in the water supply. This is because beliefs about what is poisonous do have an important role to play in directing how one lives one's life, and this would be especially true if one thought that a deadly toxin was pouring out of the taps. Note, though, that this is very unlikely to be a decisive reason for not putting fluoride in the water supply; it is more likely to be grounds for taking measures to placate the fears of those who do hold these beliefs.

Relevant Reasons in Moral Argument

Not all uses of abstraction in moral reasoning result in this degree of dissonance between an individual's reasons for rejection, from her point of view, and how these reasons ultimately figure in moral argument. Consider, as an instance of the second kind of case, an example where abstraction does not introduce this kind of dissonance to an individual's deliberations. It would be unreasonable for someone to deny that being able to form intimate relationships is an important part of living a worthwhile life; yet there is deep disagreement on the value of different forms of intimate relationship. To a certain extent, these differences can be overcome by appealing to more abstract characterizations of what constitutes an intimate relationship. By emphasizing the constitutive features of valuable intimate relationships, individuals can be brought to see that some of forms of intimate relationships, that they previously thought to be valueless, do in fact fit their own understanding of what constitutes an intimate relationship. Some of the disagreements will, however, be intractable. If someone is convinced that there can be no value in a homosexual relationship, no characterization, however abstract, is going to convince her that this is the kind of intimate relationship that can be a constitutive part of a good life.

This might be a problem if the point of appealing to higher levels of abstraction was to bring about a consensus on the value in question, e.g., if the point was to convince everyone that if they think heterosexual relationships are valuable, then they are simultaneously committed to the view that homosexual relationships are also valuable. But that is not the point. Rather, the point of subsuming what are, from some individual's points of view, practices whose value is very different, under broad, general categories of value, is to show that these practices are in a *morally relevant* way, similar.[25] For instance, a homosexual seeking to reject principles which would make it permissible for the state to interfere with his or her relationships, could appeal to the value of being able to protect one's intimate relationships from public scrutiny, and the value for a person of being able to choose her own sexual partners. These are the kinds of freedoms that make intimate, personal relationships *possible*, as part of what we understand to be a healthy intimate relationship is that both parties chose to enter into it, and that it be private. Since it would be unreasonable for anyone to deny the value of being able to pursue intimate relationships, it would be unreasonable for anyone to deny that a principle which might result in some not being able to pursue such relationships, if they chose to, would be one

---

[25] In this case, showing different practices to be similar in a morally relevant way involves arguing that the principle in question prohibits pursuit of the good in question in a way that anyone, no matter how they chose to pursue that, would find objectionable. This will not be the grounds of moral similarity in all cases. Rather, what counts as a moral similarity depends on both the good in question and the details of the principle being assessed.

that there is *pro tanto* reason to reject. One does not, in other words, have to endorse, or see the value in, homosexual relationships, in order to see the relevance of these reasons for rejecting principles which would result in their prohibition.

The method of abstraction, it appears, provides consensualism with the necessary resources to diffuse any *a priori* threat that widespread disagreement, where questions of value are concerned, might pose for its plausibility as an account of moral reasoning. The extent to which agreement on the relevance of different values can be achieved using this approach is a matter of straight forward moral argument.

(d) Individuals disagree not only about what values are relevant for moral argument, but also about how important these values are in moral argument. These disagreements are not always due to individuals attaching disproportionate weight to certain values; many differences can be accounted for by simple variables like physiology. If I get cold easily, I have greater reason to value warm clothes than someone whose metabolism makes them relatively resistant to low temperatures. It is important for a theory like consensualism, though, that there be an agreement on the importance of the values that carry weight in moral argument, as consensualism relies heavily on the informal comparison of the force of different reasons in reaching conclusions about the rejectability or non-rejectability of different principles (Scanlon 1982,128).[26]

How might a consensus be reached on the relative importance of different values, for purposes of moral argument? A device that Sen suggests, the *intersection approach*, offers part of a plausible account.[27] The intuitive idea behind the intersection approach is this: in cases where there is disagreement over the ranking of different goods, we can construct an index for comparison by appealing to common fixed points in our judgments. Though we may disagree about the comparative ranking of liberty and safety, we can all agree that the loss of liberty from having to wear seat belts is comparatively small compared to the gain in safety from being required to wear seat belts. Through

---

[26] Scanlon mentions this problem in passing, but does not discuss it in detail. He contrasts *individualized value*, which is the weight an individual should attach to a given value, given his or her other values and propensities, with *normalized value*: "a rough assignment of values to categories...which we take to be a fair starting point for justification...we do this despite the fact that there may be some who would not agree with this assignment of values" (see Scanlon 1988b, 182-83). Also see Scanlon 1993, where he notes that the relative weights attached to different categories will probably not correspond to the relative weights these categories would receive in individual outlooks (pg.199).

[27] See Amartya Sen, *Inequality Reexamined* (Oxford:1993), sec. 3.4; Thomas Hurka expresses what appears to me to be an identical idea, which he refers to as the "supervaluation approach". See Hurka 1993, pg. 86-88. (esp. 87 for use of the term "supervaluation").

appeal to intuitive judgments like this, we can construct, for any comparison of two goods, *a* and *b*, a set of *acceptable* principles, where each acceptable principle makes a claim about how *much* more important *a* is to *b*. On the basis of these sets of acceptable principles, we can make *rough* comparisons of value. We can, say, make claims to the effect that *a* is a greater burden than *b*, and have this be true on the basis of every acceptable principle, while making the degree to which *a* is a greater burden than *b* quite rough, so that this comparison proves to be true on the basis of every acceptable principle for the comparison of *a* and *b*.

This method of constructing an index for comparison of important values, which has affinities with the method of abstraction, is appropriate for consensualism, as all consensualism requires is quite rough, informal, comparisons of the importance of different values:

> For the purposes of moral argument about which principles it is reasonable to reject, a system of moral goods and bads does not need to provide a very complete ordering of levels of well-being. It is enough to distinguish between those 'very severe' losses which count as grounds for reasonable rejection and those gains and losses which are not of comparable severity (Scanlon 1993,199;cf. Scanlon 1982 127-28).

As in the case of abstraction, it is the need for a mutually acceptable standard for the comparisons of gains and losses that drives parties to agree to adopt, for the purposes of moral argument, an index comparing losses that may result in comparative judgments that are at variance with the *precise* judgments (however rough "precise" judgments may be) individuals themselves would make based on the way they themselves value the goods in question.

It is also important, though, for understanding the reasons for using such rough rankings of different values in moral deliberation, that what are being considered in moral reasoning are *principles* for the *general regulation of behavior*. The role of these principles is to structure how agents see the normative situation in the various relationships they might find themselves in, both in terms of how they can be expected to relate to others, and how they can expect others to relate to them.[28] The generality and open-ended nature of the situations, and relationships, to which the principles are to apply, provide an additional reason for accepting the very rough assignment of relative weights to relevant reasons offered for or against a principle in the course of moral argument. Since detailed knowledge of what people have reasons to value, and the relative importance they are justified in assigning to different values, in each situation to which the principles are to apply, can-

---

[28] On this point, see chpt. 3, §1(c).

not be known in advance, it is appropriate, in deliberations concerning which principles no one could reasonably reject, to rely on quite general ideas about what persons have reason to value, and rough estimates of the relative importance of these values to a person's life. This remains true no matter how much specific information one knows about what other *particular* individuals value.

This last point may seem surprising, but it should not be. Consensualism demands that legitimate moral principles be justifiable to each person, within the moral domain, from her point of view. The reasons offered in justification of a principle must, therefore, be reasons which it is reasonable to think that anyone within the moral domain would have "access" to. By "access", I mean that the claims concerning what persons have reason to value that are appealed to in justifying a principle must be based on the kind of information that it would be reasonable to expect someone, in a world like the one we know, to have. Very detailed information about what particular people have reason to value is therefore excluded from moral reasoning at the level of deliberation concerning principles.[29]

Specific information about particular people is not, of course, excluded from moral reasoning at the level of judgment where one must consider what one is morally required to do in a *particular* situation. Here, specific information about particular others may be vital for determining how well a person discharges her duty to others. It may also be important for making one aware of what one's duties to another are; this would be a case of becoming aware of how a general principle specifying interpersonal duties and obligations applies to the specific relationship one stands in with another. One could say here that specific information leads one to an awareness of the normative character of the relation one stands in to another.

§III

(a) The discussion so far might lead one to believe that moral reasoning, as consensualism portrays it, proceeds in stages. First, a consensus is reached on categories of relevant values, which form the basis of a "common language" for moral argument over the rejectability or non-rejectability of principles. In the second stage, this "common language" is put to use in considering the validity of potential principles

---

[29] The informational requirements for consensualist moral reasoning fit common sense beliefs about the kind of information we take ourselves to have access to in deliberating about which principles could be the object of a consensualist hypothetical consensus. This is something I consider to be a strength of consensualism: insofar as it is a characterization of ordinary moral reasoning, it ought to make clear how it is that we are able to deliberate about what we owe one another based on the information about others we generally take ourselves to have.

for the general regulation of behavior. Such a view is certainly suggested by a comparison of the role of categories of relevant values in consensualist moral argument with that of Rawlsian primary goods, which suggests itself as a natural analog to consensualism's categories of relevant reasons.

This, though, is a mistake. Rawlsian primary goods are meant to be used to address principles for a *specific problem*: that of reaching agreement on principles of justice for application to the basic structure of society. They are, in themselves, a complex piece of moral theory, presupposing both a view of society as a co-operative venture, and a view about the division of responsibility between the individual and the state (cf. Rawls 1982, sec. V). There is no problem analogous to principles for the regulation of the basic structure to which consensualism addresses itself, and no set of situations, which can be defined on *a priori* grounds, that call for moral argument. As a result, there is no *fixed* list of categories of relevant values, like Rawlsian primary goods, that have a role to play in consensualist moral argument.

Rather than being two separate processes, the development of categories of values, and the consideration of the validity of different principles, proceed together. The fundamental question in consensualism is "which principles for the general regulation of behavior can no one reasonably reject?". It is in the process of considering this question, in the various situations we might encounter, that the categories are developed. As we encounter new situations, which require either the formulation of new principles for the regulation of a certain kind of behavior, or the further specification of ones we already have, or we gain new insight into familiar situations, we become aware of the moral relevance of different sorts of considerations, some of which can be subsumed under familiar categories, while others will lead to the development of new categories. The categories of values are, in fact, fairly fluid and open-ended.

(b) These categories of relevant values are also, to a certain extent, socially relative. This is a result of the *formality* of consensualist characterization of moral reasoning, which portrays moral argument as involving appealing to what persons generally have reason to value. But what persons have reason to value, and the importance they are justified in attaching to these values, is dependent on the prevailing natural and social conditions of their society.

This is important for several reasons. First, though there is much that can be said at a socially transcendent level, appealing to a normative account of human nature, about the sorts of things persons have reason to value, the specific practices through which persons engage with these values, or incorporate them into their life, will differ according to time and place (e.g., the differences that exist across time and place in the nature of family life).[30] The effects of these differences in how the same goods are made available within a society tend to be diffuse, but will be crucial for the evaluation of specific moral principles that apply to that society. For instance, differences in the character of marriage have implications for the character of divorce (i.e. how easy or difficult it is to dissolve a marriage).

Secondly, the sorts of goods that are thought to be important will differ according to time and place. This is so in two respects. A similar good may be valued in two different societies, yet the importance attached to this good may differ between societies, where divergences could be explained by even very simple considerations, such as climatic differences. Or, it might be that there are goods which are valued in one society, but not valued in another (consider the good of *assurance* whose provision Scanlon cites as central to understanding the practice of promises, a good he himself notes one could well imagine not having any particular currency in a society; cf. Scanlon 1990). There is no reason to believe that every society will make exactly the same range of goods available to its members.

This does not, however, result in an account of moral reasoning that is at base, relativistic. For consensualism posits only one standard of moral validity, or appropriate process of reasoning, for the impartial identification of valid principles and the considerations relevant to the justification of those principles. What categories of value, and what principles, will be validated by this procedure will, however, potentially differ across time and societies. It is a strength of consensualism that the proposed characterization of how categories of relevant reasons are developed is able to explain the relevance of these sorts of differences for moral argument, and the substantive moral principles that apply to a particular society at a particular time, without collapsing into a form of moral relativism.

§IV

(a) The discussion so far has been limited to examining how the consensualist conception of impartiality can be applied to the problem of the identification of values and considerations that are in fact relevant for purposes of moral argument. Nothing has been said about the kinds of values and considerations that are identified as relevant. To a certain extent, this is as it should be. What values and considerations come to

---

[30] On the sorts of things that can be said at a socially transcendent level about what individuals have reason to value, appealing to a normative account of human nature, see Thomas Hurka. *Perfectionism*. Oxford Ethics Series. Oxford: Oxford University Press, 1993 and Thomas Scanlon. "Preference and Urgency." *Journal of Philosophy* LXXII (19 1975): 655-669.

be seen as relevant is a matter of straight forward moral argument, over specific principles for the general regulation of behavior.

There is, however, a temptation to assume that consensualism will be similar to utilitarianism in the considerations it identifies as relevant, insofar as all morally relevant considerations will be considerations concerning, directly or indirectly, individual well-being. The route by which a morally relevant conception of well-being is developed may be different than that favored by utilitarians, but the result, it may seem, is the same.[31]

This is a temptation that needs to be resisted, for it ignores the importance of the consensualist rejection of the asymmetry between well-being and other morally significant notions, which allows it, potentially, to account for the moral significance of considerations that utilitarianism has always had difficulty giving a clear account of, such as the distinction between intended and foreseen harm.[32] The temptation is understandable, however, as some of what Scanlon says actually encourages this way of understanding consensualism. In particular, he makes certain claims about what will be true if a person has a valid ground for rejecting a principle that have substantive implications for the sorts of considerations that can be legitimately appealed to in moral argument. He claims that,

> A set of principles can be reasonably rejected if general acceptance of that set of principles in a world *like the one we are familiar with* would cause *that* person *serious hardship,* and there are alternative principles, the general acceptance of which would not entail comparable burdens for anyone (cf. Scanlon 1993,196;emphasis and italics added).[33]

For purposes of discussion, this characterization can be divided into three central claims:

---

[31] This objection was suggested to me by Wayne Sumner, at a presentation of this material at a University of Toronto seminar.
[32] That the distinction between intended and foreseen harm can be defended as morally significant in a consensualist framework is a claim that cannot be argued for here, though it will be assumed at various points that such a distinction is defensible on the basis of principles no one could reasonably reject.
[33] The point of the "like the one we are familiar with" proviso is to make clear that (a) moral deliberation takes place from the here and now, and (b) that principles for the general regulation of behavior are meant as practical guides for action for us, in this world. This proviso also fixes an appropriate empirical basis from which facts can be drawn for evaluating the consequences of a principle as part of a system of rules for the general regulation of behavior .

The importance of the role that this proviso fulfills stands out more clearly if one contrasts the consensualist principle with Kant's famous Kingdom of Ends formulation of the categorical imperative, a standard objection to which is that it provides standards of behavior for a world of ideally rational beings, not a human world, with all its imperfections. Scanlon's proviso allows him to overcome this difficulty.

(a) a claim that reasons for *wanting* to reject a principle, even if they are not decisive, will all concern the implications *for that person* of the potential acceptance of that principle for the general regulation of behavior.

(b) a claim that the only relevant implications a person can appeal to concern the potential *burdens* that may result for her if a principle is accepted (the *well-being* restriction).

(c) a claim that in reasonably rejecting a principle, one must take into account not only the implications for oneself of the acceptance of the principle, but the implications for others if some other principle, more favorable to oneself, is adopted. The grounds for rejecting a principle, one could say, are sensitive to considerations of *symmetry*.

Discussion of claim (a) will be set aside until the discussion of aggregation (chapter 4). Claim (c), which I have referred to as *the symmetry condition,* was discussed and defended at length in chapter one, and I will not repeat that discussion here. Here, I want to focus specifically on claim (b), the well-being restriction.

This restriction states that all the relevant implications for a person of the acceptance of a principle for the general regulation of behavior concern the burdens that a person may be forced to bear as a result of that principle's acceptance. Consensualism here seems close to utilitarianism. Even though it does not identify the relevance of considerations of well-being in the manner favored by utilitarians, it is similar to it, in identifying all relevant considerations to be considerations of well-being. This is suggested by the emphasis on importance of being *burdened*.

Though Scanlon accepts claim (b) (in Scanlon 1982), I believe that it should be rejected.[34] In order to see why there is reason for thinking this, consider the following example:[35]

In the midst of a drought, the community agrees to a rule that restricts water consumption to one bucket a day per household. Dudley, the local altruist, notices that at the end of every day, there

---

[34] To quickly summarize the thrust of the objection to come: I believe that Scanlon's remark that one of the strengths of consensualism is that it breaks down the theoretical asymmetry between well-being and other moral notions (Scanlon 1982,119) is in tension with the claim that reasons for rejection must concern serious burdens. Agreeing with Scanlon that the displacement of well-being to the status of other moral notions is a strength of consensualism, I argue that what needs to be rejected is the well-being restriction.

[35] This example is loosely based on an example Scanlon offers in sect. III of his "Rights, Goals, and Fairness". The point he makes there against certain utilitarian views is one that I believe has considerable force against his own interpretation of what is true if a person has reason to reasonably reject a principle.

is a bucket of water left in the well, after everyone has taken their fair share. Dudley *takes it upon himself* to take this extra bucket of water and use it to water the public garden, in hopes of encouraging good cheer amidst difficult circumstances.[36]

When Dudley's activity comes to light, he comes under intense criticism for having *broken the rule*. Dudley, appalled by what strikes him as rule-fetishism on the part of his critics, claims in his defense that the rule needs to be re-examined, for he has done nothing objectionable. The water did not represent anyone's entitlement, and he did not use it for himself, but put it to work for the public good. Dudley's claim is that in acting as he did, he acted on the basis of a sound moral principle, one that *no one could reasonably reject*. Outspoken members of the community claim, *contra* Dudley, that they certainly could reject the principle Dudley proposes, in favor of one that required Dudley to bring the excess water to the attention of the community, so they could decide *together* how the water is to be used. Dudley fails to see what possible rationale there could be for rejecting his proposed principle.

If one accepts the well-being restriction, it would appear that Dudley has an excellent case. His action has not cost anybody anything: in fact, they are better off (assuming they are not foliage haters) than they would have been if he had acted otherwise. His action has certainly not generated any sort of serious (or not so serious) burden for anyone.

Limiting the reasons for rejection to the implications for one's well-being, though, leads one to overlook an important objection to Dudley's action, one that draws attention to the fact that he *unilaterally* gave himself the authority to decide how a jointly owned resource should be put to use. The objection is not to what Dudley did *with* the water. It is an objection to Dudley *deciding* what to do with the water, without consulting all those who have an interest in how the excess water should be used. If Dudley had some particular expertise in the optimal use of excess water, that would make him an ideal person for others to decide to appoint, on their behalf, to decide how the excess water should be used. But, this is not the case, and in the absence of any asymmetry between Dudley and the others, that would be recognized by all as the kind of asymmetry that might justify Dudley's actions, it is difficult to characterize Dudley's actions any other way than as a case of him privileging himself over others, by giving himself the authority to *decide on their behalf* how the water is to be used.

Note that this case is not an emergency scenario, in which a decision needs to be made quickly, and there is no time to consult others on

---

36 For the purposes of this example, assume that surplus water does not evaporate by the beginning of the following day, but simply accumulates.

what should be done with the surplus. If that were the case, Dudley's actions would have a very different character: it would then be more plausible to characterize the situation as one in which a decision had to be made, and Dudley just happened to be the only person on the scene, so he made the decision. As it stands, there is in fact no reason for any one person to have the power to decide how the water should be used; a joint decision is clearly what is appropriate.

The objection to the maxim of Dudley's action, then, or the kind of reason cited to reject a principle that would vindicate Dudley in favor of one which condemns his act as wrong, is that in acting as he did, he has assumed an authority to decide for others, one that there is no valid reason for him to have (which is not the same as objecting to not having had a say in how the water should be used). The objection, in other words, is interpersonal, concerning the character of the *relation* which would be set up between Dudley and the other members of the community were his action not to be condemned as wrong.[37]

Can this objection be characterized as one that draws attention to the implications of a principle for a person's well-being? It is reasonably clear that it does not.[38] One might try and argue that this objection does draw attention to some aspect of well-being, but that would naturally beg the question of why it matters, for purposes of consensualist moral argument, as to whether this objection can plausibly be defended as drawing attention to the implications of a principle for well-being. All that is required by consensualism to identify a consideration as relevant for moral argument is that the consideration be one whose relevance for moral argument no one (suitably motivated) could reasonably reject. It would certainly be unreasonable for anyone to deny the validity of an objection to a principle on the grounds that it allowed one person to make a decision on the behalf of another, or others, on a matter in which she (or they) have an interest, without consulting her, when there are no circumstantial reasons that would make a demand for consultation unreasonable. Unreasonable, in light of the normative characterization of parties to the hypothetical consensus as being concerned to live *self-directed* lives.

The consensualist procedure for identifying morally relevant considerations for the assessment of a principle will certainly identify the consequences of a principle's general acceptance for aspects of a person's well-being as being amongst the considerations that need to be

---

[37] Which is not to say that the others think ill of Dudley for his actions; what he did was well meant, but in their view, still wrong.

[38] On this topic, two recent papers by Shelly Kagan are of particular interest. See Shelly Kagan. "The Limits of Well-being." In *The Good Life and the Human Good*, ed. Fred. D. Miller Jr. Ellen Frankel Paul and Jeffrey Paul. 169-189. Cambridge: CUP, 1989; and Shelly Kagan. "Me and My Life." *Proceedings of the Aristotelian Society* XCIV (1994): 309-324.

taken into account in assessing a principle. Not taking into account such considerations would certainly constitute a failure to take the status of others as persons seriously. But considerations of well-being are not the only morally relevant class of consequences that may be relevant for the assessment of a principle. The case of Dudley points to one such consideration: persons can legitimately claim that their status as persons will not be respected by a principle that permits a person to make a decision on behalf of others, in the absence of a good justification for granting her the authority to do so. Consensualism does not require that this complaint be assimilated into the notion of well-being, in order for it to carry weight in moral argument.

Now, nothing said here precludes someone from arguing that the grounds of the objection to Dudley's principle can be assimilated into a plausible account of well-being, and thus characterized as a serious burden. I take the explanation offered to be preferable, though, on three counts. First, it is consistent with the consensualist attack on utilitarianism, part of which is to offer an alternative explanation of the moral relevance of considerations of well-being, an explanation that makes claims about well-being part of an (open-ended) set of morally relevant considerations, whose relevance is not to be explained by reference to human well-being.

Second, I believe that this sort of explanation respects the common sense notion of what it is for a person to be burdened, which tends to be more naturally associated with a person being put under some kind of pressure, or stress, be it physical or psychological, or being subject to some kind of demanding responsibility. Many morally important considerations, such as a person's sense of being *violated*, do not fit this sort of characterization.[39] The kind of explanation offered for the relevance of the objection to Dudley's actions makes room for these sorts of considerations, without distorting our intuitions about what it is for a person to be burdened.

Third, there doesn't appear to be anything lost in claiming serious burdens to be one, but not the only, kind of consideration that can be

---

[39] One piece of anecdotal evidence that partially persuaded me of the plausibility of this line of thought is a recent article in the Guardian discussing date-rape trials. The author pointed out that in many cases of date rape, the trauma usually associated with violent rape by strangers, is not present. Further, date rape victims rarely require the kind of psychological counseling that victims of violent rape require in order to help restore their psychological health. What date rape victims tend to complain of is the sense of betrayal and violation, and an associated need to have the perpetrator admit that, in acting as he did, he *wronged* his victim. The kind of evidence that courts seek in date-rape trials, however, usually concerns symptoms of physical or psychological illness (emotional instability, compulsive bathing, fear of men, etc.) or some kind of disruption to everyday life, that can be plausibly argued to have been caused by the rape. Courts, in my terminology, are looking for signs of burden, while victims are not complaining of being burdened, but violated, which is a different, but just as important, notion. [author Sarah Dunant:; reference has been mislaid]

cited for reasonably rejecting a principle. Considerations of serious burden still have a role to play, when appropriate, in moral argument. A restriction of relevant objections to serious burdens suggests an interpretation of consensualism that brings to the theory the same asymmetrical relationship between well-being and other morally relevant considerations that is characteristic of utilitarianism. The rejection of this asymmetry, as has previously been pointed out, is something that consensualism sees as one of its strengths.[40] That its rejection allows consensualism to explain the moral relevance, in an intuitively plausible manner, of considerations that do not seem to be easily assimilated into the notion of well-being, provides one good reason for thinking the initial rejection to be thoroughly justified.

(b) The rejection of a form of consensualist moral argument that involves only the comparison of potential burdens (however calculated) that individuals might incur, as a result of the acceptance of different potential principles for the general regulation of behavior, is the first step in distancing consensualism from a form of moral argument that is commonly associated with consequentialist moral argument: this view I will refer to as "appealing to costs". What is central to this style of argument is that it involves appealing to the burdens, or costs (however defined), that will result if a particular principle is adopted, rather than some other principle, *without* any attention being given to the nature of the *source* of the burden. The view is not that the identification of legitimate ways of being burdened do not matter. Rather, it is that once the sources of burden are identified, by developing a plausible account of what well-being consists in, what is required for moral argument to progress is that the *magnitude* of burdens generated by a proposed principle be compared in some way. In a consensualist account, one might say that who has the strongest reason for rejecting a principle is determined by comparison of the potential burdens a proposed principle might result in; the source of the burden is not relevant to assessing the strength of the reason. Scanlon, in fact, suggests that some form of the "appeals to costs" view is appropriate for consensualism (cf. Scanlon 1982,123;116).[41] I believe, though, that this is a mistake.

To get a clearer idea of the form of moral argument that is under scrutiny here, consider a line of argument offered by one individual to

---

[40] Stripping the notion of well-being of its explanatory primacy is, I believe, the core of what Scanlon has in mind in his discussion of *philosophical utilitarianism* (cf. Scanlon 1982, sec. I.).

[41] These examples appear in Scanlon 1982, but in no way resembles the portrayal of consensualist moral argument in his most extended application of consensualism, which is his discussion of principles governing promise keeping in his article "Promises and Practices" (Scanlon 1990). As an interpretative strategy, I have taken the style of argument in "Promises and Practices" to be the canonical example of consensualist moral argument. Here, however, I will consider the style of argument suggested in Scanlon 1982,

another, in, for simplicity, a two-person world. It goes like this: in considering a principle for the general regulation of a certain kind of behavior, an alternative principle to the one being considered is either (a) better for me and no worse for you, or (b) better for me and worse for you, but not as bad for you as the initial principle was for me, then my rejection of that principle, on the grounds that the alternative is better for me, is valid.[42] Whether this line of reasoning is sound depends on the sorts of considerations that can be offered in defense of its central, substantive, premise:

> [*Fact A*] the fact a person (k) can be spared an amount of burden (x), at either no cost to anyone else, or at a cost to someone else that is less than x, by the adoption of a principle for the general regulation of behavior other than the one that results in k having to shoulder burden x, is always a reason that k can offer for rejecting the principle which results in her having to shoulder x.

Notice that what is required here is a justification for fact A always being relevant. For the suggestion is that the relevance of fact A is one of the structural features of consensualist moral reasoning. It isn't enough, therefore, to claim that in certain cases, because of substantive features of the kind of problem under consideration, fact A is relevant (i.e., because of the kind of good, or value, at stake in the problem). One could claim, of course, that every kind of situation for which consensualist moral deliberation is appropriate has certain common substantive features, which justify the salience of the kind of fact under consideration, but this would be a very difficult, and largely implausible, case to make.

If the relevance of fact A is a structural feature of consensualist moral argument, this must be because recognizing fact A in moral argument is a necessary component of the minimal consideration persons owe one another, if they are to interact on terms that respect one another's status as persons. And this, in fact, is a plausible claim. Can one really claim to respect the status of another as a person if one does not accept as reasonable a principle which will establish a requirement that benefits her, when this requirement either costs one nothing, or costs one less than the magnitude of the benefit to her? Isn't this a clear case of giving one's own interests more moral importance than the interests of another?

This thought requires careful evaluation. Though one can say that doing something which will result in either some benefit accruing to someone else, or someone being spared a certain burden, at either no

---

and suggest some reasons this discussion is flawed. Note that this style of argument is discussed again in chapter III, where it is referred to as the *complaint model*.
[42] I am assuming here that *how* burdens are calculated is not relevant for the argument I am considering here.

cost to oneself, or a cost to oneself that is less than the benefit that person will receive, or the burden she will be spared, can be done out of respect for that person's status as a person, it doesn't follow that not doing so is a *failure* to take that person's status as a person seriously in how one relates to them, or indeed, that doing this act is part of the minimal requirements of respecting that person's status as a person.[43] This last point is particularly important, as consensualism characterizes the morality of duty and obligation as specifying the *minimal* requirements one must guide one's behavior in light of, if one is to take the status of others as persons seriously.[44]

Whether or not providing this person a certain benefit, at either no or a lesser cost to oneself, is required as part of the minimal respect one owes that person, given their status, turns on questions of: (a) what the benefit in question is, and (b) what the implications for the person of having, or not having, this benefit are for her ability to see herself as a person with a certain status. Such questions cannot be evaluated independently of consideration of what the benefit in question is, and what role it plays in her life. The same, of course, can be said of burdens: what we would want to know in evaluating a person's grounds for wanting to reasonably reject a principle is not just that a person will (potentially) face a certain burden if a principle is accepted, one that

---

[43] Here I distinguish between *being benefited* and *being spared a certain burden*. In his presentation of how substantive moral argument in consensualist framework proceeds, Scanlon (in Scanlon 1982) does not distinguish between the two. Nor, I believe, can he. On that view, not being benefited can be claimed to be a burden, as the magnitude of burdens are determined by a function that appeals to both one's level of well-being, and the difference between how well off you would be under one principle, compared to another plausible alternative principle (the *complaint model*; see Parfit *forthcoming* chpt. 6). Whether your improved state under the alternative is due to being relieved of a burden, or having received an additional benefit, is not relevant to judging the magnitude of the burden. Intuitively, though, I take being burdened to be different from having failed to receive a certain benefit. Though the two may, in certain examples, overlap, this is not always so. It is only the special features of Scanlon's favored interpretation of consensualism (in Scanlon 1982) that makes distinguishing the two otiose.

[44] This argument presupposes a version of consensualism in which the idea of respecting the status of another as a person has a prominent role to play, an idea that is not part of Scanlon's original statement of his contractualism in Scanlon 1982. However, it is doubtful that *Fact A* could be a structural feature of moral argument even on Scanlon's original statement of the theory. For there Scanlon claims that "The range of things which may be objects of my rational desires is very wide indeed, and the range of claims which others could not reasonable refuse to recognize will almost certainly be narrower than this" (Scanlon 1982,119). One implication of *Fact A*, though, is to deny that a burden could ever just *not count* in moral argument because of the source of the burden, unless one was prepared to deny that source of burden really does pick out a way in which one can be burdened. In other words, *Fact A* denies the possibility of refusing to recognize a burden in moral argument on the grounds of moral, though not prudential, irrelevance, in the very way that Scanlon wants to be able to do in his original statement of his contractualism. Those passages in Scanlon 1982 which suggest that *Fact A* is a structural feature of consensualist moral argument represent an important source of tension in that statement of Scanlon's view.

she will not have to face if an alternative principle is adopted which distributes burdens in a way that no one has to face as great a burden. We will want to know how being forced to carry this burden affects a person's life, and whether or not lessening this burden by adopting an alternative principle will be significantly less inhibiting to that person being able to live her life in a way that is appropriate to her status.

Following this line of thought, one might question whether or not the fact that, if a proposed principle is accepted, you will be worse off than you might otherwise be under a proposed alternative principle, under which no one's burden (however calculated) is even potentially as great as your own, in any way undermines your status as a person. The acceptance of *Fact A* as always being relevant would imply that this is so. But is this plausible? For it is one thing to claim that being worse off *in any respect* than one could be *always* undermines one's status as a person, but quite another to claim that being worse off than one could be *in a certain respect* undermines one's status as a person. The second claim seems more plausible, but it relies, for its plausibility, on the character of the respect in which one is worse off than one could be, and the connection between this dimension of evaluation and a person's status as a person.

For example, Sen has suggested that, in evaluating principles, we should be concerned with the resulting *capability* set that it is reasonable to assign to each person. By a *capability* set, Sen means a person's freedom to achieve various valuable states of being, and to pursue various valuable activities (e.g., what he refers to as *functionings*, which he defines in terms of valuable *doings* and *states of being*).[45] If a person is worse off in a way that significantly impedes her freedom to achieve certain valuable functionings, the fact that she is worse off will certainly be significant. But it will be significant because the way in which she is worse off impedes her ability to achieve certain valuable functionings. The claim of being worse off than one otherwise might be is not enough to establish a significant ground for rejecting a principle.

There are reasons, then, for doubting that *Fact A* is always morally relevant in consensualist moral argument, and that, *a fortiori,* the version of consensualist moral argument that incorporates the idea of 'appealing to costs' ought to be rejected. This is an important conclusion for consensualist moral argument, as will be seen in the next chapter, where it becomes important for understanding how one might explain the rationale for various deontological features of common sense morality within a consensualist framework.

---

[45] Sen's "capability" approach may be of great importance for understanding consensualist moral argument ; but this possibility cannot be adequately assessed here.

Chapter Three
Consensualism and Non-Consequentialism

§I

(a) Non-consequentialist moral theorists (also referred to as deontologists) make at least two important claims about the content of morality. First, they claim that it contains *permissions* or *options*, such that agents sometimes have a *choice* of whether or not to pursue a course of action that there are morally good reasons for pursuing.[1] For instance, if one of my flatmates is obviously lonely, I am not *morally required* to try and befriend her, perhaps by including her in gatherings with my friends, even though I know that she would fit in well. Not to do so is to expose myself as lacking a basic kindness and sympathy with others, but there are still sound reasons as to why whom I befriend should be up to me.

Second, non-consequentialists claim that there are *constraints* on action, such that it is sometimes morally wrong to pursue a course of action, even if there are good reasons for pursuing that course of action. For instance, it would be wrong of me to deliberately humiliate a lazy student in front of his equally lazy classmates, in order to scare them into working harder, which I know will result in them all achieving a much higher degree standing than they otherwise would. Or to take a simple example, killing someone is still thought to be wrong

---

[1] It is important here to distinguish between strong and weak options. Weak options concern situations where an act is permitted, or not required, because there are no good reasons for pursuing one course of action rather than another. Strong options concern situations where there are good reasons for doing a certain act, but the individual has the authority to decide whether or not to act for these reasons. What is being discussed here are strong options, which is the target of those who wish to attack the common sense belief in options.

even if it is done with the intention of saving three others from being killed in an identical manner.

To these we can add a third claim that is often, though not exclusively, associated with non-consequentialist views: that morality should not be a disaster for the agent. A moral theory that portrays the demands of morality and the requirements of leading a reasonably good life as almost always pulling in opposite directions is, on this view, deeply flawed. Morality, it is claimed, is not that *demanding*.[2]

Defenders of consequentialism[3] have long been skeptical of the non-consequentialist's claim that these are valid features of morality. According to the consequentialist, there are only moral requirements, and what one is always required to do is what will best promote well-being. In this discussion, I will assume that, to a certain extent, the consequentialist is correct in her belief. If we start with a broadly consequentialist conception of impartiality, there is no way to defend the validity of those features of morality that non-consequentialists draw attention to. To make progress in explaining the role of options and constraints in morality, we need to start with an alternative conception of impartiality. Consensualism, I believe, provides that needed alternate starting point.

In this discussion I will consider a strategy for developing a plausible rationale for options and constraints, using the resources of consensualism, one that also has important implications for the question of how a characterization of morality's demands that is less extreme than that offered by consequentialism, might be defended. In order to argue for options and constraints in a consensualist framework, though, certain features of consensualism need to be clarified. In particular, the role of *legitimate expectations* and *principles for the general regulation of behavior* within the theory require careful explication.

(b) The thought that an alternative conception of impartiality may supply the defender of non-consequentialism with the tools she needs to

---

[2] On many views, the role of options in morality just is to lower the demands that morality makes on the individual. I have distinguished the question of options from the question of how demanding morality is, on the grounds that I believe it is important to leave open the possibility that there are morally important reasons why persons might value *having a choice* in certain situations, which have nothing to do with how demanding a morality would be which required one to do, in that kind of situation, what would be for the best.

[3] By consequentialism I have in mind *act-consequentialism* (unless otherwise noted), and specifically a version which specifies the good to be promoted in terms of human well-being. In this chapter, I depart from the convention I have adopted in the rest of the book of speaking of utilitarianism and different forms of utilitarian normative theory. I have done so in order to remain consistent with the terminology that it is now standard practice to use in discussions about options and constraints. I make no attempt, in this discussion, to do justice to the diversity of theories that identify themselves as broadly consequentialist.

defend her view is not a new one. Shelly Kagan, in his *The Limits of Morality*,[4] in fact offers an explicit argument as to why characterizing impartiality in terms of a hypothetical consensus will not help the non-consequentialist justify those features of common sense morality for which she seeks a justification. His argument, which I will refer to as the *no options* argument, is worth considering in detail, as the assessment of it will set the stage for the investigation of the justification of options and constraints using the resources of consensualism.

The argument is directed specifically at characterizations of 'impartiality as consensus' that use a veil of ignorance device (i.e. Rawls and Harsanyi), but it also has implications for consensualism. Kagan envisions a hypothetical consensus situation, suitably specified to prevent any party to the consensus, in offering justifications and considering justifications she is offered, from attaching special weight to her interests because they are *her* interests. What the parties seek is a consensus on principles that will constitute a system of morality that each of them can reasonably be expected to abide by. The *no options* argument is that the system of principles to which everyone has agreed *may* contain rules that specify certain constraints on action, but they will not contain principles that make the pursuit of the greater good, on certain occasions, optional. Any moral system that can be justified by a hypothetical consensus conception of impartiality, as it won't allow for options, will be, to use Kagan's term, *extremist*.[5] This is a result that non-consequentialists who appeal to this kind of characterization of impartiality hope to avoid.

Why no options? The argument runs as follows. Each party to the hypothetical consensus is concerned to find principles that both advance her interests as well as possible, and that all can agree on. Now, it may be that all can agree to principles that allow for both options and constraints. But such principles are not, out of all the sets of principles the parties could agree on, the most likely to best advance each person's interests. For if a person agrees to principles that sometimes allow one a choice of whether to act in the way that best promotes well-being, she will be agreeing to principles that reduce the likelihood of others helping her advance her interests, as others will, in some instances, not be required to help her advance her interests. Her life under a system of principles with both options and constraints *might* not, therefore, go as well as her life lived under a system with only constraints and no options. Since each of the parties to the hypo-

---

[4] Shelly Kagan. *The Limits of Morality*. Oxford: Oxford University Press, 1989. pg. 39-46.
[5] The *extremist* denies that morality contains options, while she is neutral on the question of constraints. The *moderate* believes that morality contains both options and constraints. The *minimalist* believes that morality contains only options. Non-consequentialists hope to defend the position of the moderate, against attack from the other two positions.

thetical consensus is concerned to get the best deal for themselves as they can secure agreement on, there is no reason to think that the principles agreed to will allow for options.

One could argue that parties to the consensus would, in fact, agree to principles that allow for options, as options free up the agent from burdensome requirements, making her better able to pursue her own good. Kagan considers this argument, but rejects it, on the grounds that it is only sensible for a person to agree to principles which allow for options if the principles give her, *and no one else*, permission to choose, from amongst those courses of action not explicitly forbidden by constraints, whether or not to pursue the course of action that will best promote well-being. It is true that the chances of a person's life going well are better if it is lived within the bounds of a system that allows her more, rather than less, opportunity to pursue those courses of action that are conducive to the advancement of her own ends. However, these potential benefits of options for a person are offset by the fact that others, exercising the same options to reap the same kind of benefit, will no longer be required to assist her in the pursuit of her projects. In a world where everyone is not required to do as much in the service of others, she can expect that her interests will not be advanced as well as they would be in a system which is more demanding in its requirements of individuals. It is only if a person can establish an asymmetry between herself and others that will justify her, but not others, having options, that it is clearly better for her to agree to a moral system which contains principles that allow for options. Since it is hard to imagine how such an asymmetry would be justified, there still is no decisive reason to reject the *no options* argument.

There is a better objection to the *no options* argument, though, that Kagan does not consider. Kagan assumes that his argument is sound no matter what conception of well-being, be it hedonism or a substantive goods conception, is judged most plausible. But this claim is untenable. Some conceptions of well-being may be incompatible with a moral system that contains no options. This is most plausible in the case of conceptions of well-being that emphasize the importance of valuable forms of interpersonal relationship as part of a good life. Maintaining friendships and family relations may often require that one act in a way other than that which bests promotes well-being, but instead act in the way that will result in some specific benefit to a friend or family member. It may also be important that one have the option of choosing to act in a way that favors those one stands in a special relationship to, just because one wants to do so. This kind of spontaneity, where one acts not on a perceived requirement, but on an affectionate impulse, is an important aspect of many forms of valuable interpersonal relationship.

Options, according to this argument, may not only allow a person to better promote her well-being, but may in fact be a required feature of any moral system under which that person is able to have a good life. Having options, it would seem, is a precondition for pursuing many sorts of valuable good. That a plausible conception of well-being is one that will emphasize the importance of interpersonal relationships for having a good life ought not to be a controversial assumption. There is, therefore, a case for the claim that Kagan is wrong, and that parties to a suitably specified hypothetical consensus, each concerned to best advance her own good, will choose principles for the constitution of a moral system that allow for both options and constraints.

(c) Central to this promising line of argument is the thought that, once we start to think about the sorts of things parties to the hypothetical consensus care about, and in particular, the importance they may attach to certain kinds of valuable relationships, a plausible rationale for options and constraints begins to emerge. The consensualist characterization of impartiality takes this thought a step farther, portraying the parties to its hypothetical consensus as each concerned, not with advancing her own good, but with agreeing to mutually acceptable (or non-rejectable) principles that will structure how individuals are to *relate* to one another. What moves them is not the thought of securing their own interests, but the value, or desirability, of living together on a basis of mutual respect. Parties to the agreement thus seek principles, for the general regulation of behavior, that define the kind of consideration they owe one another if they are to live together on such a basis. Each, as Scanlon puts it, is motivated to be able to justify her actions to others on the basis of principles that no one, provided they are also motivated to be able to justify themselves to others, could reasonably reject.

Consensualism sees the importance of the morality of duty and obligation (which encompasses constraints and options) as lying in its social role of structuring relations between individuals, a concern that is alien to (or at least not emphasized by) consequentialism. Morality, on this view, provides a framework in which individuals can relate to one another and form valuable relationships with one another, on a basis of mutual respect for one another's status as a person.[6] It does so by specifying, through principles of duty and obligation, what sorts of claims individuals have on one another, claims that each party must respect if she is to stand in relations of mutual respect with others. What claims individuals have on one another differ, of course, with the

---

[6] See chpt. 1 for the discussion of the normative ideal of the person that is relevant when speaking of a person's *status*.

character of the relationship.[7] Regardless of the character of the relationship, though, the principles of duties and obligation serve the same purpose within that relationship: that of setting the standard for what persons can *legitimately expect* of one another, against which they judge the appropriateness of having various *reactive attitudes* towards one another.[8] Resentment, moral indignation, forgiveness, feeling betrayed, love—the range and subtlety of reactions we have towards others with whom we are involved in some kind of interpersonal relationship is inexhaustible—all *presuppose* beliefs about what we can reasonably expect from others.[9] The possibility of having legitimate beliefs about what it is reasonable to expect from a person enables us to form many of our reactions to others; and it is the differences in what it is reasonable to expect from one another are, at least partly, constitutive of different forms of valuable relationship in which we might stand to another. Morality enters into the very definition of the various relationships which structure our lives, not in the Hobbesian sense of *restraining* certain kinds of anti-social impulse, but in (partially) defining what it is to stand in different sorts of relationships with another.

Principles that specify what we owe one another are, in this account, assigned the special role of providing a basis for legitimate expectations between parties. Some points should be noted, though, concerning how the term is being used. First, not all legitimate expectations one might have of another can be grounded on principles for the general regulation of behavior. Principles, in consensualism, specify the *minimal* consideration one is owed by another, depending on the character of the relationship, out of respect for one's status as a person. A person may have other legitimate expectations for how another might treat her, though, based on considerations having to do with considerations specific to an individual relationship and its history. She might not see herself as being *owed* this kind of consideration, but one does

---

[7] Where questions of obligation are concerned, it will also matter whether or not the relationship was freely entered into.

[8] The term "reactive attitude" is from Strawson's "Freedom and Resentment", and refers to our moral reactions (indignation, resentment, etc.) to the attitude towards us expressed in the actions of others (though, following Scanlon 1988b, pg.167 these attitudes should be read as cognitive, insofar as it is appropriate to ask for a person's reasons for these reactions and attitudes). Such attitudes are an expression, according to Strawson's example, of the failure of others to express a degree of good will towards us that we can legitimately demand. This could also be expressed as a reaction to the failure of others, revealed in their maxims of action, to take our value as persons seriously.

[9] Of course, we can be mistaken about what it is reasonable to expect from others, either because we have made a mistake about the content of morality, or because we have made a mistake about the character of the nature relationship in which we stand to the other person, both of which would render our reactions inappropriate. The point here is that our emotional reactions are often dependent on our moral beliefs; we can have false beliefs, but this does not change the dependence relation.

not have to see oneself as being owed something as a precondition for a legitimate expectation of it.

Second, the idea of having legitimate expectations of another has a natural, intuitive home in discussions of contractual relationships. Juridical metaphors, however, aptly characterize only a very limited class of human relationships. For instance, though they are appropriate for relationships based on legal contracts or promises, it is hard to see how they are appropriate for relationships built on the basis of trust. Talk of legitimate expectations, one might argue, is inappropriate when speaking of relationships that lack this juridical character.

The intuition that this objection draws upon, I believe, is that the expectations between parties who stand in some kind of contractual relationship are clearly defined and delimited, while this is not true of non-contractual relationships. This is, to a certain extent, true. What each party can expect of the other in a contractual relationship is quite often written down. The significance of this point, though, is limited. First, written contracts, or verbal agreements, presuppose many background norms that fix legitimate expectations between parties that are not specifically written down. For instance, if I reach a commercial agreement to have a product delivered to my home at such and such an hour, I can legitimately expect this to occur. But I can also legitimately expect that the product be handled with appropriate care by the person delivering it, without having to have this written down in the contract. Second, it is a mistake to think that parties to non-contractual relationships, based on values like trust, do not have legitimate expectations of one another. It only means that the principles governing their legitimate expectations of one another, because of the open ended and partially malleable nature of such relationships, cannot, except perhaps in a very general way, be codified.

There may be another thought, though, that those who press this objection have in mind. It is that many things we believe we owe another, because of the relationship we stand to them in, are not things the other person *consciously* expects. For instance, when you live with someone, and haven't done anything special in a long time, you can often come to see yourself as owing it to the other person to do something special, however symbolic, even though she may not consciously expect you to do anything special. The importance of such gestures lies, perhaps, in the importance of indicating recognition of the character of the ongoing relationship between you. Here there is an important asymmetry between contractual and non-contractual relationships; in contractual relationships, the expectations usually are conscious. To the extent that legitimate expectations are usually thought of as *conscious* expectations, the term, as it is being used here, can be understood as a term of art, as there is no requirement here that a legitimate expectation be for something another consciously expects or relies upon in the way suggested by the example of contractual obligations. However, it should be noted that it isn't obvious that legitimate expectations, to be conscious, need be explicit. For instance, one's partner might not explicitly expect a special gesture of some sort, but may come to feel, in the absence of such a gesture, somewhat neglected for reasons that are difficult to explain.

The question of how individuals should *relate* to one another is not so central in the consequentialist picture, where the *aim* of morality is to promote well-being; morality, according to the consequentialist, will of course have implications for how we should relate to one another, but this is a trivial consequence of the action-guiding character of morality. The 'aim' of morality should not here be understood to be some goal that is external to morality, which morality is organized to realize, but an aim that is internal to morality, one that is part of the explanation of why moral demands are such as they are. Consequentialism claims that the pursuit of this aim requires that one always do whatever is necessary to promote well-being. This makes what one is morally required to do at any given moment dependent on how things happen to be in the world. The idea of legitimate expectations plays no essential role in this kind of theory.

This is not to suggest that how things happen to be in the world have no significance for working out what we owe one another. Rather, the difference is that, in consensualism, changes in the circumstances of the world (such as a local natural disaster, or a serious economic downturn), will change what we owe one another, because there are certain things that others can, depending on the details of the situation, legitimately expect of one another in the face of changes in circumstances, depending on the kind of relationship they stand in to one another. On the consequentialist view, the circumstances of the world determine for us how best to direct our energies if we are to promote well-being. The circumstances of the world are, therefore, of a direct relevance for understanding morality's demands, in a way that is not true in consensualism.[10]

Whether or not consequentialism allows one to make long term plans for one's future, or to maintain the kind of interpersonal relationships and commitments to others that are thought to be so important to a worthwhile life, is a complex question. One might be inclined to claim that it does not. Morality, in this case the promotion of the well-being, is a full-time project that leaves no room for anything else; this *sounds* extreme, but becomes less so the more one moves away

---

[10] The significance of this contrast will become clearer in the discussion of specific examples, in §III(d).

from hedonism and towards a sophisticated perfectionist account of well-being. It is also open to those who favor some form of indirect consequentialist theory to claim that morality does allow room for a degree of morally legitimate partiality for the maintenance of one's projects and personal relationships, making it justifiable that we sometimes not do what would best promote the good. A moral system, they may claim, in which individuals are given some latitude to shape their lives according to their own choices, being allowed (morally) to develop and maintain personal relationships, and long term projects of their own choosing, is a system which, if generally followed, will in the long term best promote well-being. This view does not represent a departure from indirect consequentialism; rather, it rests on empirical assumptions (about the circumstances of the world, and human motivations) to reach conclusions about how the moral system ought to be designed if it is to best realize its aim.[11]

On a very abstract level, the contrast between consequentialism and consensualism can be drawn as follows: consequentialism is concerned with what we *do*, but only because what we do affects what *happens*. The primary concern in that theory is with the promotion of well-being. Consensualism is concerned with what we *do* in a more basic sense, as what we do expresses an attitude towards others that we believe to be appropriate, given their status as persons.[12] The primary concern here is with the character of the relations that individuals stand in with respect to one another.

§II

(a) If parties to the consensualist hypothetical consensus are concerned with relating to others on terms of mutual respect, why should they be concerned with agreeing to *principles for the general regulation of behavior*? Part of the answer has already been touched upon in the earlier part of the discussion: principles for the regulation of behavior set a standard for the legitimate expectations for conduct that individuals, given their status as persons, can have of one another.

---

11   A response to the rule-consequentialist argument, that she can also give a role to legitimate expectations in her theory, would follow these lines. Consensualism claims that legitimate expectations are important as guidelines for how individuals should conduct themselves if all are to live together on a basis of mutual respect. Rule consequentialism may give legitimate expectations a role because a system in which individuals can only have demanded of them what they could legitimately have expected to have demanded of them is a system with which individuals are more likely to comply, and is therefore more likely to best promote the good. The rationale for legitimate expectations between the two theories is, therefore, very different.
12   The contrast I draw here appears in Thomas Nagel's "War and Massacre", §V, and Christine Korsgaard, "The Reasons We Can Share", 24-25 and §V.

There is, however, a further important, though perhaps more obscure, connection between the importance of principles for the general regulation of behavior in consensualism, and relating to others on terms of mutual respect.[13] In order to explore this connection, it is necessary to introduce a new idea to the discussion, that of how the *relationship* between two individuals shapes how the interests of one figure in the deliberations of the other.[14] Scanlon briefly touches upon this point, claiming that,

> The *fundamental* question of *right* is: what authority (and duty) to act is it reasonable for us to assign to each other? (Scanlon 1988a,136;italics and emphasis added).

The core of the idea is this: treating another with respect for her status as a person requires that, in interacting with this person, one act on certain kinds of reasons, *not* on the basis of certain other reasons, and be authorized to act on yet other sorts of reasons, in one's relations to her. The reasons one is required, authorized to, or required not to act on, if one is to relate to the other on terms of mutual respect, must be reasons that no one could reasonably reject as reasons that, given the character of the relationship, one should be required to act or not act on, or be authorized to act on. Note that the idea of *authorizing* someone to act on a reason is here quite different from that of *requiring* them to act on a reason. Authorizing someone to do something is akin to the idea of putting the decision in her hands; it is a notion that is fundamental for understanding options. A requirement that a person act or not act on a certain reason, though defeasible, sets out a course of action that a per-

---

[13] Scanlon claims that rules, or principles, are *fundamental* in contractualism: "they do not enter merely as devices for the promotion of acts that are right according to some other standard. Since it does not establish two potentially conflicting forms of moral reasoning, contractualism [consensualism] avoids the instability which often plagues rule utilitarianism" (Scanlon 1982,120). He does not, however, offer a further explanation of this cryptic remark. What is being offered here is one way of understanding the importance of this remark for consensualist moral theory.

[14] The consensualist view of morality is that of "a system of co-deliberation. Moral reasoning is an attempt to work out principles which each of us could be expected to employ as a basis for deliberation and to accept as a basis for criticism" (Scanlon 1988b,166). What is emphasized here, which is not prominent in Scanlon 1982, is that the system of rules the parties agree to are principles of practical deliberation, which serve to structure their practical deliberations. Notice that the way Scanlon has characterized the role of principles, their role is to isolate various considerations that someone concerned with the justifiability of her actions to others should take into account in assessing what she has most reason to do. This moves the consensualist view closer, in one way, to a form of Kantian rationalism, in which there are not two points of view, one of morality and another of prudence, but just one point of view, from which one assesses the various reasons that apply to oneself in deciding how to act. This obviously raises questions about how to account for the importance we intuitively attach (to the extent we do attach) to those considerations that are isolated by moral principles; this question will be (obliquely) discussed in the next section.

son must (or must not) pursue, where a failure to comply constitutes an instance of having done something wrong.

To take a practical example that will help to clarify this idea, consider friendship. Friendships are partly constituted by certain duties that friends owe each other. If my friend is upset and needs to talk, it is my duty to put aside what I am doing and take the time to listen. My friend's need, one can say, changes the normative situation that faces me: her need is a reason for me to respond to her need, and a reason to ignore other considerations, such as the fact that a favorite program of mine is on the television. If I fail to respond to her need, I must offer a very good reason for doing so whose importance I believe my friend would be unreasonable to deny. Or if I lack such a reason, I must later express remorse at having failed my friend. To do neither is to risk undermining the friendship, by expressing, through my actions, a lack of respect for my friend.

The same would not be true if it were a stranger who sought my time to discuss her problems; though her need may be just as great, she would not be in a similar position to demand my attention.[15] Not wanting to discuss her problems with her is sufficient reason for not doing so, whether or not I'm busy. What is being suggested here is that what accounts for the difference in the two cases is not the intensity, or importance, of the person's need. Nor is the difference to be accounted for by what one can do to satisfy the other's need. What explains the difference, between the two cases, in what counts as a morally acceptable response to a person's need, is the difference in the *character of the relationship between the parties*. The principles governing legitimate expectations between friends require that friends give a certain degree of deliberative priority to certain morally relevant aspects of one another's situation, a priority that is not owed to strangers. My duty to my friend, one I have because of the character of our relationship *as friends*, expresses itself, one can say, in my practical deliberations by certain aspects of my friend's situation taking deliberative priority over similar potentially reason giving aspects of the situations of others, and other competing considerations.

By giving morally relevant aspects of another's situation *deliberative priority*, what is meant is this: how the relevant aspects of another's situation and which aspects of her situation figure in one's deliberations about how to act are determined by the character of the relationship one stands in to the other. If aspects of a person's situation

---

15 One might be tempted to say that the difference between the case of the friend, and the case of the stranger , is that in the case of the friend, one is in a position to do something to help the friend, while one can do nothing to help the stranger. But this isn't a convincing explanation of the felt difference between the two cases. Often, what people need is just someone to talk to. The listener does not require any intimate knowledge of the person she is listening to in order to listen.

have deliberative priority, one has reason to be moved by that person's situation, and reason not to be moved by the situation of others, or by other reasons for action, *even if* being moved by the plight of others, or acting on other considerations, would better promote well-being.[16] In situations where there is more than one person involved, which aspects of a person's plight take priority over other relevant reasons in one's deliberations, reasons that arise from considering the plight of others, will be justified by the circumstances of the situation and the characters of the different relations one stands in to those involved.

It is important to keep in mind here that the 'justification' of the relative deliberative priority of relevant aspects of one person's plight over relevant aspects of another person's plight will involve the further specification, through consensualist moral argument, of the relevant principles that govern the various kinds of relationships one stands in to those whose plight, under the circumstances, is relevant. For in giving one person's plight deliberative priority over another's, one is still acting impartially. The way in which one prioritizes the reasons that arise from considering the plight of the different individuals in the situation must, therefore, be justifiable to anyone on grounds that no one could reasonably reject.

This view can be contrasted with the consequentialist conception of impartiality, which recommends that each person's morally legitimate interests figure in one's deliberations in exactly the same way, regardless of differences in the character of the relations between oneself and each of the others. Some forms of indirect consequentialism may come closer to the consensualist view, recommending taking into account one's relation to another in determining how that person's interests should figure in one's deliberations, but unlike consensualism, this will be justified on the grounds that this pattern of deliberation better promotes well-being, in the long run.

One should not be misled by the last example into thinking that, because one has no duty to listen to the woes of strangers, the relationship between strangers does not sometimes justify giving deliberative priority to the reasons that concern the plight of a stranger. For part of what is implied by the thought that the subject matter of morality concerns how we ought to *relate* to one another is that a relation between friends and a relation between strangers (more aptly described as a simple relation between *persons*) are both morally relevant relations, which can be cited, in a consensualist framework, as a justification for giving aspects of the plight of the other, with whom one stands

---

16 Many qualifications are needed here, particularly concerning the defeasibility of the priority given to reasons that are thought to take deliberative priority. These issues will be returned to after a more technical apparatus for examining the notion of deliberative priority is introduced, in section §II(b).

in that kind of relation, a certain degree of deliberative priority. The *morally relevant* difference between the two kinds of relationships is that relations between friends are characterized by a greater degree of vulnerability and intimacy than relations between strangers. As intimacy grows, vulnerability increases, and with it increases the possibility of treating another in ways that fail the minimum requirements of respecting her status as a person. Or, put simply, there are more ways in which one person can be wronged by the other. Hence the more complex set of duties that characterize friendship, and the greater range of aspects of a friend's life that might give one reasons for action that take deliberative priority over other considerations.

Aspects of a stranger's plight do, however, sometimes take deliberative priority, where this priority is justified by what is required for relations between strangers to be characterized by mutual respect. It should be noted that in such situations the stranger is not seen under the description of a 'stranger', but some other impersonal characterization that makes clear why a certain aspect of that person's situation is a source of reasons for action that have priority over other reasons e.g. one doesn't see the drowning child as a 'stranger', but as a *drowning child*. For instance, say I am on my way to give a piano recital at the Sheldonian, where hundreds have gathered to hear me play, but on route I see someone collapse in the street. If I do not make some effort to help her (if only to call an ambulance), I have *wronged* that person. Her interest in being aided is a reason for me to aid her, and not to pursue some other course of action, *even if* my ignoring her plight by going on to give the piano recital would do much more good.[17]

Notice that one theoretical implication that has emerged as a consequent of consensualism's emphasis on the importance of duties and obligations for governing relations between individuals, is a rejection of the popular distinction between *general* obligations and *special* obligations.[18] General obligations are usually thought of as duties that we owe everyone, such as the duty not to cause unnecessary suffering, or the duty to donate to charities like Oxfam, while special obligations are usually thought to depend, in some way, on a special relationship that exists between the agent and the person to whom the obligation is owed. Duties that exist between family members is the most common example of what those who employ this distinction have in mind. Consequentialism, it is often argued, can give a compelling account of

---

[17] In none of the examples I offer do I want to suggest that a consequentialist cannot construct an explanation of the example within her own framework. What is important here are the differences in how the consensualist, as contrasted with the consequentialist, reaches the result she does, and not whether the example is one that cannot be explained on other grounds.

[18] Obligation is not, for purposes of this contrast, being used in the technical sense defined in chapter 1.

general obligations, but special obligations are difficult to account for. The difficulty they encounter with special obligations is this: comparing how well well-being can be promoted by devoting a disproportionate amount of one's attention to the well-being of one's family members, and devoting the equivalent amount of time to the well-being of strangers reveals no obvious rationale for devoting more time to promoting the well-being of family members. If anything, the comparison makes devoting the kind of attention to friends and loved ones we judge to be appropriate morally very dubious.

According to consensualism, the only important distinction between types of duties is one between the duties a person has because she has *voluntarily* undertaken that duty (obligations), and duties a person has which have no voluntariness condition that must be fulfilled in order to legitimately claim that a person is under such a duty (ordinary duties).[19] That there are differences in the duties we owe to strangers and the duties we owe to family members requires no special explanation in consensualism, as what we owe one another is said to be determined by the character of the relationship we stand in to another, not by how much we can do to promote well-being by treating that person in one way rather than another.

(b) In accepting certain principles as the basis of her practical deliberations, each party to the consensualist hypothetical consensus structures her practical deliberations such that the way in which the relevant aspects (and which aspects) of another's situation figure in her deliberations is determined by the *character* of her relationship with that person. *How* principles are able to serve in this role is best elucidated through the idea of an *exclusionary* reason.

An exclusionary reason is a kind of second order reason; in this case, a reason not to act on the basis of certain first order reasons. The idea can be made much clearer by way of a simple example:

> My father asks me to cut the grass this afternoon, and I vaguely indicate, without promising, that I will try. Before I set out to cut the grass, my friend rings and suggests that we go to the pictures. Going to the pictures will bring me and my friend a great deal of pleasure. I know I can cut the grass tomorrow morning (it's not going anywhere). Even though my father would like the grass cut this afternoon, no dire consequences, other than not having this desire satisfied, will follow (for him, at least) from the grass not being cut this afternoon. He has not, for instance, invited the neighbors over that evening to admire our splendid, freshly cut, lawn.

---

[19] Specifying the voluntariness condition that must be fulfilled to claim that one is under an obligation is a tricky business, raising substantive issues about free will. On this topic, see Scanlon's *The Significance of Choice*, esp. 177-201.

I decide, after due consideration, to go to the pictures.

Now, changing the example slightly, let us say that I *promised* my father that I would cut the grass this afternoon. The normative situation that now faces me has changed: there is a new factor to be taken into account, that if I go to the pictures, breaking my promise to my father, I will have *wronged* him. I may still decide, on the balance of reasons, to go to the pictures. But if I do go, it seems that I must either have a particularly good reason for going, one that my father would be unreasonable to reject as valid grounds for releasing me from my promise, or be prepared to have the trip to the pictures tainted by both feelings of guilt at having wronged my father, and concern over what justified criticism will await me the next day. Notice that it doesn't matter whether or not I believe my father *will* say anything; he may be very easy going about these things, or may be too preoccupied by important matters to even notice that I failed to keep my promise. What is important is that I will know that I have put myself in a position in relation to my father where he can justifiably criticize my actions.

The notion of my having *wronged* my father clearly does a lot of work in this example. But it isn't clear how the fact that, by breaking my promise, I will wrong my father changes the normative situation that confronts me. One strategy is to claim that an act being *wrong* is a reason of great, perhaps absolute, weight. But this strategy is too crude to make sense of the phenomenology of the situation. If I don't cut the grass, I will have wronged my father, but this is certainly a fairly trivial wrong. Claiming that an act being wrong is always a reason of great weight will not be able to make sense of the kind of judgments we make concerning gradations of wrong doing.

A consequentialist account of what the judgment of an act being wrong consists in does not help here, since on such an analysis it isn't clear what grounds there might be, in this case, for claiming that it would be wrong not to cut the grass, and instead go to the pictures, let alone claiming that it would be a serious wrong. Perhaps, since I promised to do so, my father formed a legitimate expectation that the grass will be cut, and will be disappointed if the grass isn't cut. But this disappointment can hardly be a serious, or crippling, disappointment, since it's only the grass, and nothing of significance rests on it being cut today. Or it could be, that by not keeping *this* promise, I will be considered less reliable in the future (though this is dubious, since it is just one instance of breaking a promise, and not a pattern). And in a similar vein, the damage my not keeping this promise will do to the institution of promise keeping seems trivial. There is no obvious basis, on a consequentialist analysis, in this example for claiming that the wrong of not cutting the grass would be a reason of great weight; in fact, it is difficult to see why not cutting the grass would be wrong at all.

An analysis of wrongness, such as the one offered by consensualism, does not have to claim that wrongness is a reason of great weight. An act is wrong, on this view, because it is disallowed by rules for the general regulation of behavior that no one can reasonably reject.[20] Central to this explanation of wrongness is understanding rules to have independent reason giving force, as *exclusionary reasons*.[21] What the rule does is alter the normative situation, by acting as a *second order reason*, a reason for acting on the reasons the rule recommends, *and* a reason for not acting on other reasons that, given the situation, are valid reasons for pursuing different courses of action than that which the rule recommends.[22] The rule itself is justified by further reasons, which justify the need for a rule that changes the normative situation that faces an agent in the way the rule is designed to do.

By altering the balance of reasons in this way, rules are able to give special prominence to certain reasons, not by changing their weight, but simply by introducing further reasons for not acting on competing reasons.[23] This allows the gravity of the wrong to be determined by consideration of the importance of the reasons that the rule does not rule out acting on (including the reasons it prompts one to act on, if it

---

20 Notice that this analysis results in a very straightforward explanation for the cognitivist character of moral claims like wrongness.

21 On exclusionary reasons, see: G.J. Warnock, *The Object of Morality* (London:Metheun & Co.) 1971. pg. 53-70; Joseph Raz, *Practical Reason and Norms* (Princeton:PUP) 1990. sect. 2.2,2.3 & 3.1; Raz, "Promises and Obligations" Hacker & Raz ed. *Law, Morality and Society* (Oxford:OUP) 1977. chpt. 12.

22 Much more needs to be said to do justice to the role of rules as exclusionary reasons in practical deliberation. For instance, it could be that what is important is that one does a certain act *for a certain reason*, one that the rule recommends, rather than some other reason that would result in the same act. To take a common example, giving money to charity because you feel you owe something to those less fortunate than yourself can be understood to be an act of compliance with a moral rule of beneficence. Giving money to charity because it will provide you a tax deduction, while it does the same amount of good, is mere conformity with the rule. One has done the right thing, but for the wrong reason. The point here is that sometimes the second order reasons that justify not acting on other considerations are not always meant to direct the agent away from a particular action. In some cases, the point of the rule may be to direct the agent to act *for a particular reason*, as acting for that reason is integral to the value of the act. For purposes of this discussion, these complexities are not essential, and I do not fully explore the many possibilities that need to be considered.

23 Again, there are important qualifications to be made here. Sometimes the reasons that justify the exclusionary rule might justify not *considering* reasons for certain courses of action in one's deliberations, while in other cases what may be important is not *acting* on those considerations. There is, for instance, nothing wrong in my considering breaking my promise to my father; it is only wrong to do so. On the other hand, there does seem to be something wrong in *contemplating* murdering someone, in order to advance one's goals, even if one decides not to do so.

24 An exclusionary rule could: (a) introduce first order reasons for doing a certain act, while bringing in second order reasons for not acting on (or considering) certain other first order reasons. (b) introduce only second order reasons for not acting on certain considerations, while leaving what ought to be done to the balance of remaining first order reasons (c) introduce second order reasons that would establish a *permission* for not being *required* to act on certain reasons.

prompts one to act on certain reasons), and by consideration of the degree to which not following the rule compromises the values that justify the rule.[24]

Reconsider, in light of this analysis of wrongness, the case of my father's lawn. When I *promise* my father that I will mow the lawn, I place myself in a relation to him in which he can legitimately expect me to mow the lawn. The moral rules that govern the intentional creation of legitimate expectations for one's own behavior in another are such that, in having put myself in a relationship with my father to which such rules apply, I now have reasons for fulfilling my father's legitimate expectations, and not acting on other considerations.[25] Breaking my promise, though wrong, is a trivial wrong. This can be explained by the fact that though my father is entitled to expect me to cut the grass, this is not something he attaches great importance to, especially as what matters to him is that the grass be cut, not that it be cut at a particular hour. Further, there are good reasons for me to do something else, namely go to the pictures.[26]

The role of rules (or principles), in practical deliberation, as exclusionary reasons, explains how it is that principles, adopted for the general regulation of behavior that no one can reasonably reject, shape our judgments of what we have reason to do. We see the interests (broadly conceived) of the person with whom we stand in a certain relation as providing reasons for us to do (or not do) certain things, while other considerations (themselves valid reasons) do not move us *because* of our relation to this person. Consider, for example, Bernard Williams's much celebrated "one thought too many" example:

> surely it would be absurd to insist that if a man could, at no risk or cost to himself, save one or two persons in equal peril, and one of those in peril was, say, his wife, he must treat both equally, perhaps by flipping a coin (Williams 1982,17; citing Fried, *An Anatomy of Values*).[27]

Williams's remarks that follow this passage suggest that he understands the man's rescue of his wife as beyond moral justification (Williams 1982,18). Part of the argument for this view consists of an attack on theoretical attempts (he mentions rule-utilitarianism) to offer a moral

---

[25] The reasons that justify such rules, and how best to specify such rules, is a complex matter. For an excellent discussion, see T.M. Scanlon, "Promises and Practices", *Philosophy and Public Affairs* Summer 1990.
[26] There is a gray area here as to when the competing reasons that pull against compliance with the rule serve as justification for being excluded from the requirements for the rule, and when those reasons explain the wrong doing in a sympathetic light , but do not justify the claim that the act, within the terms of the rule, was not wrong.
[27] Williams 1982: Bernard Williams, "Persons, character and morality", repr. in *Moral Luck* (Cambridge:CUP), 1982 1-19.

rationale for this decision, by citing a valid moral principle which made the man's rescue of his wife, in situations of the sort he found himself in, at least morally permissible (*ibid.*). This kind of view will, according to Williams, end up attributing to the man, as his *motivating* thought, one thought too many. For his motivating thought in saving his wife will be, not 'she is my wife', but 'she is my wife, and in situations of this kind it is permissible to save one's wife'.

It isn't clear why Williams thinks that fully spelling out the man's *motivating* thought will require mentioning 'in situations of this kind it is permissible to save one's wife'. Consensualism, for example, could claim that the man has internalized, as the basis of his practical deliberations, certain rules for how we should relate to one another, which in this case authorize (or perhaps require) him to save his wife *because* she is his wife, and justify his not being moved to act by the equally pressing interest in being saved of the other, who is a stranger to him.[28] In acting as he did, therefore, the man was simply being motivated by what he saw himself as having reason to do. What the rule explains here is how the man saw the normative situation that confronted him, including how he prioritized the various relevant reasons for acting. In reconstructing his thinking about what he has reason to do, then, there is no need to attribute to him any awareness, or thoughts, about the rules which structure his deliberations about what he has reason to do. This does not mean that he might not refer to those rules in moments of cool reflection, perhaps in the course of an argument with someone concerning the appropriate way to treat one's partner. It only means that a moral theory need not attribute to him any higher order thoughts about the appropriateness of being guided by certain rules at the time of acting.

Williams may have further reasons for believing that a moral theory is bound to distort the phenomenology of the situation in its attempt at reconstructing the example; those lines of argument cannot be pursued in this discussion. More pressing, though, is the consequentialist argument that the consensualist response to Williams relies on certain features of rules as exclusionary reasons, and not on any features of the theory that are distinctive of it.[29] A rule consequentialist, for example,

---

[28] To repeat a previous point: nothing in this is meant to suggest that there *is* a valid moral principle which will justify the rescuer's behavior. What is important is that consensualism allows for the *possibility* of such a principle. Evaluating the question of whether one would be required to save one's wife would require detailed consideration of principles governing mutual aid in multi-person scenarios.

[29] This is an objection that someone like Peter Railton, given his sophisticated consequentialism, might justifiably press. See his Peter Railton. "Alienation, Consequentialism, and the Demands of Morality." In *Consequentialism and its Critics*, ed. Samuel Scheffler. 93-133. Oxford: OUP, 1988. It is also one that Conrad Johnson could press; see his interesting discussion of rule consequentialism, which exploits the notion of an exclusionary reason to defend his version of rule consequentialism. Conrad Johnson, "The Authority of the Moral Agent", in Scheffler *op. cit.* pg. 261-287.

might agree with consensualism that there is a valid rule that explains why it is that the man's deliberations were, morally, in good order when he saved his wife, as what he had reason to do (or at least what it was permissible for him to do) was to save his wife. The consequentialist could claim, though, *contra* consensualism, that the justification for this rule is that it is a better world in which, in situations of the kind Williams is concerned with, a person sees herself as having reason to save her spouse, rather than a stranger.

What the indirect consequentialist has a harder time explaining is the thought, latent but not explicit in Williams's discussion, that something has gone wrong when, even in moments of cool reflection, the man pointing out that it was his wife he saved is not a sufficient justification for acting as he did. According to the indirect consequentialist, what justifies being motivated by the thought 'it's my wife', is that individuals being motivated by this thought results in the better promotion of well-being. The promotion of well-being, not the fact that it was his wife, does the justificatory work here. Consensualism, concerned with how individuals relate to one another, can attach a more immediate significance to claim that it was his wife as a justification for the man's actions. For in pointing out the relationship between himself and the person he saved, he draws attention to a principle, that no one could reasonably reject, that governs relations of that kind. The character of the relationship between husband and wife is what does the justificatory work here.

A distinction Raz offers may help clarify this point.[30] A person *conforms* with the reasons that apply to her if, by being motivated by considerations other than those reasons, she better achieves what she has reason to do. A person *complies* with reason if she is motivated *directly* by the thought of what she has reason to do. The indirect consequentialist justifies the man's motivating thought by the fact that this pattern of thinking results in him coming closer to achieving the goal that morality sets him, which is to promote well-being; in being moved to save his wife, then, the man conforms with reason. Consensualism can claim that the man is *complying* with reason, for in saving his wife because she is his wife, he is treating his wife with the kind of consideration that is owed her according to a principle, that no one can reasonably reject, governing the duties owed between spouses.[31] In saving his wife, the man is, according to consensualism, simply complying with the general aim of morality.

Exactly what considerations one can act on, and which must remain motivationally inert, if one is to comply with a rule, is an exer-

---

[30] Raz. 1990 pg. 178. The distinction is not a new one; Railton also expresses the idea, though his terminology of subjective and objective is more unwieldy.
[31] Of course, there may be no such principle; that is a matter for substantive argument.

cise in careful judgment and deliberation. Rules require judgment in order to perceive what facts about the particular situation one finds oneself in are relevant for compliance with the rule. Deliberation is required when one comes across new, unfamiliar, situations, or circumstances have changed such that the rule needs to be fine-tuned.[32] These are all situations in which what is called for is *further specification* of the rule, in which we re-consider how certain reasons ought to figure in our practical deliberations.[33] In other words, these are situations where we stop following the existing rule, and engage in moral argument to reach a consensus on a refined rule (or perhaps a successor rule), which will then be followed. Rules, in consensualism, may be fundamental, but they are not rigid.

Finally, the connection between rules and legitimate expectations can be further clarified. Rules for the general regulation of behavior are a basis for forming legitimate expectations about the conduct of others, as they provide a basis for anyone to judge what reasons there are for him to conduct himself in certain ways, given the kinds of relationships he stands in to others, and what reasons there are for others to conduct themselves in certain ways, depending on the kind of relationship they stand in to him. They also provide each person a basis of assessing, and if need be, arguing with others, concerning what reasons she has, and what reasons they have, to do certain things, or refrain from certain kinds of action.

§III

(a) Understanding the *aim* of the parties to the consensualist hypothetical consensus, and the role of rules in shaping a person's practical deliberations, are both necessary for defending the view that an adequate account of the role and importance of constraints and options in morality can be developed in a consensualist framework for moral argument. The task of presenting a complete account of this kind goes well beyond the scope of anything that can be presented here. In this part of the discussion, I will only sketch how the resources of consensualism can be harnessed to develop such an account.

I will approach this task by considering the question of what considerations are relevant for formulating within a consensualist framework valid principles to guide the reasoning of actors, with a simple example. Specifically, I will consider two lines of reasoning, the first of

---

[32] Recall here the connection between the adjustments to categories of relevant values in consensualism and the further specification, or fine-tuning, of rules.

[33] As Scanlon puts the point, "Principles represent complex, incompletely articulated pieces of [moral] argument about what authority to act it is reasonable to grant (and refuse to grant) one another" (Scanlon 1988b,136).

which suggests both that consensualism cannot offer an adequate explanation of options or constraints, and that moral principles that are defensible within a consensualist framework will be extremely demanding. The second line of reasoning, which emphasizes the importance of structuring our practical deliberations in such a way that we relate to one another on terms of mutual respect, suggests a strategy for understanding how options, constraints, and limits on the demandingness of morality might be justified in a consensualist framework. The first line of reasoning is, I believe, flawed, but exploring why this is so reveals much of the potential of consensualist moral argument for explaining the basis of the non-consequentialist features of morality.

The case I want to consider is one in which one person (call her Allie) will lose her life unless another person (call him Geoff) loses his arm.[34] On the first interpretation, which I will call the *complaint model* interpretation of consensualist moral reasoning, it seems that Allie can reasonably reject any principle that results in Geoff keeping his arm and her losing her life, as long as the causal connection between her not losing her life and Geoff losing his arm holds.[35] Geoff may complain that he doesn't want to lose his arm, but he cannot deny that it is worse for Allie to lose her life than it is for him to lose his arm.

Intuitively, this story seems underdetermined. What are the circumstances under which Allie is in danger of losing her life? How is Geoff's arm caused to be severed? Many will think that it does make a moral difference as to whether Geoff's arm was deliberately severed in order to save Allie's life, was severed in the process of saving Allie's life, or was not saved from being severed in order that Allie's life be saved. But the point of the example is that such details are not relevant if one accepts the *complaint model* interpretation.

---

[34] The details of the case are kept deliberately vague, especially concerning the circumstances under which Geoff loses his arm. This is necessary because on one straightforward reading of Scanlon's claim that, in rejecting a principle, one can only appeal to the potential effects of a proposed principle's adoption on oneself, no information other than that offered in the vague characterization of the situation is necessary. Non-consequentialists would insist that we need more information to judge this case. I agree, but want to argue that the relevance of these details can be justified *as relevant* within the consensualist framework for justification, and need not be *presupposed* by it as additional moral content.

[35] The term *complaint model* is borrowed from chpt. 6 of Parfit's *On Giving Priority to the Worse Off*. The *complaint model* interpretation, which has clear affinities with the "appeal to costs" view of moral argument that was criticized in chapter II §IV (b), combines three ideas: (a) that in consensualist moral argument, what one focuses on is the justifiability of particular *acts*, not *principles*, (b) that justification always involves appeals to potential losses (however calculated), and only potential losses, and (c) that only considerations concerning individual well-being are relevant for moral argument. (see chpt. II for discussion of the difference between (b) and (c)). Note that my use of the term *complaint model* is not identical to Parfit's, as his discussion emphasizes a particular way of appealing to losses, one which requires that calculation of a loss take into account both a person's absolute level and the difference between how well off she will be under the proposed principle and her proposed alternative. For purposes of this discussion, this aspect of the *complaint model* can be set aside.

The understanding of consensualist moral argument at work here is one in which consensualism, like consequentialism, appeals to the consequences that result from a principle being adopted, as the grounds for the principle's justification. Rather than judging these outcomes by ranking their potential aggregate value relative to the potential aggregate value of outcomes that would obtain from the adoption of some other principle(s), consensualism judges outcomes by considering their acceptability to each person, judging the best outcome as one which is least unacceptable to the person to whom it is most unacceptable.[36] By this standard, the best outcome is surely one in which Geoff loses his arm and Allie preserves her life. The other possibilities, principles which result in Geoff, perhaps, keeping his arm, will all result in outcomes that are more unacceptable to Allie, since they are outcomes in which she faces the prospect of death.

Before accepting this conclusion, though, it is worth reconsidering the way the *complaint model* approach works, in order to assess whether the line of reasoning that leads to the conclusion that Geoff's arm is forfeit is really as sound as it appears to be.

It starts by considering a situation in which one person must lose his arm if another is not to lose her life. The question is then asked "can anyone reasonably reject a principle (for application to our imperfect world) which justifies the loss of her arm in order that someone else's life be saved?". The conclusion is supposed to be "no": no one can reject a principle under which she loses her arm if the complement set of principles all result in someone else losing her life. This conclusion follows from comparing the possible outcomes that might follow from the initial situation in which the question was posed. In one possible outcome, one person is dead and another keeps his arm, while in the other, both are alive but one lacks an arm. It is reasonable to judge that anyone would find an outcome in which she is dead more unacceptable than an outcome in which she is alive but missing an arm, and so it follows that Geoff cannot reasonably reject a principle under which he loses his arm, if on every alternative principle Allie loses her life.

Is this conclusion as sound as it appears? Perhaps not. The first move in the argument—in which the question of whether or not a principle that morally justifies the loss of the arm can be reasonably rejected—is sound, in so far as consensualism is an account of *moral reasoning*, and there is certainly no reason in principle for not engaging in

---

[36] An interpretation suggested by Nagel's discussion of unanimity in his "Equality" pg. 117, in Thomas Nagel. "Equality." In *Mortal Questions*, 106-127. Cambridge: Cambridge University Press, 1979. Scanlon, in "Contractualism and Utilitarianism" pg. 123 , also suggests a view along these lines. I have argued, in chpt. 2, that this view is not an essential feature of consensualism, and there are good reasons for rejecting it as part of the theory.

critical reflection about moral requirements in a difficult situation, where the stakes are obviously high.

The second move is more questionable, as it does not clearly distinguish between considering which act no one could reasonably reject, and which *principle for the general regulation of behavior* no one could reasonably reject. The two notions are quite different. For in considering the rejectability of different principles it is appropriate to consider, not the different *outcomes* that may result from an action, but the different *social worlds* that would result from the adoption of different principles for the general regulation of a certain kind of behavior. This points to the range of considerations that are potentially relevant for assessing whether or not principles can be reasonably rejected being much wider in scope than *complaint model* approach would suggest. For instance, if his arm is lost because it is required by a morally authoritative principle, Geoff will justifiably be concerned about the broader implications for the kind of world it is he will live in, in which principles for the general regulation of behavior justify his arm being severed. He will be concerned, for instance, both with what individuals being morally required to act for certain reasons will require of him, and what might happen to him as a result of those principles being accepted, both as a direct *effect* of the principle and as a consequence of the kind of world that *results* from the general acceptance of such a principle.

The breadth of the types of considerations that might be judged relevant in considering what a social world would be like should not be underestimated. For instance, as an agent, Geoff will not only be concerned about how the relevant principle affects his pursuit of his goals and projects, but how he is likely to behave, or treat others, in an effort to comply with the principle. Depending on what the principle requires of him, or allows him to do, Geoff, in his efforts to comply, may end up systematically undermining his relations with others, by continually wronging them. This would not be due to any maliciousness on Geoff's part, but due to Geoff's average, and thus limited, ability to make fine grained discriminations in a short time, his natural tendency to sometimes panic and thus misjudge a situation, and the limited amount of information that Geoff is able to marshal at his fingertips at short notice.[37] This concern is only compounded in considering what social relations would be like with everyone acting on this principle.

There is a third move in the argument that also deserves scrutiny. It is the move which directs our attention, in evaluating the reasonable

---

[37] Here, I agree with the rule consequentialist, who claims that general facts about human capabilities, and their *limitations and frailties* will have an important influence in shaping the principles that fix what is right and wrong. The fact that moral reasoning is concerned with principles for application to the world as we know it makes these considerations particularly relevant.

rejectability of a principle that requires that Geoff's arm be sacrificed, to the potential consequences, from general acceptance of that principle, for each person's well-being. This would be a legitimate move *if* one could help oneself to the claim that each individual should judge the non-rejectability of a principle by the implications (broadly construed) of its acceptance for her well-being. But this is something that cannot be presumed. A person may care about more than the consequences of the general acceptance of a principle for her well-being; she may, for instance, be concerned with the character of the principle itself. In particular, it is perfectly reasonable for her to take into account, in her assessment of whether or not she has reasonable grounds for rejecting a principle, to consider the kinds of reasons the principle endorses (or rules out) acting on. For example, if Geoff's arm is severed in order to save Allie's life, he may find the loss of his arm more justifiable than if the causal connection between the loss of his arm and the saving of Allie's life is more indirect, as in a case where the saving of Allie's life is not intended but is merely a foreseen side effect of chopping off his arm.[38]

The *complaint model* interpretation of how moral argument proceeds in a consensualist framework, then, should be rejected on two counts. First, it fails to respect the importance of the fact that the principles are for the general regulation of behavior. Second, it limits, without justification, the sorts of considerations a person might take into account in assessing a principle to the *consequences* of the acceptance of that principle for her well-being. This is an unduly restrictive requirement: it is morally relevant to the assessment of principles that individuals care about more than just what happens, they also care about how it happens and the degree to which they are able to control what happens to them. An adequate interpretation of how consensualist moral argument works should not, without justification, exclude these sorts of considerations from the class of reasonable considerations that a person might cite in rejecting a principle.

(b) What is appealing in the *complaint model* interpretation becomes clearer if one considers the following problem: suppose we decide that, in fact, Geoff is not required to forfeit his arm so that Allie's life may be spared. How can one justify the principle which leads to this conclusion to Allie? What reasons can we offer for her to accept a principle whose general acceptance results in her death, while some other principle would result in her living and someone else merely los-

---

[38] Geoff justifying the loss of his arm to himself by the thought that at least it was lost in the name of saving a life is not, in an important sense, the same as Geoff thinking "well, at least the loss of my arm did some good". "Doing some good" might involve small benefits accruing to large numbers as the result of the loss of his arm. This might be thought to be no justification at all.

ing his arm? Though it may seem an unfair question to press, there is certainly nothing which says that one cannot engage in consensualist moral reasoning in moments of crisis. Further, valid moral principles are principles that must be justifiable to each person, from her own point of view, with no informational restrictions. In Allie's case, this requires that a justification be available, to be offered to Allie, that will justify to her a principle, for general acceptance, which she knows results in death. Appealing to what she *would* accept if she didn't know that she was about to die is, therefore, ruled out as a justificatory strategy.[39] If this strategy is blocked, a principle whose validity could be justified to Allie does not appear to be available. The *complaint model* interpretation, even it arrives there in the wrong way, does seem to reach the inevitable conclusion.

There is a way of vitiating this conclusion, for a strategy for justifying to Allie the principle that results in her own death is available if one employs what I will refer to as the *alternative social worlds* approach to consensualist moral argument. This approach emphasizes the idea that consensualism is concerned with principles for the general regulation of behavior, which structure how the relevant aspects of another's situation are to figure in a person's practical deliberations. The acceptability of the principles is evaluated according to the kinds of relations between individuals such principles both establish and allow. On this approach, the relevant question in assessing a principle is not 'what are the implications of this principle for me *at this moment*', but 'what will the world be like, and what kinds of life will be possible in this world, compared to a world in which some other principle is accepted as part of the general regulation of behavior?'.[40,41]

The explanation that this approach suggests of why Allie does not have reason to reject a principle which potentially results in her death, is that her reasons for accepting the principle in the first place concern the desirability of relating to others in the way that the principle makes

---

[39] Judith Thomson uses such a strategy in her discussion of the Trolley Problem. See Judith Jarvis Thomson. *The Realm of Rights*. Cambridge: Harvard University Press, 1990, pg. 187-196.
[40] Scanlon says that an act is wrong if it is disallowed by any *system of rules* for the general regulation of behavior. Though I haven't made much of this point, it is important to note its significance. Since the unit of assessment is the character of the life that can be led, the interlocking (or holistic) character of rules in structuring what is possible becomes very important. For instance, how one assesses rules governing divorce depends in part on the rules governing marriage; the two cannot be separated from one another in moral assessment.
[41] This approach clearly makes sense in a theory like consensualism, which emphasizes the importance of rules for the general regulation of behavior. Others have also found it appealing, though harder to motivate. For instance, see Scheffler's latest thoughts, concerning the importance of evaluating the costs of permissions at the level of a *practice* of individuals having such a permission, rather than on a case by case basis. Samuel Scheffler. "Prerogatives without Restrictions." In *The Rejection of Consequentialism*, 167-192. 2nd ed. Oxford: OUP, 1994.

possible, and living her life in the kind of world that will result from the general acceptance of that principle. Comparing what the quality of life for a person (evaluated from the point of view of the person's concern to live a rationally self-directed good life), as a *patient* and as an *agent*, would be like in two alternative worlds, one in which there is a valid principle requiring one to sacrifice limbs in order to save others from death, and another in which there is no such principle, Geoff might claim that the quality of life for a person is better in a world without such a requirement than with such a requirement.

If Geoff is right about this, it is open to him to argue that there are reasons that justify a principle, as one that no one can reasonably reject, that does not require Geoff to volunteer his arm. Allie's imminent death does not change the fact that, even from her point of view, these are reasons that justify the principle as valid. Allie would, of course, contest this claim. If Geoff is right, she cannot deny that there are good reasons that favor a principle that does not require him to make a sacrifice, but she can argue that the importance of these reasons, in comparison with the importance of securing conditions in which the evil of an early and unwelcome death is minimized, have been vastly overestimated. For the argument to be completely impartial, of course, she would have to argue that no one can deny that it is more important to be as secured against the prospect of an early and unwelcome death as possible, than it is to avoid the kinds of consequences that, as Geoff has pointed out, would be a consequence of living in a world with this kind of security. This is important if she is to avoid the charge that she has only arrived at this view because she faces an imminent death.[42]

There may also be other implications of a practice of not requiring that limbs be sacrificed for lives (of the kind surveyed earlier) that Geoff may have ignored, that may contribute to the force of Allie's argument in favor of a suitable principle that would make it wrong for Geoff to not be required to give up his arm. This points to a virtue of this approach to consensualist moral argument: it makes the circumstances of a person's death relevant to moral assessment of a person's death, which is in line with common sense morality.

---

[42] Having to argue in terms of the importance that anyone attaches to avoiding an early and preventable death, where prevention does not actually require that another life be sacrificed, will mean that the full importance for Allie (who is facing an imminent departure) of not dying will not carry over into moral argument (see related comments in chpt. 2, §II(d)). This may be thought to introduce a kind of 'veil of ignorance' into consensualist moral reasoning. The term, however, is not apt. For though parties to the consensualist hypothetical consensus are required to employ a degree of abstraction in their reasoning about principles, they are not required to reason as if they did not know who they are (which is what Scanlon criticizes Rawls for in his use of the veil of ignorance device). The use of abstraction in consensualism is not, therefore, susceptible to the same criticisms of the veil of ignorance device that leads Scanlon to reject Rawls's employment of it.

(c) The *alternative social worlds* approach to consensualist moral argument allows consensualism to fulfill its promise of explaining some of the features of common sense morality that non-consequentialists draw attention to. That this is so becomes clear by considering different variants of the initial Geoff and Allie scenario, in which the circumstances under which Geoff loses his arm vary. These circumstantial details are relevant under the *alternative social worlds* interpretation, and are crucial for the justification of options and constraints.

Let us say that the situation is one in which Geoff and Allie are both being threatened by a large dog, who is about to bite one of them. Some third party can save one of them from being bitten, but not the other (with 100% reliability). Allie is allergic to dog bites: if bitten, she will die, while if Geoff is bitten, he will only lose his arm. Can Geoff reasonably reject a principle that requires that the person who is aided be the one who has the most to lose from not being aided? It isn't clear what kind of argument he would offer for reasonably rejecting such a principle. The situation of the two parties is completely symmetrical, so here it seems appropriate to authorize the third party to decide whom to aid by comparing potential losses.

Notice, though, that the principle Geoff cannot reject is one which says (very roughly) "when separate parties are in symmetrical positions in relation to a source of aid, help the one who will gain the most from being aided".[43] This is a crude principle; further examples could be considered to direct its elaboration. But crucial to it is that the parties are in *symmetrical positions in relation to aid*. This is, to use the language of the deontologists, a case where the harm that will arise to one of the parties, from not being aided, is foreseen, but not intended.[44]

---

[43] Note that in consensualist moral argument, there is no prima facie requirement to *promote* anything. The fact that an action will do some good may well be a reason to do that action; what consensualist moral argument tries to establish is whether or not one is required to act on that reason, or one is required not to act on that reason, or whether it is permissible for one to be indifferent to that reason. One way of describing this is that consensualism here exploits a contrast between the right and the good.

[44] This might suggest that the relevance of a distinction between foreseen harm and intended harm is being imported into consensualist moral argument. This is not so, if this is a claim that the intending/foreseeing distinction cannot be defended as morally relevant, through consensualist moral argument. What is being assumed here is that a principle recognizing the relevance of the intending/foreseeing distinction can be produced as a product of consensualist moral argument, and this principle is being brought into moral argument over the formulation of a principle for a different kind of situation. There is nothing wrong with bringing into an argument over one kind of principle other principles of the moral system; one is simply assuming the truth of those other beliefs whose truth one has no reason to doubt, while trying to determine the truth of a matter over which there is confusion and doubt. In this way, moral argument in consensualism bears some resemblance to questions of distributive justice, familiar from the writings of Rawls and Dworkin, where no distributive entitlements are assumed, but principles specifying personal responsibility are assumed in the background of the process of working out what each person's entitlement is.

Consider another variation of the core scenario. This time, Allie is being threatened by the infamous dog, and will die if bitten—and she surely will be bitten unless something happens. Geoff happens to wander on to the scene. There is no prior relationship between him and Allie, and Geoff occupies no special role, such as being a policeman (a necessary assumption to avoid complications that might arise in considering duties of police officers to citizens). Geoff is made aware, by her pleas for help, of the potential implications for Allie's being bitten. The only way the dog can be prevented from biting Allie is if Geoff puts himself between Allie and the dog, in which case the dog will satisfy himself by biting off Geoff's arm. Can Geoff reasonably reject a principle which *requires him* to put himself between Allie and the dog?

Now, on a straight comparison of potential losses (as the *complaint model* approach would recommend), the situation has remained unchanged from the previous scenario. But the principle under which Geoff loses his arm is quite different. It is no longer a principle specifying the duty of a third party in a situation where she can help one but not both. Rather, it is a principle of mutual aid, requiring Geoff to make a sacrifice in order to prevent another person's loss. Such a principle can very roughly be glossed as follows:

> *Rough Mutual Aid Principle:* Each person is *required* to always do what is necessary to prevent another from incurring a significant loss, provided she can do so at a cost to herself that is less significant.[45]

Does characterizing the situation as one of mutual aid make a difference to the sorts of arguments Geoff can offer for reasonably rejecting

---

[45] This principle in some ways resembles an act-utilitarian principle of beneficence. It can, plausibly, be argued that the appropriate principle to consider here is a much more specific principle, applicable to the specific situation that Allie finds herself in. Such situations are *so* rare, that it isn't obvious how Allie could lose her argument with Geoff over what is morally required of him. This is an important point, as it focuses attention on a point about the role of principles in consensualism that it shares with many rule-consequentialist theories: one of the benefits of rules in practical deliberation is that they make us immediately responsive to morally relevant considerations, without having to engage in time consuming deliberations. If this benefit of "deliberative economy" is to be realized, the rules need to be general enough to help guide our actions in the *general* sorts of situations we encounter. Generating many specific rules to cover specific situations would result in the loss of this benefit. Parties to the consensualist hypothetical consensus are concerned to preserve this benefit of being guided in one's actions by rules. Hence I think it more plausible to discuss the Geoff and Allie scenario in terms of a fairly general rule which is being *applied* to this specific case, as this is closer to the kind of rule that the parties are likely to agree to. Further, nothing rests, in this example, in Geoff winning the argument with Allie: what is important to see here is that there are many considerations that are potentially relevant that the *complaint model* interpretation does not account for. (on the benefit of rules in deliberation for ordinary life, see R.M. Hare's "Ethical Theory and Utilitarianism", repr. in Sen and Williams ed. *Utilitarianism and Beyond* (Cambridge:CUP) 1982. 23-38).

a principle that results in the loss of his arm? Intuitively it does, for most would see Geoff's act of intervention as *supererogatory*. If Geoff intervenes to save Allie's life, citing as his reason for doing so the fact that it is worse for Allie to lose her life than it is for him to lose his arm, then we can say that Geoff acted for what are clearly morally sound reasons. But we don't think that Geoff was *required* to act for these reasons; rather, most would intuitively say that he had a *choice* as to whether or not to act on those reasons.

What argument could Geoff give for not being required to act on the reasons cited, but instead having a choice of whether to act on these reasons? One set of considerations, directly relevant given Geoff's normative status as a person, concern autonomy: it is reasonable for people to want to have sufficient control over the course of their lives, that they are able to make and execute plans, and to some extent have the course of their lives dictated by choices they make. A principle requiring one to intervene at significant cost to oneself, in order to save another from a greater cost whenever one is in a position to do so, would seriously jeopardize this important interest. This is not only due to the cost to oneself of no longer having an arm, which will require some serious changes in one's future plans, but the costs of constant diligence as one moves about in the streets, keeping one's eyes open for situations in which one can intervene to save someone from a loss at a lesser loss to oneself. Not to mention the insecurity and worry of not being able to make plans for the future, never knowing what situations one might encounter in the execution of those plans which will require either a major deviation from them, or abandonment of them, and the stress induced by constantly having to make rough estimates of comparative costs.

It is important here that the action required is at a *significant* cost to oneself, for it is the significance of the cost to oneself that, in part, gives weight to the appeal to autonomy-type interests. Losing one's arm seriously affects a person's future life. This suggests that the principle should be altered, to say

> Mutual Aid Principle #2: a person must do what is necessary to prevent a significant loss to someone else when she can do so at a *much less* significant cost to herself.

On this principle, the kind of intervention that is required of Geoff may involve him signaling for a policeman, yelling for assistance, or using a gun in his possession at the time to shoot the dog before it bites Allie; his case for here reasonably rejecting the principle would appear to be weaker. This is because, though he would still have a claim to reject the principle on the grounds of autonomy interests, the seriousness of the infringement of autonomy interests would be significantly weakened, strengthening Allie's case for a right to be aided.

Geoff, however, could attack this principle on the grounds that his autonomy interests only *appear* to constitute a less serious objection to this principle *in this case*, as what he has to do in order to save Allie's life is fairly minor, not constituting much of an interference with his life. However, the mutual aid principle is still one that he has to live with long after Allie has been saved, so other kinds of situations he might encounter throughout his life should be considered in assessing the reasonable rejectability of mutual aid #2. For example, let us say that Geoff is a world renowned experimental psychologist, who has a deserved reputation for his skill as a critic. Younger psychologists, struggling to make a name for themselves in the field, frequently send him papers to read and comment on. It doesn't require much effort on Geoff's part to comment on these drafts, and his comments will, in most cases, *dramatically* improve the quality of a paper. The improvement in the quality of a paper, though it costs Geoff little, is very significant for the young researcher whose paper it is, as the difference between a good paper and an excellent paper, early on in one's career, could mark the difference between establishing a reputation and not having a reputation as a good researcher.

Now, Geoff could object that mutual aid #2 will *require* him to comment on all such papers that pass his desk. But this, he can plausibly argue, is a principle he could reasonably reject, on the grounds that his incurring a duty to every young researcher who sends him a paper, *just* by that researcher having sent him a paper, constitutes an unreasonable interference with his life. It should be up to him whether or not he comments on the paper; others should not be able to obligate him *just* by sending him something to read through the mail.

The difficulty with mutual aid #2, that Geoff's example draws attention to, is that the question of whether a person is under a certain duty is determined solely by comparing costs. The greater the difference between what it costs one to help, compared with what the other stands to gain (or avoid losing), the more likely it is that one will be under a duty to help. In some cases, this leads to the intuitively right result, but in other cases not. Given that it is more likely that Geoff will frequently have papers sent to him than he will encounter people whose lives are in peril, it appears that Geoff has a strong case for reasonably rejecting mutual aid #2, in favour of a principle which gives him a *choice* of whether or not to aid Allie.

Allie here has a powerful reply available to her. Geoff's example gains much of its plausibility from both the fact that his abilities are such that it costs him (in time and effort) very little to help others a great deal, and there are a great many who could profit a great deal from his devoting a very small amount of time and effort to helping them. Most, however, will not be as gifted as Geoff, so the general acceptance of mutual aid #2 will not result in the needs of others generating so many valid claims on their time and resources that they are unable to effectively pursue their own projects. If anything, general acceptance of mutual aid #2 has the potential to greatly enhance each person's life, as each will be assured of a greater degree of assistance from others in the pursuit of her goals. This isn't to deny that Geoff, and those in a similar position, do not have a valid grievance against mutual aid #2. But the appropriate response to this is not its outright rejection, but the emendation of the principle by the addition of a clause which places a limit of the cumulative amount of good that a person can be required to do by this principle. The addition of this clause will prevent mutual aid #2 from becoming particularly burdensome for those in Geoff's position, who are unusually capable of benefiting others with little effort.

There are serious objections to this proposal as stated. Let us say that Geoff lives in a leafy suburb, located on the edge of a large artificial lake, and home to an unusual number of families with very young children. Unfortunately for Geoff, rarely a week goes by where he does not encounter, on his way to the lab, a child drowning in the lake, who will die if he does not rush to her aid. Since Geoff is a strong swimmer, with a good grasp of basic lifesaving techniques, he is able to save drowning children with little risk to his own life. Now, under Allie's proposed revision to mutual aid #2, Geoff will quickly reach the threshold over which more cannot be demanded of him on the basis of this principle. He will then be in a position to justify not even trying to save further drowning children he may encounter by citing the number of children he has already saved. But this is clearly an unacceptable conclusion. Geoff may be very *unlucky* insofar as fate continuously puts drowning children in his path, but that does not *excuse* him from his duty to make an effort to save every drowning child he encounters.

What has gone wrong in Allie's reply to Geoff is that it assumes that Geoff's objection to mutual aid #2 appeals to the cumulative effect on his life of the burdens he may potentially be required to bear as a result of its general acceptance. But that is not Geoff's only concern. What he is concerned about is the character of the social world that will result from the general acceptance of mutual aid #2, one in which the number of *involuntarily acquired* duties that persons owe one another will increase dramatically. For many, though perhaps not for Geoff, the increased number of duties will not be an overall burden; as Allie has pointed out, many stand to benefit a good deal from the assistance they will be in a position to demand of others. What will be true for all, however, is that each will have less control over their responsibilities to others, or the extent to which they can be held accountable by others for their actions.

This is what worries Geoff. It is not just the burden of having to read all those papers that he is concerned about, but the fact that another can change the normative character of the relationship between them in way that increases his degree of accountability to her, *without* his consent. She need only drop an envelope in the post to bring about such a change. Given their normative status as persons who value control over their lives, this is something that parties to the hypothetical consensus certainly have reason to be alarmed about.

One does not, of course, always have control over how accountable one is to others. Geoff's encounters with the drowning children are an example of this. He has a duty to help them, even though he does not choose to put himself in a position where he is able to help: he literally stumbles into situations where he involuntarily acquires the weighty duty of trying to save another's life. A duty to save someone's life when one is in a position to do so with little or no risk to one's own life, though, is a duty that can be understood to be one that is owed another out of minimal respect for her status as a person. And this fact is essential for justifying to Geoff (or anyone) why no one could reasonably reject a principle which placed them under a standing, non-voluntary, duty of this form. It is also one that is not available for use in the justification to Geoff of the principle which allows young psychologists to impose a duty upon him to read their work; while death undermines the self-directed pursuit of a good life, not benefiting from another's expertise will, at worst, result in one's life being less successful than it otherwise might have been. But mutual aid #2 is insensitive to this difference, as on that principle what one is required to do for another as a matter of duty is determined by appealing only to relative costs.

Not all duties we owe one another concern matters that are basic to the rationally self-directed pursuit of a good life. However, these sorts of duties are duties we tend to owe to another as part of voluntarily entered into relationships, such as contractual obligations, or ongoing valuable relationships e.g. duties we owe to family members or friends, distinguished by a shared history from the kinds of relationships that obtain between strangers. Another implication of mutual aid #2 that Geoff can object to, is that it will result in a social world in which the boundaries between these different valuable ways of relating to one another are blurred. It may even be that certain kinds of relationships will no longer even be live options, as the duties that once distinguished those ways of relating to others no longer distinguish them as particular types of relationships. For example, it may be that reading and offering detailed comments on the work of a younger colleague is something Geoff chooses to do as a way of entering into a relationship of friend and mentor to that young colleague. Mutual aid #2, by requiring Geoff to comment on all papers he can easily improve, will eliminate the relationship-creating significance of his commenting on another's work. As someone concerned to lead a good life, Geoff can certainly object to a principle which reduces the ways in which he can form valuable relationships, and may even eliminate some valuable forms of relationship that can obtain between individuals.

In light of these criticisms, Allie may want to put forward a more plausible mutual aid principle, which avoids the objections that Geoff's second example raises, such as

> *The Restricted Mutual Aid Principle*: Each person is required to intervene to prevent a very significant *harm* befalling someone else, even if there is a *potential* for significant harm to oneself, or one *will* incur a *much* less significant harm to oneself, than the harm the other person faces, in circumstances where (a) one just happens to encounter someone in a desperate situation, and (b) there is no one else who can help that person.[46]

Here she has a much stronger case, as this principle, though still very crude, has a great deal of intuitive plausibility. It may still require that Geoff sacrifice his arm, but the best thing to say about that may be that the problem is not with the principle, but with the unfortunate, and rare, circumstances the world has thrown in Geoff's way. The principal improvement to this principle, which defuses Geoff's previous objections, is that it has moved away from *just* appealing to costs, and towards imposing a duty on Geoff only when certain values are at stake. Formulating this principle in terms of harm is still very crude. Further elaboration of it would require considering more examples, on the basis of which specific categories of relevant harm may be identified. The task of developing plausible principles of mutual aid, within a consensualist framework, is too large a task to be pursued in this discussion. But the discussion so far points in the direction that such a task should proceed, away from principles which appeal to costs, *contra* the *complaint model* approach, and towards principles which appeal to specific goods and values.[47]

Notice that the kinds of considerations, canvassed as relevant in trying to develop a non-rejectable principle of mutual aid, suggest the direction that it would be most plausible to take when considering the best formulation of other moral principles which, potentially, could be very demanding. Consider, for example, principles concerning what we

---

[46] I am assuming here that no one else is in a position to help. Further specification of this principle would have to consider the issue of *if*, and if so, *how* the presence of others who are in a position to help change one's duty. In particular, the question of how the willingness of others to help affects one's duty would need to be considered.

[47] Recall here the conclusions of chpt. 2. §IV(b).

owe others in nations stricken by famine, overpopulation problems, and natural disasters.[48] Utilitarian theorists have long argued that our present levels of aid to these nations hardly scratch the surface of what we must do if we are to fulfill our duties to the people of these nations. Consensualism need not dispute this claim (as it's hard to believe that there isn't a great deal of truth in it). What can be insisted upon, though, is that principles governing what we owe to others in these nations be at least reasonably compatible with one's own self-directed pursuit of valuable projects. Such a compatibility is possible when all are aware of what can be reasonably expected (i.e. demanded) of them in, for instance, their contributions to third world aid organizations like Oxfam. Once legitimate expectations have been fixed, and assuming that the demands are not so onerous that they force everyone to pursue high wage careers in order to fulfill their duties, it is perfectly reasonable to expect each person to organize her pursuits in a way that will allow her to fulfill her duty.

The emphasis on compatibility becomes particularly relevant when considering the formulation of principles concerning our duties to others at times of *disaster*, compared with our duties to others who are the victims of systemic poverty. A consequentialist, when the numbers victimized by the disaster are suitably large, cannot distinguish the two kinds of case. But a consensualist can argue that our duties to disaster victims are, arguably, lower than what we owe to those who live in conditions of endemic poverty, even though their level of well-being, relative to our own, may be identical. This is because principles which required us to respond to sudden shifts in the quality of life of large populations in other nations, by making charitable contributions that would make it possible for those populations to be restored to a decent standard of living, may frustrate our abilities to conceive, with the reasonable hope of being able to succeed in, the kinds of valuable projects that require long-term planning and resource management. Principles that make our duties to others overly sensitive to the bad luck of others can, plausibly, be reasonably rejected.

This argument may strike some as surprising: isn't it more plausible to argue that one is required to contribute more heavily to disaster cases, but less in the battle against systemic poverty? After all, it is more likely that contributing only in disaster cases will end up costing a person less, over the course of a lifetime, than giving money to fight poverty. The difficulty with this argument, though, is that the relevance of what contributing costs a person has yet to be established. The original argument is based on the importance of being able to avoid disruptive

---

[48] I am grateful here to Tim Mulgan, who pressed me to say something about this question. This is a very cursory treatment of this subject, as there are many other issues that need to be addressed, such as what difference, if any at all, the distance makes in our duty to aid.

duties; contributing only in disaster situations may be less costly, but it is not less disruptive.

Another difficulty with this argument that will strike many as important is that it suggests that the moral principles that can be justified on consensualist grounds may still be very demanding. This is quite plausible, if what is meant by 'demanding' is that compliance with certain principles may be very costly. But on this view, compliance will at least not be incompatible with many of the pursuits and relationships that give life meaning. Or, at least, not as incompatible as the two are on many utilitarian accounts of morality.[49]

Finally, it is important to be clear that the argument does not suggest that there are not very good, and forceful, reasons for contributing as much as one is capable of when disaster strikes. All that is being claimed is that what is required of one by the standards that regulate interpersonal conduct in disaster cases is less than what is required of one in the ongoing war against systemic poverty.

Much more needs to be said about principles of mutual aid to even begin to adequately develop plausible principles in a consensualist framework. The reason for sketching how such arguments may proceed is that they show, first, why it is reasonable to think that a moral system constituted by principles no one could reasonably reject could include *permissions*. Second, it shows that consensualist moral argument is most plausibly thought of as not appealing to costs in the way the *complaint model* interpretation suggests it does. One does not have to find the suggested principles and arguments concerning mutual aid convincing to accept these conclusions.

(e) The kind of justification that it has been suggested Geoff should offer to Allie, as grounds for her acceptance of a principle that will result in Allie *not being wronged* if Geoff does not help her, appeals to the importance of autonomy. The importance of not adopting a principle that seriously compromises an individual's autonomy is something that it is thought that Allie, from her point of view, cannot reasonably deny.

Now, someone may be willing to accept the plausibility of this line of argument, yet insist that it does not do enough to explain the puzzling features of common sense morality that non-consequentialists struggle to defend. For what the above argument establishes is that there are reasons why Geoff should not be morally obligated to *intervene*. This does not establish that there are limits on what might be

---

[49] Arguably, if the initial argument is plausible, the pursuit of many sorts of goods and activities will not be compatible with compliance e.g. certain kinds of resource intensive artistic endeavours. This may well be true; whether it is an objection requires more detailed consideration of principles of aid than can be pursued in this discussion.

done to Geoff *in order to help Allie*. The contrast might be put as follows: though reasons (such as those canvassed above) can be offered for options and certain limits on the stringency on the demands of morality, there do not appear to be similar reasons that will justify constraints.

To focus on the issues that the constraint case raises, consider another variation on the basic scenario, in which Allie, in order to *save her life*, grabs Geoff, and propels him in front of the villainous, and this time, *very hungry* dog, knowing that he does not have to fear death from a dog bite, but, at worst, the loss of his arm.[50]

Allie, in her defense, claims that she has not wronged Geoff in acting as she did. For it was an emergency situation, and if she had not acted as she did, she would have died. There does, however, seem to be something wrong in Allie having acted this way. It is one thing for *Geoff* to sacrifice himself to the dog's jaws in order to save Allie, but quite another to have Allie volunteer him as her hero without consulting him first.

What reasons are there for thinking that Allie's action was wrong? Following the previous strategy, what is sought here are reasons, that no one could reasonably reject, for a principle which, in situations such as the one we are considering, requires that Geoff have a certain amount of control, or authority, over what may be done to him, or how he may permissibly be treated by others. This principle would allow Geoff to claim that Allie has wronged him by *acting as she did*, even though it was in pursuit of the worthy goal of saving her own life.[51]

It is not clear, however, what reasons Geoff would have for objecting to a quite limited principle which made it permissible for one person to harm another, either directly or through the use of some tool, in an emergency circumstance, where harming the person is the only way to prevent a loss of life. Such a principle need not fall directly afoul of the autonomy considerations canvassed earlier. For the principle does not require Geoff to be on the lookout for possible occasions where he may be required to help, nor will it, if carefully stated, leave Geoff in a constant state of low level panic, expecting some kind of harm to befall him at any moment, in the name of preventing an even greater harm befalling someone else. A carefully stated principle would make the probability of anyone actually being harmed to prevent another from

---

[50] The proviso that the dog be *very hungry* is crucial for Allie's act to be one which can be characterized as her having intended that Geoff's arm be sacrificed to the dog; without this stipulation, one might say that the harm done to Geoff was foreseen, but not intended harm, which may, potentially, offer Allie lines of defense that cannot be adequately explored in this discussion.

[51] Note that the character of Allie's action is crucial here; it is, intuitively, harder to say whether Allie would have wronged Geoff if, for instance, she simply jumped back, out of harm's way, without first warning Geoff of the impending danger.

befalling a greater harm fairly low. Certainly low enough that no one need feel unable to form and pursue complex projects because of the constant fear of having to give them up, or radically revise them, because of some harm that has befallen them in the name of preventing a greater harm from befalling someone else.

Geoff's grounds for rejecting such a principle, though, need not concern the threat of harm, or the effect of such a principle on his ability to pursue valuable goals. He can appeal to the consequences for how he will see himself as a result of the relations between individuals that result from a moral system in which it is permissible for Allie to *commandeer* his body in order to save her life.[52] Specifically, what Geoff objects to is the moral permissibility for Allie to consider, as a possible course of action she might take in saving her own life, the use of his body, as a kind of defensive shield, *without his consent*. This is an objection to the way the moral system allows Allie to *see* Geoff. One might also characterize this as an objection to how Allie is allowed to *relate* to Geoff—using his body to save her life in the same way that she would use a convenient stick of wood to bludgeon the oncoming dog— treating him as an object, not a person. But the objection just isn't to Allie treating Geoff this way, but to it being permissible for Allie to *consider* using Geoff in this way. Geoff, one might say, objects to it being permissible for him to be thought of as on par, for practical purposes, with a convenient piece of wood.

Allie can readily respond here that Geoff is exaggerating his case; he is certainly not being thought of as *a piece of wood*. That would be to think of him as a *mere* means. If she thought of him that way, she would not even consider the consequences of his being used in the way she proposes in the justification of the principle she has offered in her defense. It is true that she used Geoff as a means, but she has presented a clear justification for doing so, that does take into account the implications of her actions for him: it was an emergency situation, and if she did not use him as a means, her life would have been forfeited.

---

52 Here I have benefited enormously from reading, and largely agree with, Warren Quinn's inspired discussion of the rationale for this kind of constraint. See his Warren Quinn. "Actions, intentions, and consequences: The Doctrine of Doing and Allowing." In *Morality and Action*, ed. Phillipa Foot. 149-174. Cambridge: Cambridge University Press, 1993. Frances Kamm also emphasizes the importance of how a person sees herself as a result of the design of the moral system; see Kamm. "Non-consequentialism, the Person an End-in-Itself, and the Significance of Status." *Philosophy and Public Affairs* 21 (4 1992): 354-389. Where I disagree with both Quinn and Kamm is in the suggestion that it being wrong to treat persons in certain ways is *constitutive* of them being able to see themselves as independent beings. While I agree that the importance of being able to see oneself as an independent being justifies certain constraints on how persons may be treated, I do not see why a person could not understand herself to be an independent being in the absence of such constraints, in a world in which there was never any reason to believe that anyone would treat others in a way that would undermine their sense of themselves as independent beings.

Geoff may dislike the fact that it is morally permissible for her to think of him as a means (though not a mere means), but that isn't a good reason for rejecting a principle that permits her to commandeer his body. After all, it being permissible to think of him this way does not affect his rationally self-directed pursuit of valuable projects. So why should his dislike of being thought of this way be taken seriously as a legitimate (though perhaps not decisive) ground for Geoff's rejection of Allie's proposed principle?

Geoff's objection to Allie's proposed principle is not, however, based on a dislike of being thought of a certain way. For the same principle which allows Allie to think of him in the way he finds objectionable also affects the way he sees himself; more specifically, the principle affects the way he *relates to his own body*. His sense of himself as an independent being, whose body is *his*, to the extent that he has sole authority in deciding how it will be used, abused, or developed, will be undermined by Allie's proposed principle. Geoff can claim that Allie would be unreasonable in denying that this constitutes a direct assault on his status as a person.[53,54]

It is important to be clear here that Geoff's objection is not based just on the *loss of control* over his body that may result if Allie's proposed principle is adopted. If this were the case, Geoff's objection would be an objection to anyone causing his arm to be severed, whether or not his arm being severed was intended (as it is in Allie's case), or merely foreseen, an unfortunate consequence that is in no way relevant to the advancement of the goals of the person who caused his arm to be severed. His objection to Allie's principle is that it makes it permissible for a person to *commandeer* his body, for another to assume authority over what happens to his body in order to further advance that person's aims, which there is no reason for that person to think *are shared by him*. Geoff's losing his arm due to the foreseen consequences of a person's act may result in his losing control over what happens to his body, but as long as the sacrifice of Geoff's arm has no role to play in the

---

[53] A more everyday example of the importance of this kind of value is to be found in the importance we attach to organ donor consent cards. At present, it is thought wrong to remove the organs of a clinically dead person, for transplant or research purposes, unless they have indicated their consent on the donor consent card. To remove the organs without consent, though not *harmful* to the dead, is thought to be an *insult* to the dead. The importance, for a person, of being able to control her own body is also often raised as an important consideration in discussions of the ethics of abortion.

[54] Though I cannot pursue the matter in any detail here, this account of why Geoff is wronged can be used to explain the cases that Nagel discusses, in which it is necessary for a third party to harm one person to prevent a greater harm befalling someone else. He suggests an explanation which locates the grounds for judgments of wrongness in the point of view of the person *doing the wronging*. The explanation of why Geoff is wronged, developed here, locates the grounds for judgments that someone has been wronged in the more plausible location of the implications *for the person who is wronged* of it not being wrong to treat her in certain ways. See Thomas Nagel. *The View From Nowhere*. Oxford: Oxford University Press, 1986 pg. 175-85.

advancement of that person's goal in acting as she did, he still has sole authority over the use of his body as a means. For no one has presumed to take a decision on Geoff's behalf concerning how his body will be used. Allie's principle also results in Geoff losing control over his body, but with a difference: she is arguing that it is permissible, under the circumstances, for her to decide how Geoff's body will be *used*. It is a decision about how his body will be used, rather than a decision that has implications for what happens to Geoff, because it is essential for Allie's purposes that Geoff's arm be lost (it is the only way to satisfy the hungry dog). It is the possibility of it being permissible for Allie to decide for Geoff how his body will be used that Geoff is specifically objecting to.

Geoff's objection to Allie's proposed principle, it is important to emphasize, is to the adoption of the principle *for the general regulation of behavior*; an objection, one might say, to incorporating such a principle into the very design of morality itself. For the basis of Geoff's objection to Allie's suggested principle is not to the harm that might befall him if the principle is adopted, but to what this granting of permission to think of him as a means without him volunteering himself as such *says* about him.[55] What Geoff's claim suggests is that a revision to Allie's proposed principle, one that would require Allie to seek Geoff's *consent* before implicating him in saving her life, would be more appropriate. Such a requirement would provide the appropriate recognition of the importance of Geoff having sole authority over the use of his body by others, that Allie's previous principle lacked.

A complete discussion of this case would have to consider the reasons Allie could produce for her initial proposed principle to be one that Geoff, despite the reasons he has offered as grounds for wanting to reasonably reject her principle, cannot reasonably reject. What has hopefully been shown by the discussion so far is that consensualism does contain the kinds of resources that are necessary to argue for constraints as part of a justified moral system.

(f) Notice that this kind of argument for constraints does not question the claim that physically harming someone is sometimes the only way to prevent an even greater harm from befalling another. That may be true; what is questioned is the *relevance* of this claim. The argument for the kind of constraint that is considered in this argument rested on the importance of it being impermissible for agents to consider treating others in certain ways, for certain reasons, on the grounds that granting all agents discretion to harm others for these reasons undermines an agent's own sense of herself as an independent being who controls her

---

55 As the common saying puts it, 'actions *speak* louder than words'.

own body. Preventing an even greater physical harm from befalling another falls into the relevant class of excluded reasons.

This does not mean, though, that constraints are not defeasible. There may be some reasons that would justify harming another without her consent, whose recognition by a valid principle would not undermine an agent's sense of herself as an independent being who controls her own body. In particular, an agent's viewing herself this way *may* be consistent with it being justifiable to harm her, without her consent, to prevent a greater harm from befalling each of a *great many* people. When very large numbers are at stake (I leave it to intuition how large the number should be), harming one without her consent, to perhaps *save* those people may be justified as permissible (perhaps sometimes required). Why its being permissible to harm a person in these situations *might* not undermine her sense of herself as controlling her own body is a complex question, which will be discussed in detail in the next chapter, concerning aggregation (chpt. 4).

Chapter Four
Unanimity and Aggregation

§1

(a) If there is one feature of common sense morality that it would be very convenient for the non-consequentialist to discredit, it is the thought that, at least in some cases, the numbers of people who stand to benefit by one's choice of action is a relevant consideration for deciding what one morally has reason to do. It has always been a strength of utilitarianism that it has an explanation for the relevance of numbers that is well motivated by its account of what agents who are moved by moral considerations care about, while those who oppose them have no such account.[1] Numbers, says the utilitarian, are thought to be relevant because they are a useful (or practical) indicator of the amount of good that can be done by pursuing a particular course of action, i.e., to benefit the greater number is, in most cases, to do more good.

Some will find this explanation of the relevance of numbers unsatisfactory, in part because it has considerable revisionist implications. The most plausible cases in which we believe the numbers are clearly relevant are cases such as one put forward by Anscombe:

> *The Rocks:* You are in a boat, equidistant from two rocks. On one rock, there are six people. On the other rock, there is one person.

---

[1] By utilitarianism I have in mind meta-ethical utilitarianism. For purposes of this discussion, a utilitarian theory should be thought of as any consequentialist theory where the good to be promoted is exhausted by an account of human well-being.

The water is rising, and there is only time to get to one of the rocks and save its occupant(s), before water engulfs both rocks.[2]

In this case, the intuitively right thing to do is to save the six. The utilitarian explanation of the relevance of numbers, though, leads one to the suspect conclusion that numbers are always relevant for moral deliberation, as the question of what one, morally, has reason to do always leads one to consider the question of how best to promote the good.[3] For example, if I am on my way to give a lecture, but I happen across someone kneeling in the street who has just had a stroke, the utilitarian will claim that the number of people I could benefit through my lecture if I proceed, leaving the person in the street, is at least in principle a relevant consideration for deciding how morality requires me to proceed. The difficulty here is not just with the fact that trivial benefits to a large number may justify acts which strike us as abominable. This result might be avoidable by a combination of a sufficiently complex value theory, and a function for calculating the amount of good that might be done by pursuing different courses of action that takes into account all the considerations we take to be relevant.[4] Such tactics make the utilitarian view more plausible, by ensuring that trivial benefits will almost never outweigh, and thus never justify, acts which impose serious costs on one, or a few.

The problem here is not that the benefits are thought to be too small to be taken into account. Rather, it is intuitively hard to believe that, in a context where a person's life is at stake, the kind of benefit that a person may receive if the lecture is delivered, regardless of how many stand to benefit, is of any moral relevance at all. Yet the utilitarian, assuming that entertainment and some understanding of philosophy are plausible components of the human good, is committed to the view that it must be relevant. She is committed to this claim by the fact that utilitarian justifications involve appealing to the aggregate value of outcomes, where any consideration relevant to well-being is relevant in the assessment of the aggregate value of an outcome.

This case should be distinguished from one in which the kind of benefit or burden to which the utilitarian draws attention is agreed, in the context, to be relevant, but what is thought to be counter-intuitive

---

[2] To avoid any complications here, assume that all are strangers to one another, and the person doing the life saving does not occupy any special role that might change her relationship with any of those she is in a position to save. Further, assume that there is no time for any consultation among the individuals involved.
[3] This is always true in considering the question of how morality requires one to decide how to act. It need not be true as a prescription for individual decisions on a day to day basis.
[4] On value theory, see, for example, Thomas Hurka's *Perfectionism*; on the function used to calculate the amount of good that could be produced, see Parfit, *On Giving Priority to the Worse Off*, chpt. 8, particularly the discussion of weighted beneficence.

is what the utilitarian believes can be justified on the basis of these considerations. Consider a case in which three could be saved from certain death by intentionally killing one. The fact that three lives are at stake is undeniably relevant. What is intuitively dubious is that preventing three deaths could justify taking a person's life as the means of preventing their deaths. Like the problem of irrelevance, this difficulty is a consequence of the aggregate value of outcomes being the only thing that ultimately matters in utilitarian justifications. In this case, though, the counter-intuitive implications of the theory are a result of attaching moral relevance only to what happens, while the problem of irrelevance is a result of the theory not having any principled grounds for distinguishing the relevant aspects of an outcome from those that are, in the context, intuitively irrelevant.

Further, it seems that if the choice is between saving the one and the six, in the absence of any other extenuating considerations, it would be wrong not to save the six, because they are six. That is, the fact that we can save six rather than one strikes us as a reason for saving the six that even the one who will not be saved could not reasonably reject as a valid reason for saving the six. The utilitarian wants to characterize this judgment as a matter of comparing quantities of well-being. But this does not seem quite right: it is important that the choice is between saving *one* or saving *six*. The numbers are intuitively significant in a way that the utilitarian explication of this significance, relegating them to the level of pragmatic indicators for how well different courses of action may promote well-being, fails to capture. Though, admittedly, it is not obvious how to justify to the one the fairness of saving the six, and not her, just because there are more of them, without invoking some notion like 'doing more good', or 'avoiding what is worse', in the explanation of the justificatory significance of the fact that 'there are more of them'.

Now, the utilitarian explanation of why numbers count may have revisionist implications, but this can be of little comfort to the non-consequentialist, as the few non-consequentialists who have discussed this issue have tended to deny the relevance of numbers altogether, even in cases where denying their relevance is highly counter intuitive.[5] John Taurek, for instance, has argued that, in a case like *Rocks*, there is no more reason to save the one then there is to save the six. This is because values cannot, on his view, be added in a way that would make it a

---

5   The noteworthy exception here is represented by Frances Kamm's pioneering work in this area. See, in particular, her Frances Kamm. "Equal Treatment and Equal Chances." *Philosophy and Public Affairs* (3 1986): 177-194. andFrances Kamm. *Morality, Mortality*. Vol. 1. Oxford: Oxford University Press, 1993, particularly chpts. 6-8. I am much indebted to her excellent discussion of aggregation and the theory of right.

morally worse outcome for six to die rather than for only one to die.[6] Elizabeth Anscombe, arguing a less extreme position, has claimed that it would not be *wrong* to save the one, rather than the six, though there are certainly good and bad reasons, that do not have a direct bearing on determining right and wrong, for saving the six rather than the one.[7] Central to her line of reasoning is the thought that the six being grouped together makes no difference to the strength of each individual's claim to be saved. No *one* of them has a greater claim to be saved than any of the others.

Both these proposals are, intuitively, extreme. What a plausible non-consequentialist moral theory should aim for is to be able to provide a cogent explanation of why numbers count, in those scenarios, such as *Rocks*, where we clearly do believe they do count, without endorsing the utilitarian view, in which numbers (as pragmatic indicators) are always relevant. It is worth emphasizing here that to be plausible, such an account need not explain the relevance of numbers in every case where there is reason to think they may be relevant; it is enough to be able to explain the relevance of numbers in those cases, such as *Rocks*, where our conviction that the numbers do matter is quite strong.

It is also important to note that a plausible account of why numbers are relevant in some instances need not be a theory of limited aggregation. This point is not merely terminological. When the utilitarian claims that it would be wrong not to save the six, she need only invite the critic to weigh up the relevant reasons. There is a reason of a certain weight to save the one, but there is a reason of a greater weight to save the six. The comparative strength of the reasons depends on the aggregate value of the outcomes that would be produced by pursuing one course of action rather than the other. But there is no reason, at the outset, for thinking that a non-consequentialist need appeal to notions like aggregate well-being, or even consider the value of different states of affairs, in developing a plausible account of why it would be wrong

---

[6] See John Taurek. "Should the Numbers Count?" *Philosophy and Public Affairs* 6 (1977): 293-316. Taurek appears to endorse the view that one should be guided in one's choice of action by the potential value of the states of affairs that might be produced by different courses of action. Christine Korsgaard commits herself to what may appear to be a similar view concerning the additivity of values: "My happiness is good for me and yours is good for you, but the sum of these two values is not good *for* anyone, and so the intersubjectivist will deny that the sum, as such, is a value" (Korsgaard 1993,29). The argument here is somewhat cryptic. It is not a straightforward argument against consequentialism, as consequentialism does not need to claim that the sum of values is good or bad *for* anyone; she need only claim that the sum of values is relevant for judging the aggregate value of different *outcomes*. Korsgaard's argument appears to rely on a claim in the first section of her paper (24-25), that the only morally relevant claims are claims about what is good or bad for *an individual*. The value of outcomes is morally irrelevant. This claim explains the relevance of the later claim concerning the additivity of values.

[7] See G.E.M. Anscombe. "Who Is Wronged?" *The Oxford Review* (5 1967): 16-17.

not to save the six. Which is not to say that the best account of why it would be wrong not to save the six will not, or should not, appeal to the notion of aggregate well-being. The point is just that the case should not be prejudged, in the way terms like 'limited aggregation' make it easy to do.[8]

(b) Though Scanlon's original presentation of consensualism at times suggests that the theory is able to explain the relevance of numbers, no such explanation is offered (cf. Scanlon 1982,120,123) . In fact, the substance of the theory provides some grounds for thinking that an explanation for the relevance of numbers cannot be developed within its parameters.

The place to begin considering how one might be led to this conclusion is by recalling the distinction between the kinds of considerations that may be appealed to in the justification of a principle (meta-level considerations), and the kinds of considerations to which a valid principle may draw attention as morally relevant for deciding how best to conduct oneself (normative considerations). A rule-utilitarian, for example, would be someone who believes that the only relevant meta-level consideration is aggregate well-being, yet accepts that, at the normative level, morality has the kind of non-consequentialist structure that our common sense intuitions suggest it does.

Consensualism is diametrically opposed to utilitarianism at the meta-level. The only considerations that can be invoked in the justification or reasonable rejection of a principle are *personal reasons*. Personal reasons are considerations having to do with the implications of the acceptance of a proposed principle for the general regulation of behavior *for the individual*.[9] What is ruled out, therefore, as a legiti-

---

[8] Scanlon claims that "It is quite possible that, according to [consensualism], *some* moral questions may be properly settled by appeal to maximum aggregate well-being, *even though this is not the sole or ultimate standard of justification*" (Scanlon 1982,120; emphasis added). Scanlon's point here, I believe, is that though consensualism is foundationally anti-aggregative, a principle for cases such as *Rocks*, which would justify appealing to aggregate well-being in deciding to save the six, might be one that no one could reasonably reject. Though I am sympathetic with the thought that there must be a principle, that no one could reasonably reject, in virtue of which it would be wrong not to save the six, I am less comfortable with the thought that such a principle will authorize the life saver in *Rocks* to decide who should be saved by an appeal to aggregate well-being.

[9] The personal reasons restriction is close, but not identical to, the restriction on the grounds for rejection that Scanlon introduces in his complaint model interpretation of contractualist moral argument. As he states it, "one noteworthy feature of contractualist argument as I have presented it so far is that it is non-aggregative: what are compared are individual gains, losses and levels of welfare" (Scanlon 1982,123). The difference is that, on the version of consensualism defended here, one may appeal to more than just the implications for one's well-being as valid grounds for rejecting a principle.

It is important to be clear here that both these positions are substantive interpretations of contractualism. As David Brink has noted, the general formula "an act is wrong if it is one that no one can reasonably reject" does not imply any conclusions about what kinds of considerations to which a person may

mate grounds for reasonably rejecting a principle, is a direct appeal to the aggregate value of the outcomes that might result if the proposed principle is accepted.[10] This does not mean that the aggregate value of states of affairs can have no role to play at the normative level; they are only excluded at the meta-level.[11]

Why the restriction to personal reasons? The explanation is to be found in the fact that the aim of the parties to the consensualist hypothetical consensus is to work out principles for the general regulation of behavior, which will govern what individuals *owe* one another if they are to *relate* to one another on terms of mutual respect. Each person will assess principles, therefore, by considering both the implications for her of the general acceptance of a principle, and the justifiability to other individuals of her relating to others, to whom she may stand in a variety of different relationships, and the way that the proposed principle would direct her to (or at least make it permissible for her to) relate to them. The restriction to personal reasons can therefore be understood to be a consequence of the central importance, in consensualism, of the character of the relations between individuals.

Restricting reasons for reasonably rejecting a principle to personal reasons may strike some as being damaging to the theory's potential explanatory power. Concerns may be voiced here about a pernicious 'individualism'. The validity of this concern requires careful assessment. One reason one may think it justified is that the restriction does not appear to allow a person to appeal to the implications of a principle which are just bad, but not bad for anyone in particular. These are implications for what is of impersonal, or intrinsic, value. For instance, one might claim that a principle which made it permissible to destroy the tropical rain forest on Vancouver Island should be reasonably rejected, on the ground that the rain forest is intrinsically valuable, so its destruction would be bad. That is, the value of the rain forest cannot be adequately accounted for by its contribution to the quality of

---

appeal in reasonably rejecting a principle other than the exclusion of direct appeals to the aggregate value of outcomes. The formula still allows for the possibility that a person may reject a principle on the grounds that she is a member of a group of people whose *collective* complaint is greater than anyone else's complaint. It only implies the complaint model (and *a fortiori*, the personal reasons restriction) if one accepts additional substantive premises that the acceptance of the general formula does not commit one to accepting (cf. Brink 1993,278-81).

[10] For a discussion of the way states of affairs are appealed to in consequentialism, seePhilippa Foot. "Utilitarianism and the Virtues." In *Consequentialism and its Critics*, ed. Samuel Scheffler. 224-242. Oxford: OUP, 1988.

[11] Scanlon admits this, claiming that for all he knows, act-utilitarianism will be the normative outcome of meta-level consensualism (though he also says this is highly implausible) (Scanlon 1982,115). Such a result would require that the sole product of consensualist moral argument is the act-utilitarian principle, enjoining one to always act so as to maximize well-being. This is a very implausible outcome, and an argument, within the parameters of consensualism, would have to be produced to establish its plausibility.

human life, and the reasons there are for protecting it from exploitation have nothing to do with its contribution to human life, but with the fact that it is just valuable.[12] The restriction to personal reasons rules out appealing to these reasons, so consensualism, one might argue, cannot account for the important duty not to destroy the rain forest (assuming here that there is such a duty).

Consensualism need not *deny* that the intrinsic value of the rain forest is a reason for not destroying it, but it is true that a direct appeal to the intrinsic value of the rain forest is ruled out by the theory as a reasonable grounds for wanting to reject a principle permitting its destruction. But this does not mean that the intrinsic value of the rain forest cannot be appealed to at all in moral argument. One may, for example, appeal to this value by appealing to the importance for an individual, given her status, of being able to experience intrinsically valuable natural wonders such as the rain forest. This kind of move allows for arguments to proceed concerning the extent we *owe it to others* to protect the rain forest. Nothing in this kind of appeal, it is important to note, requires that one think that the importance of the rain forest is exhausted by its value for the enrichment of individual lives; one does not even have to think that this contribution is a particularly important aspect of the value of the rain forest.[13] What matters is that the rain forest does have a role to play in enriching human life, and this allows it to be appealed to, under this description, in consensualist moral argument.

Someone who does attach a great importance to the protection of the rain forest might argue that this way of appealing to the value of the rain forest will not allow us to make sense of many of our duties to the rain forest. For there are duties to protect it that derive, not from our commitment to respecting others as persons, but directly from our respect for the value of the rain forest itself. These are duties that consensualism cannot account for. Consensualism can concede this point, but questions the extent to which it is a failing of the theory.

---

[12] The notion of intrinsic value has been recently discussed, in the context of abortion, by Ronald Dworkin. See his *Life's Dominion*. It is also used by Scanlon in his discussion of the value of fairness and equality; see T.M. Scanlon. "Rights, Goals, and Fairness." In *Theories of Rights,* ed. Jeremy Waldron. 137-152. Oxford: OUP, 1984.

[13] Recall here the 'method of abstraction' from chpt. 2 §II(c). The details of that strategy re-emerge here as important, because there is deep disagreement on what follows for a person's reasons from something being intrinsically valuable. The argument here suggests that agreement on the significance of something being intrinsically valuable is not necessary to ground duties not to destroy what is of intrinsic value. For instance, those who bombed the Uffizi might think that Leonardo drawings are overrated, so their destruction would not be in the same league as desecrating something they take to be truly inspired. Their assessment of the value of the art has no bearing, however, on the fact that they owe it to others not to destroy what are obviously important works of art (even if they think them overrated).

Consensualism is only concerned with that class of duties (and rights and obligations) of which it is true that a failure to comply is something for which one can be held accountable by others. There may be duties that some understand to be imposed upon them by their appreciation of the value of the rain forest, but it seems unlikely that they would understand others who do not also value the rain forest this way also to have such duties. Or if they do understand others to have such duties, they are not the kind of duties to which they can demand that others comply; at best, they may pity those who do not sufficiently appreciate the value of the rain forest to appreciate the duties they owe it.

A different example may help clarify this point: many view themselves as morally required to devote their lives to serving others less fortunate in whatever way they will be able to do the most good. But this may not be something they view as the same kind of requirement as the requirement not to intentionally murder others for amusement. For the source of the requirement lies not in what they owe others, but in what is required of them if they are to live up to their own standards, or their deepest beliefs about what is valuable in life. Consensualism need not deny that these are legitimate moral requirements; just a different class of moral requirement than that of *interpersonal* standards of behavior that each can be reasonably expected to live up to, and held accountable by others if they fail to do so, with which consensualism concerns itself.

Impersonal, or intrinsic, values may also be appealed to in consensualism in the justification of principles which allow for permissions (or options), so as to allow for the accommodation of the role of impersonal, or intrinsic, values in a person's life. It is perfectly reasonable to want to reject a principle that does not recognize, as a legitimate (though not necessarily decisive) reason for non-compliance with that principle's requirements, the fact that compliance requires one to act in a way that is inconsistent with appropriately valuing what one takes to be of intrinsic value. For instance, a builder, assigned by her employer to work with a team whose assignment it is to demolish the structures at Stonehenge in order to make way for a new motorway, might legitimately claim that she can reasonably reject a principle that does not give her the option of demanding re-assignment, rather than participating in the desecration of a site she understands to be sacred. Here, moral argument recognizes the importance of intrinsic values indirectly, by recognizing the importance a person legitimately attaches to being able to guide her life in light of what she takes to be of intrinsic value. The importance of this individual interest manifests itself in moral argument by admitting as a reasonable (though not always decisive) ground for rejecting a principle, the claim that a principle may require individuals to act in ways that are inconsistent with appropriately valuing those things they take to be of intrinsic value.

Another way one might express doubts about the personal reasons restriction is to say that it prevents appeals to the implications of a principle *on us*. This is a criticism of consensualism, as it shows that the theory only appeals to values that a person can in principle pursue, or benefit from in isolation from others. Collective goods—goods, or values, which are a product of association, or interaction with others, and cannot be realized any other way—cannot be appealed to in consensualist moral argument, because they gain their value from the benefit they bring to a great many people (or at least more than one person) (e.g., the value of a common culture and language, or the value of entertaining).[14] A theory that does not allow for collective appeals to the implications of a principle as a grounds for rejection will block collective goods from having a role to play in moral argument.

This line of thinking is confused. For though the conditions that must obtain for the provision of collective goods make an ineradicable reference to others, the value of a collective good is best understood in terms of the benefits that accrue to individuals, as individuals, from the provision of such a good. Nothing about collective goods suggests that groups have interests. Nor is it true that collective goods gain their importance from the benefit they bring to a great many people. Values do not become more valuable because many people share them. For instance, it may be that each person has an interest in participating in a culture with which she can identify. If, however, there are not enough people who share a similar interest in a certain kind of culture, those who have this interest may not be able to have their interest satisfied, due to the lack of numbers necessary to constitute a vibrant cultural group. Numbers, in this case, determine the possibility of the provision of a collective good, not the moral importance of the good. There is, it appears, nothing in consensualism to prevent individuals from appealing to the importance of collective goods in moral argument.

(c) It is cases such as *Rocks* that raise the most serious concerns about restricting the grounds for rejecting a principle to personal reasons, as it appears that consensualism is forced to reach a conclusion about this kind of case that is very much in line with Anscombe's position. The core of the difficulty is that there is no obvious way for attaching any significance, in moral argument, to the fact that the choice in *Rocks* is between saving one or saving six. For in trying to formulate a principle for the general regulation of behavior that is appli-

---

14 On the relevance of collective goods in moral argument, see Jeremy Waldron. "Can communal goods be communal rights?" In *Liberal Rights*, 339-369. Cambridge: CUP, 1993.

cable to cases such as *Rocks*, each party to the hypothetical consensus can only appeal to the implications for her of the acceptance of a proposed principle. As has been previously discussed, the range of considerations that might be legitimately appealed to is quite large.[15] But it is not clear that this helps in resolving the root of the dilemma for consensualism, which is that the kind of situation for which an appropriate principle is sought is one in which parties are *symmetrically* situated with respect to the source of aid. Any reasons that one person may produce for a principle that would result in it being wrong to aid her are also reasons for others to claim that each of them would be wronged if they are not aided. Moral argument concerning a general principle to deal with situations such as *Rocks* appears to be destined to end in a deadlock.

One might conclude that what a deadlock shows is that it is not wrong to save the one rather than the six (Anscombe's conclusion). But this claim is ambiguous between two readings. There is a weak sense in which one can say that it is not wrong to save the one rather than the six simply because the consensualist standard of right and wrong fails to apply in this situation. Consensualism does not condemn the act as wrong, but neither does it claim that the act is defensible. It is just silent on the matter. There is also a stronger sense in which one might claim that it would not be wrong to save the one, which Anscombe has in mind, which says that it is not wrong to save the one because saving the one can be justified to others on grounds that no one can reasonably reject. This conclusion presupposes an agreement amongst the parties on a principle in virtue of which this would be true, and so cannot be a legitimate inference from a situation of deadlock amongst the parties.

It is not clear how moral argument is to proceed in deadlocked situations, as there do not appear to be any reasons that may be cited as a justification for aiding some (or one) but not the other(s). One way out of this dilemma that has some initial appeal is for the parties to agree upon a general principle that requires the decision be made by some form of fair decision procedure, such as a coin toss, or rolling a die. If all the situations to which the principle is to apply could be expected to be of the form of there being several potential recipients of aid, all symmetrically situated, out of which only one can be aided, this would be an intuitively satisfactory principle, e.g., if all situations were of the form of there being seven individuals on seven rocks, all situated symmetrically with respect to the life boat.

But flipping a coin in the *Rocks* case is intuitively not the right way to decide the matter, and it is a case which fits the general description of the kind of situation to which the principle is to apply. For it is hard

---

[15] In this section, the approach to consensualist moral argument that was argued for in chapter 3, the *alternative social worlds* approach, is being presupposed.

to believe that it would not at least be wrong not to save the six, even if one is more reluctant to accept the stronger claim, that many would accept as plausible, that the six will be wronged if they are not saved. There do not appear to be any reasons that would justify this belief, though, that are admissible in consensualist moral argument. Direct appeals to the aggregate value of outcomes are ruled out, as are appeals by groups to the implications for them of not being saved. And, assuming (plausibly, I believe) that it is no worse for a person to perish together with others than it is to perish alone, there do not appear to be any reasons that members of a group could appeal to, that arise out of group membership, that could be offered for a principle which requires the six rather than the one be saved.[16] Consensualism appears to be forced to side with Anscombe, and to conclude that there is no duty to save the six rather than the one. In fact, the conclusion here is even more extreme than Anscombe's, insofar as consensualism appears to fail to be able to establish that there is a duty to save anyone at all in this situation.

§II

(a) There are at least four routes that the defender of consensualism might take at this point. First, she might claim that this is the correct conclusion to reach: there is no duty to save the six rather than the one. This is not to claim, though, that there are no reasons for saving the six rather than the one.[17] Second, she could concede that, in some cases, a direct appeal to the aggregate value of a potential outcome is a legitimate ground for reasonably rejecting a proposed principle. Third, she could allow individuals to pool their individual reasons for rejecting a principle, appealing to the net benefit that will accrue to them as their grounds for rejecting a principle.[18] Or, fourth, she could accept that, intuitively, it is wrong not to save the six, but concede that consensualism simply cannot explain this duty, as it cannot account for the rele-

---

16   Even if there were such reasons, it is hard to see how they could be deployed to argue for the legitimacy of a principle (intuitively plausible) that would require that the larger rather than the smaller group be saved, when faced with a choice between the two.
17   This is the position with which both Anscombe and Fried appear to sympathize. For Fried's view, see Charles Fried. "Correspondence." *Philosophy and Public Affairs* 8 (4 1979): 393-395.
18   Brink has argued that the concerns that animate contractualism would be better represented in a theory that did not completely reject aggregation, but allowed for individuals to pool their complaints provided they are all on the same level of seriousness, offering their collective complaint as a grounds for rejecting a principle. His view, *complaint minimization*, rests on a different version of contractualism than either Scanlon's complaint model interpretation of contractualism, or the one that is under discussion here. A separate discussion would be required to adequately evaluate this view, and to show how it differs from Scanlon's view and the one under discussion here. See Brink 1993 for his position.

vance of numbers in determining what our duties are; what has been discovered is an important weakness of the theory.[19] This would be a major concession; the extent to which one thought it damaged consensualism's plausibility would in part depend on one's opinion of the plausibility of the explanation that other theories offer of the relevance of numbers.

Amongst these four options, the fourth is preferable to the second and third. Allowing outcomes to be directly appealed to (by citing their impersonal aggregate value), or allowing for the pooling of reasons, would result in the abandonment of those features of consensualism that sharply distinguish it from consequentialism. Further, it is not obvious how allowing pooling or appealing to outcomes, whose exclusion is well motivated within the theory, could be justified as other than an obvious *ad hoc* modification, to allow for a consensualist explanation of cases like *Rocks*. Whether the fourth is preferable to the first is more difficult judgment to make. Most, I believe, would accept that it is.

There is a fifth option available to consensualism, though, that tends to be overlooked. Consensualism appears to have difficulty explaining the relevance of numbers because the natural way to explain their relevance, by appealing to the aggregate value of outcomes, is excluded by the theory. That is part of what makes it a distinctive view. There is an important assumption lurking behind this way of characterizing the dilemma though, that what consensualism needs to explain is the thought that, in cases like *Rocks*, it is *worse* for six to die than for one to die. Spelling out this premise fully, one could say: it is worse for six to die than for one to die, and in situations like *Rocks*, one should be guided by a desire to avoid what is worse. If this is what consensualism needs to explain, than it is easy to see why one would think that appealing to the aggregate value of outcomes is the most straight forward way of constructing such an explanation. But there is no reason to burden consensualism with this task: what it needs to explain is why it would be wrong not to save six; it need not take a stand on the question of whether or not it is worse if six rather than one die, and the explanation of why it would be wrong not to save the six need not incorporate the idea that it is morally important to avoid what is worse.

With this in mind, the possibility that parties to the hypothetical consensus may agree to a *procedural solution* for settling cases like *Rocks*, one which yields the result that it would be wrong not to save the six, emerges as a plausible way for consensualism to explain the relevance of numbers. The idea of appealing to a procedural solution is a

---

[19] Nagel expresses pessimism about the ability of a theory that incorporates a characterization of impartiality as unanimity to explain the relevance of numbers, though he admits that "no plausible theory can avoid the relevance of numbers completely". See his "Equality" pg. 125.

familiar one from other instances of deadlocked negotiations. For instance, in labour disputes, parties who cannot agree on a compromise position, but need to reach some kind of agreement, will often agree to put the matter in the hands of a fair arbitrator (someone who is acceptable to all the parties involved), whose decision will be binding. A procedural solution in the context of consensualism works in the same way: in the absence of an agreement on who should be saved, the pressure to agree on principles no one could reasonably reject leads parties to the hypothetical consensus to agree that the matter should be decided by the outcome of a fair procedure, or a procedure for deciding on who should be saved that no one could reasonably reject.

This last requirement is of particular importance, as it ensures that those who are not saved have no reason for judging themselves to have been wronged in not being saved. That is, the fact that the decision on whom to save was made by a procedure that no one could reasonably reject ensures that a justification for the decision to the the others (or another) is available that can be offered to the person who will not be saved, and knows she will not be saved (the decision having already been made). Relations of mutual respect between herself and others are thus preserved, despite the fact that she has not been saved.

An example of a procedural solution has already been touched upon: the coin toss. In tossing a coin to decide a deadlocked case, one acknowledges the symmetry of each person's situation with respect to the source of aid by giving each an equal chance of being aided, while what decides the issue is an arbitrary element which each party can agree cannot (assuming a fair toss) be influenced to decide the issue in favor of one party or another. It appears, then, to be a procedure that no one could reasonably reject for deciding cases such as *Rocks*. This is not to defend the coin toss as the appropriate procedure for deciding the case of *Rocks*. Intuitively it is not, and settling the question is a matter for further argument concerning the form an appropriate general procedure should take for deciding how to justifiably proceed in the kind of case under consideration here. What it does suggest, though, is that the explanation of the relevance of numbers need not raise the kind of problem for consensualism that challenges its plausibility as a characterization of moral deliberation, or prompts *ad hoc* modifications to the theory, such as allowing direct appeals to the aggregate value of states of affairs as grounds for reasonably rejecting a principle. Whether or not there does prove to be a problem for consensualism here, one that can be laid at the doorstep of the personal reasons restriction, will depend on whether a suitable procedure can be developed which will help make sense of the intuition that it would be wrong not to save the six.

(b) The intuitive ground for taking a coin toss to be an inappropriate general procedure is that, in cases like *Rocks*, it may give the wrong result. If a coin is flipped, we may end up being directed to save the one, which will strike many as the wrong thing to do. But the coin toss, or some form of fair lottery, as the appropriate procedure also has a certain intuitive appeal. For many will feel that the one will be wronged if the six are saved without at least giving her some chance of being saved. And what could be fairer than giving each person the same chance of being saved? Each has the same amount to lose, and all cannot benefit: so how could fairness justify doing other than giving them all an *equal chance* to benefit? Is this not the fairest solution, short of simply wasting the good by refusing to benefit anyone at all?

In order to properly assess this thought, what needs to be considered is why giving each person an equal chance is thought to be fair.[20] John Broome offers a compelling rationale for this idea. Fairness, on his view, is concerned with a class of reasons he calls 'claims', which are "duties *owed to the candidate herself*" (Broome 1991,92; italics in original text). If a person has a claim to a good, she is entitled to that good (though Broome does not use the language of entitlement). Where a good is indivisible and scarce, everyone's entitlement cannot be satisfied. Here, according to Broome, fairness requires that "claims should be satisfied in proportion to their strength":

> the heart of my suggestion is that fairness is concerned only with how well each person's claim is satisfied *compared with* how well other people's are satisfied. It is concerned only with relative satisfaction....Claims should be satisfied....But it is not *unfair* if they are not, provided everyone is treated proportionally (Broome 1991,95).

In the sort of case that is relevant to Broome's discussion here, the good is indivisible, so only one person can have their claim fully satisfied. *Ex post* unfairness, or unfairness in the outcome of a procedure for deciding how an indivisible good should be allocated, is therefore inevitable. One way of avoiding this, of course, is to not allocate the good to anyone. Broome rules out this possibility on the grounds that claims,

> give rise to two separate requirements: they should be satisfied, and they should be satisfied proportionally....It will normally be impos-

---

[20] In the discussion of lotteries, I largely follow John Broome's excellent discussion of the fairness of lotteries, and the doubts I have about the appropriateness of lotteries for deciding all distribution of indivisible goods cases are largely directed at the rationale he offers for believing they are appropriate. For purposes of this discussion, I set aside those parts of Broome's discussion concerned with weighted lotteries. See John Broome."Fairness." *Proceedings of the Aristotelian Society* 91 (1 1991): 87-102. See also Lewis Kornhauser and Lawrence Sager. "Just Lotteries." *Social Science Information* 27 (4 1988): 483-516. They discuss a proposal similar to Broome's, but argue that the question of whether fairness demands equal chances turns on a further question of what the best interpretation is of the right to be treated as an equal, which they do not attempt to resolve (K&S 1988,502-3).

sible to fulfill both requirements completely. Consequently, the two will themselves have to be combined together in some way, to determine what should be done, all things considered (Broome 1991,96).

The satisfaction requirement, to which all reasons, not just claims, give rise is apparently meant to rule out wasting any of the good, as it requires maximization of satisfaction (Broome 1991,95,97).

Ex post unfairness is therefore inevitable. But a second best solution is available, which at least avoids *ex ante* unfairness, by holding a lottery. An unbiased lottery, though it results in *ex post* unfairness, has the virtue of avoiding *ex ante* unfairness by dividing the good probabilistically, giving each person an equal chance of having their claim fully satisfied.[21] There are two features of the lottery that account for its fairness. First, because the lottery assigns each claimant an equal chance of receiving the good, the lottery is impartial between all valid claimants. This is so because (i) each person is assigned a chance of being benefited based solely on the strength of her claim, so no one is recognized as more entitled to the good than anyone else for illegitimate reasons. It is for this reason that Broome emphasizes that fairness is concerned with relative, not absolute, satisfaction of claims (Broome 1991,95). And (ii), the 'surrogate satisfaction' that each valid claimant receives from being given a chance proportional to the strength of her claim is a way of recognizing the claim of each valid claimant in the process of deciding.[22] Claims demand satisfaction, so the partial satisfaction of a person's claim constitutes a recognition of that claim. A lottery, therefore, can claim to be a procedure that recognizes all valid claimants in the process of deciding, giving each no more importance in the process than she is entitled to.

Second, only individual claims (what is *owed* to a person) are taken into account by the lottery procedure as relevant for deciding how the good should be allocated. All other considerations are excluded. The exclusion of other considerations is important, for it ensures that claims are respected, rather than overridden (Broome 1991, 94,98). These two features of the lottery are at the heart of its claim to be a fair procedure for deciding on the allocation of indivisible goods, one that gives proper recognition to people's separateness (cf. Broome 1991,94).

---

[21] I assume throughout the discussion, unless otherwise indicated, that the lottery mechanism is unbiased.
[22] Broome claims that having a chance at the good can be thought of as itself a good, a source of 'surrogate satisfaction' (Broome 1991,97-98). This claim also plays a role in explaining how the lottery partially satisfies the satisfaction requirement to which claims give rise. On its own, though, it does not account for the fairness of lotteries.

(c) Broome's justification of the fairness of lotteries has, at times, a consensualist tone to it. Consider the example of the dangerous mission, that will probably result in death. All candidates are similar in all relevant respects, except that one has special talents that make her more likely to achieve the mission's goal, though no more likely to survive (Broome 1991,90). He comments,

> Suppose, in the example of the dangerous mission, that the talented candidate was sent because of her talents. She could make the following complaint. She has as strong a claim to staying behind as anybody else. Her claim was weighed against other reasons. But this *overrode her claim* rather than satisfied it. It was never on the cards that she might actually get the good she has a claim to. But if she was sent because a lottery is held and she lost, *she could make no such complaint* (Broome,98; italics added).[23]

A lottery, in assigning each person an equal chance of receiving the benefit, allows the beneficiary (or beneficiaries) and the person who provided the benefit to justify themselves, after the benefit has been handed out, to the person who was not benefited. The argument could be put to this person: 'you had exactly the same chance of being saved as everyone else. This indicates that your claim to the benefit was taken seriously, in a way that is consistent with the recognition of the claims of others. It's too bad that you lost. But you can't complain that you have been wronged in not being benefited'. Such a complaint would either require her to *deny* that the others each had as much of a claim to the good as she did, or the discovery of some relevant asymmetry between herself and others, that would justify her arguing that her claim to be benefited was better than that of the others. The first possibility is not available to her as the claim would be false, and the second is closed because there just is no relevant asymmetry between herself and others. If there were such an asymmetry, the lottery would have been unnecessary.

The only other possible legitimate source of complaint, that some irrelevant consideration (like talent) was taken account of in the decision procedure, is also not available here, as the lottery only takes into account *claims*, and not other reasons. There is every reason for the loser to believe, therefore, that she has been treated fairly, and thus cannot complain of having been wronged.

---

[23] It is crucial for Broome's argument that the good being distributed is the good of *being left behind* (Broome 1990,90). This is crucial because it justifies excluding as irrelevant to a fair procedure any consideration other than the fact that a person has something to lose by not being left behind (in this case, her life). This is important for understanding why taking into account a person's talent is being complained about as unfair; this would only be relevant if the purpose of the procedure was to pick the person most likely to succeed in the mission.

It is natural to think that, given the consensualist tone of Broome's justification of the fairness of lotteries, it would be a justification that could be easily adapted as a consensualist justification for the fairness of lotteries. This would establish the coin toss as a procedure for deciding whom to save in the *Rocks* case that no one could reasonably reject. This is certainly a counter-intuitive conclusion, but there is no reason to think that a plausible moral theory will not have normative implications that lead us to revise our common sense beliefs.

There are reasons, though, for doubting that Broome's analysis really can provide a consensualist justification for using the lottery as a decision procedure in indivisible goods cases. First, his arguments make use of the notion of a claim, which he glosses as a *duty owed to the candidate herself* (Broome 1991,92). But the notion of a claim can have no role to play in consensualist moral argument. Imagine the parties in the Rocks case reasoning about an appropriate procedure for deciding who should be saved. One person argues that she has a claim to be saved. If she has such a claim, consensualism tells us that this must be in virtue of a principle that no one could reasonably reject. Now, she could no doubt cite a non-rejectable principle which imposes on the rescuer a duty to save her in situations where hers is the only life at stake. However, such a principle would not extend to cases where there are many lives at stake. For each of the others whose lives are at risk could reasonably reject a principle which imposed a duty on the rescuer to save that person, on the grounds that they have as much to lose by not being saved as she does. Consensualist reasoning, one could say, is here concerned with determining what the rescuer's duty is, given that there are competing *reasons* that pull in different directions. Duties, or claims that the parties have on the rescuer, cannot serve as inputs to this process of deliberation.

Broome says little about what he has in mind in speaking of duties; perhaps he only means *prima facie* duties, in which case an argument might be offered for admitting Broome's claims as legitimate inputs to consensualist moral argument. In order to properly assess the relevant arguments, it is best not to put too much weight on Broome's use of this term. Consider, then, the substantive features of claims as a kind of reason. First, if a person has a claim, there is a reason why she should have the good. This is stronger than saying there is a reason why her interest in having the good should be taken into account. The difference can be accounted for by the satisfaction requirement: if a person has a claim to a good, she should have some of the good (Broome 1991,95).

Second, claims are reasons for providing her with a good in virtue of a kind of moral worth (or status) she has simply as a person, quite apart from considerations such as how much good she might do, or facts about her circumstances (i.e. who might be depending on her).

This is suggested by the way Broome motivates the distinction between claims and other reasons:

> Take the dangerous mission, for example. One candidate is more talented than the others. This is a reason for allotting to the others the good of staying behind. But the other candidates' lack of talent gives them no *claim* to this good. It may be right to leave them behind, but it is not *owed them* to do so. Whatever claim they have to this good, the talented candidate has it also (Broome 1991,92).

The suggested contrast is something like the following: a person has a claim to a benefit in virtue of the significance *to the individual* who has the claim (or to whom the duty is owed) of being, or not being, benefited. Other reasons, such as a person's talent or lack of talent, are reasons for benefiting that person, not because of the benefit that would accrue to the individual, but because of strategic considerations, such as the fact that some goal would be more likely to be realized if that person is benefited.

Once the language of duty is dropped from the description of what a claim consists in, claims appear to have a natural home in consensualist moral argument, which is concerned with working out what we owe one another. This is plausible, to the extent that claims are reasons why taking her into account as a candidate for a good is owed to the person, on par with other legitimate candidates for a good. What cannot be accepted about Broome's notion of a claim, if it is to have a role in consensualist moral argument, is that what is owed a person who has a claim to a good is that good, or in the kind of case that is relevant here, some chance at the good. Without this further stipulation, however, the case for a lottery cannot be made in a consensualist framework.

The stipulation is unacceptable because it presupposes a substantive account of what is involved in taking a person properly into account as a candidate for a good on par with the other legitimate candidates, one that says to take a person properly into account is to take her *well-being* into account in a way that is compatible with giving the same consideration to the well-being of the other valid candidates. The thought that to be able to justify oneself to another requires being able to show that one has taken her well-being into account is central to the *complaint model* interpretation of consensualist moral argument, and utilitarian moral theory.[24] But it is one that has no role to play in the version of consensualism that is of concern in this discussion, in which taking a person into account in the appropriate way requires taking her *point of view* into account.

---

24 See, on the *complaint model* interpretation, chpt. 3, §III(a). Also see chpt. 1, §II(a).

To further develop this line of argument, consider two versions of a scenario like *Rocks*:[25]

(1) Person A on one rock, person B on the other rock.

(2) Person A on one rock, persons B,C,D,E,F,G,H,I,J and K on the other rock.

In each case, the rescuer is in a boat equidistant from either rock, the tide is rising fast, and there is only time to reach one rock, but not both. Thus, death is clearly foreseen whatever course is chosen. If a lottery is the correct way (according to consensualism) to decide this sort of situation, what is required in each case is that the rescuer decide by flipping a coin.

Let us say that, in both cases, person A is the one who is favored by the toss of the coin. In case (1), the rescuer and person A can both justify themselves to B by pointing out that what was *owed her* was taken into account in deciding who should be saved, in a way that she cannot complain about. The implications for the well-being of both her and A of not being saved were taken into account, and since both could not be saved, each was given the same chance of being saved. The implications for one's well-being of only being given a chance at being saved are not as good as actually being saved, but at least B cannot claim that the implication for her well-being (i.e., her livelihood) was not taken seriously.

The same justification could be offered by A and the rescuer to each of the ten in (2). Each had the same chance as A of being saved, indicating that the implication for each person's well-being of not being saved was taken seriously. In other words, in giving each person a chance, each has been given the kind of consideration she is owed given her status as a person. Thus no one of them has a legitimate basis for complaint.

In each of these cases, A and the life saver's justification to others relies on the premise that in taking into account each person's potential loss if she is not saved, each has been given the kind of consideration she is owed. When the competing losses were examined, it turned out that whose losses would be averted depended on the choice between two competing outcomes. Since aggregating potential losses is ruled out as a way of deciding between outcomes, a coin was flipped to decide between them.

The premise, though, can be reasonably rejected as part of a consensualist justification for holding a lottery in indivisible goods cases. For according to consensualism, taking a person appropriately into account in choosing a course of action (assuming that that person will

---

[25] The line of argument that follows is much indebted to a similar argument offered by Frances Kamm; see Kamm 1986 pg. 181.

be implicated in whatever action is chosen) requires that the choice be one that can be shown, from her point of view, to have been done for reasons that she has reason to authorize others to act on (assuming she is concerned to be able to justify herself to others also interested in mutual justification). Put loosely, what a person is thought to fundamentally care about is not the implications of other's actions for her well-being, but that she have a say in determining what will be done in situations the resolution of which have implications for her life.

Holding a lottery allows for a justification to those not saved of the form 'you, as an individual, have been taken into account, because your *interest* in being saved has been taken into account'. But this is not the same as giving a person a say in determining what is done. This is evident from the comparison of cases (1) and (2). For purposes of the lottery, the addition of more people in (2) makes absolutely no *potential* difference to the outcome of the procedure; there is no basis in the lottery procedure for even acknowledging the addition of nine people to one of the rocks. The choice, to be decided by the lottery, is still between two competing outcomes, the choice of which determines whose losses will be prevented. This would not be an objection if taking the implications for a person's well-being into account were adequate for giving a person the kind of consideration she is owed. But if a procedure is to be defensible on consensualist terms, the addition of persons to one of the rocks must at least be acknowledged by the procedure to make a *potential* difference to the outcome of the procedure, as what is being added are additional voices to the debate over what should be done, each of which has the potential to make a difference to the resolution of the debate. A procedure that does not meet this requirement will be one that can be reasonably rejected.

There are reasons, then, for reasonably rejecting the kind of argument Broome offers for the lottery as a fair procedure for deciding how to proceed in indivisible goods cases. This might not be thought to be a conclusive case for rejecting a lottery as defensible on consensualist grounds, as better arguments for the fairness of lotteries, that do not depend on the notion of a claim in the way Broome's does, might be developed. It does provide some evidence, though, for concluding that a lottery is not the kind of procedure parties to the hypothetical consensus could agree on for deciding indivisible goods cases.

§III

(a) The lottery procedure was ultimately rejected on the grounds that the lottery fails to take into account each individual in the right way. Rather than further pursue alternative strategies for justifying a lottery that might not be vulnerable to this objection, I will here consider a different kind of procedure for deciding who should be saved. This is the *balance of undefeated reasons* procedure (to be referred to as the *balancing* procedure).[26]

To motivate this procedure, consider again the kind of principle that parties to the hypothetical consensus are trying to develop. It is one for the general regulation of behavior of situations which fit the general form of there being an individual who is able to supply some morally significant benefit, where the potential recipients are all symmetrically situated with respect to both the benefactor and to one another, and all are strangers to one another. A suitable procedure should take into account each person in a way that 'gives her a say' in deciding who should receive the benefit, and the final decision of whom to benefit based on this procedure should be justifiable to each person, from her point of view.

The *balancing* procedure claims that the best procedure that meets these requirements is one that imposes a duty on the benefactor to act as the undefeated balance of reasons directs her to act. How this procedure works is easiest to visualize if one imagines deciding a case such as *Rocks* by constructing a two column list, in which one puts down all the reasons that favour each possible course of action (assuming that doing nothing is excluded as an option). Each life that might be saved by pursuing a particular course of action is a morally relevant reason for pursuing that course of action. Comparing the lists, there are simply more reasons for directing the boat towards the rock with six on it than the rock with one person on it.[27]

Can this decision be justified to the person who is not saved? It can, by pointing out to her that her life being at stake was taken into account as a reason for saving her life, but its force was offset by an

---

[26] Here I once more follow a suggestion by Frances Kamm. See her *Morality, Mortality* Vol. 1 , 114-21; and her "Equal Chances and Equal Treatment" pg. 181-84. She labels this procedure *majority rule*. I have changed the name for two reasons. First, Kamm conducts her discussion in terms of preferences, but it is important to her view that what a person prefers to have happen is *in this case* being taken as a reason for bringing that outcome about. Nothing in her view endorses the idea that we always have reason to satisfy a person's preferences. Second, majority rule might suggest that the life saver is required to actually consult those whose lives are at stake before deciding how to act. But this is misleading; a person may choose to consult, if there is time, and she thinks there is reason to do so, but she would not be wronging anyone if she simply took the fact that a person's life is at stake as a reason for her to be saved (if possible). The procedure, as I will present it, is explicitly meant to illuminate the general form of reasoning that is appropriate for the kinds of situations under consideration. In particular, it aims to explain how it is that our intuitions about numbers can be explained without appealing to any notions of net benefit or the aggregate value of outcomes. I should also note that, though I find Kamm's suggestion compelling, the justification I offer for it makes no use of the three morally relevant perspectives that are central to Kamm's metaethic, and also play an important role in her justification of her majority rule procedure: the subjective point of view, the objective point of view, and the impartial point of view. Multiple perspectives have no role to play in consensualist moral argument.

equal and opposing reason. The two reasons simply balanced one another. Since the opposing reason is identical to her own, she cannot reasonably deny its force. And since the force of the opposing reason is also offset in coming to a decision of how to proceed, it is not clear what basis she might have for claiming to have been wronged.

She might, first, consider a complaint on the grounds that the procedure does not really give her a voice in deciding who should be saved. This is an important objection, but it can be rebutted. For it is not the case, as it was in the lottery, that the addition of extra person to one of the rocks makes no potential difference to which direction the boat will go in. Depending on how the numbers are already balanced, the addition of an extra person could tip the balance of reasons in one direction or the other.

The idea of giving a person a voice might be made more explicit in this procedure if the decision on whom to save was decided on the balance of preferences. The difficulty with this is that a person's preference is not always a morally defensible reason for deciding one way rather than another.[28] In the *Rocks* case, for instance, given the fact that all the parties are presumed to be strangers to one another, no one could reasonably deny that they have been given the kind of consideration they are owed if the fact that her life is at stake is taken to be a reason for saving her, to be balanced against the reasons for saving the lives of others. A procedure that required that her preference be taken into account may not be so defensible. A person may object, for instance, that she may be panicked in a situation like *Rocks*, and would quite reasonably not want her preference taken into account under these circumstances.

There are sound reasons why parties to the hypothetical consensus may want the principle that governs cases like *Rocks* to direct that the decision on whom to save sometimes be decided on the basis of expressed preferences. For instance, if the seven persons involved were all members of the same family, it may be that the one would rather perish, knowing that the rest of the family will live on. It is important,

---

[27] This procedure is not the same as the proposal that parties be allowed to pool their complaints. First, the 'pooling proposal' is a meta-ethical proposal, arguing that collective losses should be recognized as a kind of reason a person may appeal to in moral argument over the validity of a proposed principle. Such appeals are ruled out in consensualism (though may be admissible in other versions of contractualism). Second, on the balancing procedure, the justification offered to the one for not saving her is not "there were more people on the other Rock, so they were saved", but "your claim to be saved was taken into account, but it was *offset* by an *equal* and *opposite* claim of another on the other rock". The number of people on the other rock has no role to play in the justification offered to the one; only the existence of her 'opposite number', whose claim has also been neutralized, is cited in justification.

[28] See Chpt. 2, §II(a), concerning preferences in consensualism.

though, that this preference is one that can be rationalized as reasonable based on general beliefs about value. It is not just the fact of a person's preference that is being taken to be a reason for deciding one way rather than another.

There are also considerations having to do with the rescuer's point of view for not requiring that preferences be consulted in deciding who should be saved. There may not, for instance, be time to consult individuals on their preferences, and if there is, it may not be reasonable, especially in dramatic situations, to expect the rescuer to be so clear headed as to think of consulting all those whose lives are at stake about how she should proceed. On balance, it would not be unreasonable to formulate the principle as to grant the rescuer authority, in the absence of any clear indication to the contrary, to presume that if a person's life is at stake, the requirement that her point of view be taken into account will be fulfilled if her life being at stake is taken to be a reason to choose that course of action which should result in her being saved.

Taking a different line of attack, the one who is not saved might complain that this procedure is unfairly biased towards saving the many. There is some truth in the thought that the procedure will always favour saving the many (assuming all prefer to be saved), but this does not necessarily make it unfair. Since the procedure is for the general regulation of behavior, no one can know in advance whether or not the outcome of such a procedure will ever favour her i.e. no one knows in advance which rock she will be on. And from the point of view of any individual, acting on the balance of undefeated reasons is a suitably arbitrary basis for deciding whom to save, as no one individual can influence how the balance of reasons will turn out so as to favour herself. The one who is not saved in *Rocks* cannot, therefore, claim that the procedure was unfairly biased against her, as the way the balance of reasons turned out was due to forces beyond any individual's control.

In the *Rocks* case, the *balancing* procedure directs the life saver to save the six, as this is where the balance of undefeated reasons lies. But there will not always be an undefeated balance of reasons. In some cases, the reasons may be perfectly balanced, in which case a lottery is justified, as a *tie-breaking* procedure. It is important to be clear, though, on when and why the lottery is an appropriate tie- breaking procedure. One could, for instance, leave it up to the life saver to make a decision. This possibility can be reasonably rejected, both because of the possibility of favoritism on the part of the life saver, and because having to decide is a significant burden on the life saver that she would not be unreasonable in wanting to be spared.

One might also appeal to a *fixed rule* for breaking ties. Broome argues that this is as good a way of breaking a tie as a lottery (Broome

1991,88). On his analysis, the fixed rule decides the issue by introducing some new reason, which breaks the tie:

> For life saving, the rule of picking the youngest will do this [i.e. break ties]. Age will certainly be one of the factors that helps determine which candidates are the best. Other things being equal, it is better to save a younger person than an older, because it does more good to the person who is saved (Broome 1991,88).[29]

The difficulty with this is that 'being younger' is a kind of consideration that can be reasonably rejected as a legitimate grounds for breaking a tie. If there is, for instance, only six months difference in age between two candidates, it would not be unreasonable for the older one to reject benefiting the younger candidate on the grounds that she is younger.[30] But there is an important point here. Breaking ties by appealing to a lottery might only be justifiable in the absence of some other reason whose relevance cannot be reasonably rejected. One might, for instance, imagine having to make a choice between two people on two different rocks. The icy water is rising quickly, there is not time to save them both, nor is there time to consult. However, in the water beside one of the rocks is another person, wearing a life jacket. She will be saved either way. If the person whose rock she is beside is saved, though, she will be spared the effects of severe hypothermia, which will permanently damage her health. The avoidance of severe hypothermia is a morally relevant consideration that can be appealed to in order to break the tie, assuming that it is a consideration whose moral relevance no one could reasonably reject.

A lottery is appropriate according to the *balancing* procedure, then, where there are no undefeated and morally relevant considerations that can be appealed to as the basis of a decision. This is because a lottery is a suitably arbitrary way of deciding where relevant reasons have run out. It makes each person equally a hostage to fortune, as no one has reason to think that the likelihood of their being benefited is any different that anyone else's. No one has grounds, therefore, to complain of being treated unfairly in the decision making process.

(b) The *balancing* procedure has a great deal of intuitive plausibility. First, it explains why it is that the numbers involved actually are sometimes relevant in justifying our acts to others. Unlike the utilitarian explanation of the significance of numbers, which tells us that citing numbers is an elliptical way of referring to the amount of good that may be done, this explanation claims that, in citing the numbers, we are

---

[29] Broome offers this point as part of an argument against the view that the lottery is a uniquely just way of deciding how to proceed only in tie-breaking situations.

[30] This leaves open the possibility that a difference in age of a sufficient magnitude may be legitimate reason for favoring the younger over the older.

drawing attention to the number of reasons for pursuing that action, compared to the number of equally forceful reasons for pursuing another available course of action.

Second, it is consistent with the requirements of consensualism, insofar as it offers an explanation for the significance of numbers that does not in any way appeal to the aggregate value of states of affairs. Only personal reasons and the number of personal reasons have a role to play here.

Third, the *balancing* procedure offers an explanation for why we sometimes judge that the greater number should be benefited, while at other times a lottery is judged appropriate for deciding on the allocation of an indivisible good, i.e., in the special circumstances of there being no undefeated relevant reasons.

Notice, though, that discussion of this procedure has thus far proceeded using examples in which all the relevant reasons have been of the same strength (except in certain tie-breaking cases). An adequate account of our intuitions about the relevance of numbers in moral reasoning should not have to rely on this assumption for its plausibility, as we often judge that numbers are relevant though the relevant reasons are not all of equal strength:

> if the choice is between preventing severe hardship *for some who are very poor and deprived*, and preventing *less severe but still substantial* hardship for those who are better off but *still struggling for subsistence,* then it is very difficult for me to believe that numbers do not count, and that priority of urgency goes to the worse off however many more there are of the better off (Nagel 1979, 125;emphasis and italics added).[31]

The intuition that Nagel expresses in this passage has a great deal of force, and a plausible explanation of the significance of numbers should be able to offer some account of it. It isn't clear, though, that the *balancing* procedure can offer such an account, as the kind of balancing of reasons that is central to the procedure does presuppose that the reasons to be balanced are all symmetrical in force. The explanatory power of the procedure, it seems, is much more limited than has thus far been suggested.

This conclusion can be challenged. For it assumes that symmetrical reasons must be of *exactly* the same weight. This, however, is at the very least a tendentious way of understanding what must be true for reasons to be symmetrical, as reasons can be *roughly symmetrical*, or more to the point, *symmetrical for moral purposes*. The reason for pre-

---

[31] I have used this passage for my own purposes, ignoring the question it raises concerning distributive justice: what is the justification, if there is one, for giving priority to the worst off? This is an important question that cannot be considered here.

ferring the later term to the former is that *rough* symmetry suggests that there is some kind of difficulty in making fine grained judgments concerning the symmetry of reasons, having to do with the nature of reasons or perhaps due to our epistemic position: we simply can't determine the strength of each reason with sufficient precision to make fine grained discriminations between the strengths of the various reasons that a situation presents us with.

This may or may not be the case. Consensualism need not presuppose a view on this question in order to claim that, for purposes of consensualist moral argument, fine grained discriminations between reasons on the basis of their strength are unnecessary. For the importance of such discriminations are relative to the kind of information that is sought, and why such information is sought. If I have three cups of coffee before me, two quite large, and one smaller, and am feeling in need of a big shot of caffeine to wake me up, I don't need to know exactly how much coffee each cup holds. A very rough comparison of cups is all that is required to make a decision to choose one of the large cups. Which of the large cups to choose is a matter of indifference to me; for my purposes, either will do the job. On the other hand, if I was employed by a magazine to discover where in Oxford one gets the best deal for the money on a cup of coffee, the volume of the cups would be of a much greater significance.

Consensualism deploys a similar form of argument to argue against the relevance of fine grained discriminations of the strength of reasons. Such discriminations would only matter if appeals to the precise strength of a reason (no matter how precise that may turn out to be) matter for the kind of question that is addressed in moral argument. For example, on a negative utilitarian view, that we can judge one person to be in very intense pain, but another person to be in more intense pain, would be of direct moral relevance, especially in circumstances where we could only alleviate the pain of one, but not both. On the consensualist view, what matters is that the judgment that one person's pain is more intense than another's pain constitutes a stronger reason for benefiting that person be justifiable on the basis of a principle, for the general regulation of behavior, that no one could reasonably reject. This requires that the judgment be justifiable to each person from her own point of view (provided she is suitably motivated). As was discussed in chapter two, this requirement results in only quite rough comparisons of the strengths of different reasons being justifiable as morally relevant; claims based on precise judgments fail the test of being justifiable to any person's point of view.[32] In comparing the pain of the two individuals, then, it is enough, for purposes of moral argument, to be able to judge that both are in intense pain, to justify the claim that

---

[32] See on this point, chpt II, sec. 2(d).

the reasons for alleviating their suffering are symmetrical. More finely discriminated comparisons may be possible, but are not relevant.

This conclusion, it should be noted, is in line with the consensualist general rejection of appealing only to comparisons of magnitudes of harm and benefit in moral argument. What persons appeal to, and compare, as reasons for and against different principles are specific ways of being harmed and benefited, where comparisons and judgments of the strengths of different reasons are conducted in qualitative terms. Levels of pain, for example, could be distinguished by terms such as "acceptable", "bearable", or "completely unacceptable", discriminations that are suitable for consensualism's rough comparisons of reasons.

With a better understanding of what is involved in judging reasons to be symmetrical for purposes of moral argument, the initial objection to the *balancing* procedure can be reassessed. Consider the example from Nagel: here, all those concerned are struggling for subsistence. The fact that someone is struggling for subsistence is a good reason for helping that person; how *much* they are struggling can, I believe, be plausibly judged to be not relevant to judging the strength of the reason to help them. To justify the degree of struggle as relevant, there would have to be a consensus on the importance of different degrees of struggle, which is implausible. If this is accepted, it is then reasonable to judge that relevant reasons in Nagel's example are, for moral purposes, symmetrical, and the example is much less threatening. For it is precisely the differences in degree of struggle that Nagel cites as the grounds for distinguishing the worst off from the better off; once the degree of struggle has been set aside as relevant, the *balancing* procedure can be used to illumine the reasons for judging that the many, rather than the one, should be helped in Nagel's example.

(c) There is another important objection to the balance of reasons procedure that has yet to be considered. This objection draws attention to the 'all or nothing' character of the procedure. It seems to tell us that *if* what you stand to gain from receiving the indivisible good is important enough to be judged as important as what others stand to gain from receipt of the good, the reason to benefit you will be included in the set of reasons to be balanced against one another. However, if the strength of the reason for benefiting you falls below the threshold set by the strength of reasons there are for benefiting others, your reason counts for nothing. It is as if the strength of reasons were all ranked on a scale of 1-100; if the strength of the reason to benefit you falls in the 80-100 band, it is counted as a reason, to be balanced against the others, no matter where in that band its strength falls. However, if the strength of your reason is 75, it does not count at all. This is very counter intuitive—surely a reason whose strength is 75 should count for something! The balancing procedure appears committed to denying that this is so.

This is a difficult objection to assess, as it is most plausibly, and vividly, stated in a form that involves (explicitly or implicitly) appealing to magnitudes of benefit or harm. Consensualism, however, rejects appealing to magnitudes as having a general role to play in moral argument. They may have some role in specific cases, but this can be explained by considering the kind of good (or value) in question, which makes appealing to magnitudes appropriate in those cases. Without such appeals, though, the force of the objection can become elusive.

To clarify why this might be so, imagine two individuals arguing about who should be counted as a potential beneficiary for a specific indivisible good, say a bread roll.[33] Appealing to magnitudes, one person can say to the other 'How can you possibly claim that the reason to benefit you should be put on the balance, while the reason to benefit me should not be put on the balance? After all, only one unit separates us on the hunger scale!'. It isn't clear, however, how this argument is to proceed if it is conducted in terms more appropriate to consensualist moral argument. One person may say to another 'how can you deny that my hunger should count, since I am *almost* as hungry as you'. Or, she might say 'how can you deny that my hunger should count? Though I am not *starving* like you, I am still *hungry*' (perhaps because the person has not eaten for 12 hours). If the judgment of 'almost as hungry as' is plausible, there is little point in arguing: the person has established the rough symmetry of her reason with that of others. In the second formulation, though, the objection appears to have little force. Hunger is terrible, but it does not carry with it the same implications as starvation. Faced with a choice between alleviating hunger and alleviating starvation, and limited resources, most would, I believe, agree that the starving should be helped and the hungry ignored.[34]

Many will object to this last claim. Before objecting, though, it is important to consider the question of how one represents 'being hungry' to oneself in reflecting on this example. There is a rich evaluative vocabulary that can be used to distinguish different states that fall under the general description 'being hungry'. It is hard to deny that hunger, in some instances, will be of trivial importance in the face of starvation, but in other cases this will not be the case. The point that needs to be pressed here is this: in considering how to understand

---

[33] Bread rolls are divisible, but assume for purposes of argument that a person has to eat the whole roll in order to derive any benefit from it at all.

[34] Mill puts this point elegantly in noting that where the moral assessment of burdens is concerned, " the difference in degree (as if often the case in psychology) becomes a real difference in kind" *Utilitarianism* para. 24.

'being hungry' for purposes of the example, it seems that we either move towards understanding 'being hungry' as similar to starvation, in which case it can be counted as roughly symmetrical to starvation in its force as a reason, or we construe it as trivial in the face of starvation (e.g. being hungry because it's morning and one has yet to eat breakfast). The dramatic 'all or nothing' character of the initial objection appears to disappear as one further refines one's initial judgment of the comparative force of the reasons that arise from considering the plights of different persons.

This is only a partial response to the initial objection, as it will not help clarify an important set of 'gray zone' cases, where we feel that a reason should count for something, but not as much as the other reasons. Consider a case in which a drug has been developed that can extend the life of patients who are suffering from some life threatening disease. A doctor has only a fixed quantity of this drug available, and faces a choice. She can either administer all of the drug to a patient who is in the advanced stages of the disease, restoring her to full health, and a life expectancy of a further fifteen years, or divide the drug into three doses, administering it to each of four patients in the early stages of the disease, restoring each of them to full health, with a life expectancy of a further 50 years. All the patients are of the same age, let us say twenty-five years old.

This may be a case where the balancing procedure does not apply. What the argument turns on is whether or not, for moral purposes, there is as much reason to give a person the drug in the hope of extending her life fifteen years as there is to give a person the drug in hopes of extending her life a further fifty years. If this judgment is defensible, the balancing procedure can be applied to this case. It is not completely implausible: a person may have as rich a life in her remaining fifteen years as another may have in her fifty years. The difficulty here is that the more likely conclusion is that, though there is a strong reason for giving the drug to the person who will live for another fifteen years, there is a much stronger reason for giving the drug to someone who will live another fifty years. This exposes a weakness in the balancing procedure: it can only count the person who will live only another fifteen years as a potential claimant to the drug *if* her claim is judged, for moral purposes, as strong as those who may live another fifty years. If this judgment cannot be defended, she cannot be counted as a legitimate claimant at all. But this is very counter-intuitive; surely the fact that a person could have her life extended another fifteen years entitles her to some representation in the procedure?

This is an important problem for the balancing procedure, which at present I can only flag as problem that requires further work and the detailed consideration of more examples if progress is to be made towards its resolution.

§IV

(a) The discussion thus far has focused exclusively on cases where numbers are thought to be relevant for deciding how to allocate an indivisible good. Not all cases where numbers might be relevant are like this. Many believe that there are ways of treating a person that are normally wrong, but can be justified when something of importance to a great many is at stake. This is too complex a topic to be discussed here in any detail. Here, I can only sketch a general approach for understanding such cases in a consensualist framework.

First, it is important, in considering our intuitions about these matters, to consider carefully whether or not numbers really do have a role to play in our judgments. Consider, for example, a case where one is forced to lie to another to save several lives. When lives are at stake, the prohibition against lying is certainly weaker, if it doesn't dissolve completely. The explanation of the change in the force of the prohibition against lying, though, does not draw attention to the *number* of lives at stake. What matters is that *life* is at stake; it makes no difference whether it is one life or a thousand lives. The argument for this would go as follows: we could see the situation in the example as one that calls for further specification of the relevant principle governing the duty to tell the truth, in which the legitimacy of an exception clause to the general principle is considered, one which allows for intentional deception when human life is at stake, and deception is required for it to be saved. The new principle is arguably one that could not be reasonably rejected, as such occasions would be so rare that the values secured by the duty to tell the truth would not be compromised in the resulting social world (e.g., people would not become unduly suspicious and distrustful of one another, nor would the integrity of public sources of information be thrown into doubt), and it would be unreasonable for anyone to deny that preventing the loss of human life is a morally important value.

A similar strategy for explaining our intuitions without appealing to numbers is available to consensualism by distinguishing between the moral significance of doing harm rather than allowing harm, and intending that harm befall someone rather than just pursuing a course of action which one knows might, unfortunately, result in someone being harmed.[35] This is a strategy long favored by non-consequentialists for explaining our intuitions about various cases without appealing to claims about aggregate well-being, which the utilitarian will claim can naturally be explained on the basis of considerations of aggregate well-being.[36] Working out how these distinctions work in moral reasoning is a complex matter, but they have a powerful intuitive importance in consensualist moral argument. For what these distinctions draw one's attention to are a person's intentions in acting as she did, which, to be assessed, require asking questions about a person's reasons (or lack of reasons) for acting as she did. Consensualism claims that a person's reasons for acting are of vital importance for moral evaluation, as what an act says about, or how it affects, a person's relations with others depends very much on that person's reasons for acting. What is ostensibly the same act (judging by its consequences) may or may not be wrong, as determined by a principle no one can reasonably reject, depending on what the relevant principle says about the legitimacy of a person's authority to act on the kinds of reasons she did act on, while ignoring or discounting other valid considerations.

Finally, some intuitions may be accounted for by appealing to the reasons a person might have for valuing the prevention of certain kinds of states of affairs from obtaining. This strategy is particularly relevant for accounting for the intuition that though there are certain ways of harming a person that, if done intentionally, are wrong, the constraint on treating another in these ways is defeasible when large numbers of lives are at stake.[37] For instance, in the case of Geoff and Allie discussed in chapter three, one might agree that it would be wrong for Allie to push Geoff in front of the dog in order to save herself, but think that it might not be wrong for Allie to do this if more than her life were at stake, but lives of herself and a thousand others as well.[38] The difficulty for consensualism is how to justify to Geoff the claim that, though it may be wrong for Allie to push him in front of the dog to save herself, it may be permissible for her to do so if she is to save herself and a thousand others as well.

One thing that Allie might appeal to is what it being wrong to prevent a thousand and one deaths at the expense of intentionally sacrificing his arm to the vicious dog, without his consent, would say about the

---

[35] Once again, it is important to keep in mind that these distinctions are not being presupposed as additional moral content in the theory. What is being presupposed is that principles that justify the moral importance of these distinctions can be defended in a consensualist framework.
[36] The classic example of this strategy being Phillipa Foot. "The Problem of Abortion and the Doctrine of Double Effect." In *Virtues and Vices*, 19-32. Berkeley: University of California Press, 1978.
[37] This is a very common intuition. For example, in a seminar on Judith Thomson's *The Realm of Rights* at Harvard in the Fall of 1993, there was near unanimous agreement that though it would be wrong to kill one person to save five people from being killed, it may be permissible to kill one to save a thousand from being killed. The puzzle is how one can explain this deeply felt intuition without appealing to the aggregate value of states of affairs.
[38] To avoid complications, assume that the connection between Allie's life and those of the others is quite direct, so that if she dies, the thousand others will perish with her.

value of human life.[39] She could argue that the value of life would be cheapened, which is something that Geoff, as a human being, has reason to care about. How important is it, she may ask, that your body is your own to control—the value appealed to in the constraint against Allie pushing Geoff in front of the dog—in a social world where human life is itself not that highly valued? Note that Allie's argument here need not involve an appeal to the aggregate disvalue of the state of affairs that results from preventable deaths of the thousand and one people. One reason for thinking this construal misleading is that the phenomena Allie is concerned with drawing Geoff's attention to is not just the occurrence of a thousand and one deaths, but the circumstances under which they will perish—the fact that they will all die *together*, and the deaths were *preventable* by sacrificing his arm. These circumstances are crucial for understanding what the deaths of the thousand and one say about the value of human life, and why it is that the same implications would not follow if, for instance, the thousand and one perished together due to a freak mud slide, or if they occurred all at the same moment, but in different places due to unrelated causes.

One obvious objection to this line of thought is that Allie could invoke an appeal to the value of human life in the case involving just her and Geoff. Nothing in this argument denies this; what Allie's death will say about the value of human life will certainly be one of the factors to be taken into account in considering the grounds for the constraint against intentionally sacrificing Geoff's arm. All that the argument here claims is that, where it is just Allie's life at stake, this reason is not strong enough to overrule Geoff's reasons for a constraint against being treated in the way Allie proposes to treat him. Where a thousand and one lives are at stake, the suggestion is that Geoff's case for the constraint is not as good.

Whether or not this line of argument is finally judged persuasive, it at least shows how one might proceed in constructing a consensualist explanation of the defeasability of certain constraints when large numbers are at stake, one that makes no direct appeal to aggregate value of outcomes.

---

[39] The value of human life, in the loose sense in which the term is being employed here, is an elusive notion. Here I can only appeal to anecdotal evidence, based on time spent traveling in India. There, I definitely felt that the disregard shown for the corpses, lying in the street, of the beggars who had frozen to death in the night, contributed to a general atmosphere where the value of a human life felt significantly cheaper than in more prosperous western welfare states.

Appendix
Reasonableness in Consensualism

(a) Judith Thomson, discussing Scanlon's account of the property of an act being morally wrong, comments that,

> "Reasonably" here bears a heavy weight, and I suggest that whatever does the moral work of making it true that no one could reasonably reject a given set of rules is what does the moral work of justifying them. In short, the reference to agreement can drop out (Thomson 1990,189).

Many share the kind of concern Thomson expresses here (though few have expressed the point in print) that (a) the term reasonableness is 'morally loaded', (b) that there must be something, not disclosed in Scanlon's original statement of the consensualism (or Scanlonian contractualism), in virtue of which principles are unreasonable to reject and (c) whatever this thing is, it does all the justificatory work in the theory.

In order to evaluate these concerns, it will help to be clear on what the distinction between the reasonable and the rational in consensualism is supposed to be.[1] The distinction is an intuitively familiar one from everyday ways of speaking, both in ethical and non-ethical contexts. For example, making statistical projections of population growth requires that one make certain assumptions about appropriate values for all the exogenous variables. The choice of values for these variables may be assessed as reasonable or unreasonable, depending on how

---

[1] The clearest discussion of this distinction is W.M. Sibley. "The Rational Versus The Reasonable." *Philosophical Review* 62 (October 1953): 554-60, which I here largely follow. See also Rawls's excellent discussion, in John Rawls. *Political Liberalism*. New York: Columbia University Press, 1993, pg. 48-54. Rawls's discussion, though, is more focused on reasonableness in the context of the form of political justification that he outlines.

plausible it is to think that the conditions under which those variables will actually take those values will obtain. Assessments of reasonableness or unreasonableness made by others focus, in this context, on one's reasons for making certain choices, assessing them in light of shared information and an assumption that certain aims guided those choices. If, in light of her reasons for making the choices she did, a person's choices are judged to be reasonable, that person's reasons for making those choices are ones it is legitimate to expect that others (who have the appropriate level of expertise) would also find compelling (or at least plausible) reasons for making those choices (without having to commit themselves to the claim that those are the choices they themselves would have made).

Assessing a choice of values on the basis of their rationality is quite a different matter. A choice of a value would be irrational, for example, if it is was so unlikely that circumstances would obtain in which that variable took on that value, that the choice can only ensure that the results of the model will be of no predictive value whatsoever, e.g., it would be irrational, in forecasting the results of the next general election, to build in an assumption to the model of one hundred per cent voter participation.[2] The choice of value would also be straight forwardly irrational if the number that were chosen fell outside the range of values that the variable in question could in principle hold true for that variable, e.g., one could not have one hundred and ten per cent voter turn out in an election. But choices could well be perfectly rational, without being reasonable. Calling a choice 'overly optimistic given what is known from the experience of the past few years' is a perfect example of a choice that falls into this category.

Two general points can now be made about judgments of reasonableness. First, they involve an assessment of how well something can stand up to public scrutiny, or how compelling a tribunal of one's peers would find the reasons that one offers in defence of what is being scrutinized. Who will count as 'the public' or a person's 'peers' will vary depending on the context. In the case of population forecasting, for instance, the relevant public would be others who are informed about population forecasting, who understand both the criteria for good and bad forecasts that regulate the discipline, and are familiar with the appropriate data and literature.[3]

---

[2] I assume here that a choice is irrational. if it will clearly frustrate the achievement of one's purpose in engaging in that activity, in circumstances where a person has enough information available to her to know that her choice will frustrate her own purposes.

[3] As Sibley and Rawls both point out, persons may also be assessed as reasonable or unreasonable, according to their willingness to subject their conduct to public scrutiny, and adjust it in light of the legitimate criticisms of others.

Second, judgments of reasonableness are not free floating, as they cannot be made independently of the standards appropriate for the assessment of whatever it is that is being judged reasonable or unreasonable. There are, for example, standards and aims that govern population forecasting, in virtue of which the choices made in constructing a forecast can be evaluated as reasonable or unreasonable.

In moral contexts, judgments of reasonableness are still assessments of how defensible something would be before a group of peers, all with potentially conflicting points of view, united by a shared aim and common criteria of assessment. What distinguishes judgments of reasonableness in ethical contexts from other contexts is that the criteria by which public evaluation is conducted are those of moral impartiality. As was discussed earlier, working out what these criteria are, what the limits of their application should be, and who the constituents of the peer group are, is a matter of contention between different theories, and can only be resolved through substantive argument. The most that can be said about judgments of reasonableness in moral contexts, without making any theory-specific commitments about the requirements of impartiality, is that they imply that the implications for all within the moral domain were taken into account, treating each member as no more or less worthy of concern than any other member.

(b) In light of these points, it becomes less clear why anyone would think that there is something (perhaps some substantive property) that makes principles not reasonably rejectable, which does all the justificatory work in the theory. In consensualism, the validity of a principle turns on the reasons offered for judging that principle to be valid. Certain *formal* constraints are imposed on the sorts of reasons that can be offered as grounds for judging a principle to be valid by the criteria that consensualism specifies as characteristic of impartial moral deliberation. In particular, whether the reasons offered in justification of a specific principle do in fact justify that principle as valid turns on the question of whether or not those reasons constitute a justification for it that is defensible before others (with different points of view) assessing the justification in light of the shared aim: that of finding principles for the general regulation of behaviour that no one can reasonably reject as a basis for unforced, informed, general agreement.

Reasonableness, far from doing all the justificatory work in the theory, has a very small independent role to play in it. Rather, it is the specific commitments that consensualism makes in offering a characterization of impartial deliberation, including the reference to agreement, that are of central importance for understanding the consensualist account of moral justification. The significance of reasonableness in the theory is two-fold. First, it characterizes, in a general way, the 'public' before whom principles must be defensible as one whose constituents are already committed to the view that persons are ends in themselves, or that each person is of equal intrinsic value, and are concerned to work out how they should conduct themselves in light of this fact. This, in itself, does not distinguish consensualism from utilitarianism, but it does clearly distinguish it from reductive theories, such as Gauthier's contractarianism, which seek a justification in terms of self-interest for why one should take the value of others as sources of reasons that are relevant for one's practical deliberations.

Second, characterizing valid principles as those that cannot be *reasonably* rejected, rather than those that cannot be *rationally* rejected, is important for indicating that a commitment to being guided by standards appropriate to moral conduct and deliberation is more substantive than a commitement to be guided by norms of rational deliberation and conduct. For many of the considerations that are morally excluded from impartial deliberations are not in fact considerations that it would be irrational to take into account in one's deliberations. This would only be true if what being rational consists in is the same as what being reasonable consists in, a position many Kantians have defended, but consensualism rejects.[4]

It is harder to assess what those who claim that the term 'reasonable' is morally loaded have in mind. It is true that the criteria which guide moral argument in consensualism, in light of which grounds for rejection are judged reasonable or unreasonable, are themselves normative. Perhaps what is being objected to is the introduction of *normative* content into the foundations of the theory. If this is the objection, though, an adequate assessment cannot even be broached within the scope of this discussion. For the idea that one can reach normative conclusions from non-normative premises is, at the very least, controversial. But something like this would have to be presupposed by an objection to the introduction of normative content to the theory.

It would be more plausible to argue that what is being objected to is not the introduction of normative content, but of controversial normative content. Characterizing each party to the hypothetical consensus as initially committed to governing her conduct according to standards of rational prudence may be thought by some to be more plausible than characterizing each of them as reasonable. The plausibility of this, though, as an objection to the theory, rather than as a statement

---

[4] Onora O'Neill argues this Kantian position in two important papers. See "The public use of reason." and "Reason and politics in the Kantian enterprise." In *Constructions of Reason*, 28-50 and 3-27. Cambridge: CUP, 1989. Scanlon appears to reject the Kantian position in Scanlon 1989 pg. 2-5. The difficulty with that argument against the Kantian position is that Scanlon discusses rationality in terms of self-interest. But it is not clear whether this substantive characterization of rationality is relevant for the argument. A proper discussion of this point cannot be adequately pursued here.

of disagreement, needs to be argued in detail, as it is certainly not obvious that a commit to prudence (or self-interest) has any role to play in an account of the foundations of moral reasoning.

Bibliography

Ackrill, J. L. (1980). 'Aristotle on Eudaimonia'. In *Essays on Aristotle's Ethics* ed. A.O. Rorty. Berkeley, University of California Press. 15-34.
Anderson, E. (1993). *Value in Ethics and Economics.* Cambridge MA, Harvard University Press.
Anscombe, G. E. M. (1967). 'Who Is Wronged?'. *The Oxford Review* (5): 16-17.
Brandt, R. B. (1992). 'Some Merits of One Form of Rule-Utilitarianism'. In *Morality, Utilitarianism, and Rights.* Cambridge, Cambridge University Press. 111-137.
Brink, D. (1986). 'Utilitarian Morality and the Personal Point of View'. *Journal of Philosophy* 83: 417-38.
Brink, D. (1989). *Moral Realism and the Foundations of Ethics.* Cambridge, Cambridge University Press.
Brink, D. (1993). 'The separateness of persons, distributive norms, and moral theory'. In *Value, Welfare and Morality* ed. R.G. Frey and Christopher Morris. Cambridge, Cambridge University Press. 252-289.
Broome, J. (1991). 'Fairness'. *Proceedings of the Aristotelian Society* 91(1): 87-102.
Carruthers, P. (1992). *The Animals Issue.* Cambridge, Cambridge University Press.
Cohen, G. A. (1989). 'On the Currency of Egalitarian Justice'. *Ethics* 99(4): 906-44.
Daniels, N. (1979). 'Moral Theory and the Plasticity of Persons'. *The Monist* 62: 265-87.
Darwall, S. (1976). 'A Defense of the Kantian Interpretation'. *Ethics* 86(January).

Dworkin, R. (1978a). 'Justice and Rights'. In *Taking Rights Seriously*. London, Duckworth Press. 150-183.

Dworkin, R. (1978b). 'What Rights Do We Have?'. In *Taking Rights Seriously*. London, Duckworth Press. 266-278.

Dworkin, R. (1984). 'Rights as Trumps'. In *Theories of Rights* ed. Jeremy Waldron. Oxford, Oxford University Press. 153-167.

Dworkin, R. (1990). 'Foundations of Liberal Equality'. In *The Tanner Lectures on Human Values* Vol. 11 ed. Grethe Petersen. Salt Lake City, University of Utah Press. 1-119.

Foot, P. (1978). 'The Problem of Abortion and the Doctrine of Double Effect'. In *Virtues and Vices*. Berkeley, University of California Press. 19-32.

Foot, P. (1988). 'Utilitarianism and the Virtues'. In *Consequentialism and its Critics* ed. Samuel Scheffler. Oxford, Oxford University Press. 224-242.

Freeman, S. (1991). 'Contractualism, Moral Motivation, and Practical Reason'. *The Journal of Philosophy* 88(6): 281-301.

Fried, C. (1979). 'Correspondence'. *Philosophy and Public Affairs* 8(4): 393-395.

Hampton, J. (1991). 'Two Faces of Contractarian Thought'. In *Contractarianism and Rational Choice* ed. Peter Valletyne. Cambridge, Cambridge University Press. 31-55.

Hare, R. M. (1982). 'Ethical theory and utilitarianism'. In *Utilitarianism and Beyond* ed. B.A.O. Williams and A.K. Sen. Cambridge, Cambridge University Press. 23-38.

Hart, H. L. A. (1975). 'Rawls on Liberty and its Priority'. In *Reading Rawls* ed. Norman Daniels. Oxford, Basil Blackwell. 230-252.

Hart, H. L. A. (1982a). 'Legal Rights'. In *Essays on Bentham*. Oxford, Oxford University Press. 162-193.

Hart, H. L. A. (1982b). 'Natural Rights: Bentham and John Stuart Mill'. In *Essays on Bentham*. Oxford, Oxford University Press. 79-104.

Hart, H. L. A. (1984). 'Are There Any Natural Rights?'. In *Theories of Rights* ed. Jeremy Waldron. Oxford, Oxford University Press. 77-90.

Herman, B. (1993). 'Leaving Deontology Behind'. In *The Practice of Moral Judgment* Cambridge, Harvard University Press. 208-240.

Hill, T. E. (1991). 'Self-Respect reconsidered'. In *Autonomy and Self-Respect*. Cambridge, Cambridge University Press. 19-24.

Hill, T. E. (1991). 'Servility and Self-Respect'. In *Autonomy and Self-Respect*. Cambridge, Cambridge University Press. 4-18.

Hooker, B. (1990). 'Rule-Consequentialism'. *Mind* 99: 67-77.

Hurka, T. (1993). *Perfectionism*. Oxford Ethics Series, Oxford, Oxford University Press.

Johnson, C. (1988). 'The Authority of the Moral Agent'. In *Consequentialism and its Critics* ed. Scheffler. Oxford, Oxford University Press. 261-287.

Kagan, S. (1989a). *The Limits of Morality*. Oxford, Oxford University Press.

Kagan, S. (1989b). 'The Limits of Well-being'. In *The Good Life and the Human Good* ed. Fred. D. Miller Jr. Ellen Frankel Paul and Jeffrey Paul. Cambridge, Cambridge University Press. 169-189.

Kagan, S. (1994). 'Me and My Life'. *Proceedings of the Aristotelian Society* XCIV: 309-324.

Kamm, F. (1986). 'Equal Treatment and Equal Chances'. *Philosophy and Public Affairs* 15(3): 177-194.

Kamm, F. (1989). 'Harming Some to Save Others'. *Philosophical Studies* 57: 227-260.

Kamm, F. (1992). 'Non-consequentialism, the Person an End-in-Itself, and the Significance of Status'. *Philosophy and Public Affairs* 21(4): 354-389.

Kamm, F. (1993). *Morality, Mortality*. Vol. 1. Oxford, Oxford University Press.

Kant, I. (1785). *Grounding for the Metaphysics of Morals*. Translated by James W. Ellington. Indianapolis, Hackett Publishing Co.

Kant, I. (1797). *The Metaphysics of Morals*. Translated by Mary Gregor. Cambridge, Cambridge University Press.

Kornhauser, L. and L. Sager (1988). 'Just Lotteries'. *Social Science Information* 27(4): 483-516.

Korsgaard, C. M. (1993). 'The Reasons We Can Share: An Attack On The Distinction Between Agent-Relative and Agent-Neutral Values'. *Social Philosophy and Policy* 10(1): 24-51.

Kymlicka, W. (1988). 'Rawls on Teleology and Deontology'. *Philosophy and Public Affairs* 17(3): 173-190.

Lyons, D. (1994). 'Mill's Theory of Morality'. In *Rights, Welfare, and Mill's Moral Theory*. Oxford, Oxford University Press. 47-66.

MacCormick, D. N. (1977). 'Rights in Legislation'. In *Law, Morality and Society* ed. P.M.S. Hacker and J. Raz. Oxford, Oxford University Press. 210-228.

McKerlie, D. (1988). 'Egalitarianism and the Separateness of Persons'. *Canadian Journal of Philosophy* : 219-220.

Mill, J. S. (1993). *Utilitarianism*. Everyman Edition ed., ed. Geriant Williams. London, J.M. Dent.

Nagel, T. (1970). *The Possibility of Altruism*. Princeton, Princeton University Press.

Nagel, T. (1979a). 'Equality'. In *Mortal Questions*. Cambridge, Cambridge University Press. 106-127.

Nagel, T. (1979b). 'War and Massacre'. In *Mortal Questions*. Cambridge, Cambridge University Press. 53-74.
Nagel, T. (1986). *The View From Nowhere*. Oxford, Oxford University Press.
Nagel, T. (1987). 'Moral Conflict and Political Legitimacy'. In *Authority* ed. Joseph Raz. Oxford, Basil Blackwell's. 300-324.
Nagel, T. (1991). *Equality and Partiality*. Oxford, Oxford University Press.
Nagel, T. (1994). 'The Value of Inviolability'. *Revue de Metaphysique et de Morale*: 149-166.
O'Neill, O. (1989). 'The public use of reason'. In *Constructions of Reason*. Cambridge, Cambridge University Press. 28-50.
O'Neill, O. (1989). 'Reason and politics in the Kantian enterprise'. In *Constructions of Reason*. Cambridge, Cambridge University Press. 3-27.
Parfit, D. (1978). 'Innumerate Ethics'. *Philosophy and Public Affairs* 7(4): 285-301.
Parfit, D. (1984). *Reasons and Persons*. Oxford, Oxford University Press.
Parfit, D. (forthcoming). *On Giving Priority to the Worse Off*. Oxford, Oxford University Press.
Pettit, P. (1988). 'The Consequentialist Can Recognize Rights'. *Philosophical Quarterly* (38): 42-53.
Pettit, P. (1992). 'Consequentialism'. In *Blackwell's Companion to Ethics* ed. Peter Singer. Oxford, Basil Blackwell. 230-239.
Quinn, W. (1993). 'Actions, intentions, and consequences: The Doctrine of Doing and Allowing'. In *Morality and Action* ed. Phillipa Foot. Cambridge, Cambridge University Press. 149-174.
Railton, P. (1988). 'Alienation, Consequentialism, and the Demands of Morality'. In *Consequentialism and its Critics* ed. Samuel Scheffler. Oxford, Oxford University Press. 93-133.
Rawls, J. (1971). *A Theory of Justice*. Cambridge, Harvard University Press.
Rawls, J. (1982). 'Social unity and primary goods'. In *Utilitarianism and Beyond* ed. Amartya Sen and Bernard Williams. Cambridge, Cambridge Universisty Press. 159-185.
Rawls, J. (1993). *Political Liberalism*. New York, Columbia University Press.
Raz, J. (1984). 'Right-Based Moralities'. In *Theories of Rights* ed. Jeremy Waldron. Oxford, Oxford University Press. 182-200.
Raz, J. (1986). *The Morality of Freedom*. Oxford, Oxford University Press.
Raz, J. (1990). *Practical Reason and Norms*. 2nd ed., Princeton, Princeton University Press.
Raz, J. (1994). 'Free Expression and Personal Identification'. In *Ethics in the Public Domain*. Oxford, Oxford University Press. 131-154.

Scanlon, T. (1975). 'Preference and Urgency'. *Journal of Philosophy* LXXII(19): 655-669.
Scanlon, T. M. (1973). 'Rawls's Theory of Justice'. *University of Pennsylvania Law Review* 12(1): 1020-69.
Scanlon, T. M. (1982). 'Contractualism and utilitarianism'. In *Utilitarianism and Beyond* ed. Amartya Sen and Bernard Williams. Cambridge, Cambridge University Press. 103-128.
Scanlon, T. M. (1984). 'Rights, Goals, and Fairness'. In *Theories of Rights* ed. Jeremy Waldron. Oxford, Oxford University Press. 137-152.
Scanlon, T. M. (1988a). 'Levels of Moral Thinking'. In *Hare and Critics: Essays on Moral Thinking* ed. Seanor and Fotion. Oxford, Oxford University Press. 129-146.
Scanlon, T. M. (1988b). 'The Significance of Choice'. In *The Tanner Lectures on Human Values*. Vol. 8. Salt Lake City, University of Utah Press. 155-216.
Scanlon, T. M. (1989).'Questions About Reasonableness'. *NYU Law and Philosophy Colloquium,* NYU Law School.
Scanlon, T. M. (1990). 'Promises and Practices'. *Philosophy and Public Affairs* 19(3): 199-226.
Scanlon, T. M. (1991). 'The moral basis of interpersonal comparisons'. In *Interpersonal Comparisons of Well-Being* ed. Jon Elster and John Roemer. Cambridge, Cambridge University Press. 17-44.
Scanlon, T. M. (1992). 'The Aims and Authority of Moral Theory'. *Oxford Journal of Legal Studies* 12(1): 1-23.
Scanlon, T. M. (1993). 'Value, Desire, and Quality of Life'. In *The Quality of Life* ed. Martha Nussbaum and Amartya Sen. Oxford, Oxford University Press. 185-200.
Scheffler, S. (1979). 'Moral Scepticism and Ideals of the Person'. *The Monist* 62: 288-303.
Scheffler, S. (1982a). 'Ethics, Personal Identity, and Ideals of the Person'. *Canadian Journal of Philosophy* 12(2): 229-246.
Scheffler, S. (1982b). *The Rejection of Consequentialism.* 1 ed., Oxford, Oxford University Press.
Scheffler, S. (1992). *Human Morality.* Oxford, Oxford University Press.
Scheffler, S. (1994). 'Prerogatives without Restrictions'. In *The Rejection of Consequentialism* . Oxford, Oxford University Press. 2nd, ed. 167-192.
Sen, A. (1988). 'Rights and Agency'. In *Consequentialism and its Critics* ed. Samuel Scheffler. Oxford, Oxford University Press. 187-223.
Sen, A. (1992). *Inequality Reexamined.* Cambridge MA, Harvard University Press.
Sibley, W. M. (1953). 'The Rational Versus The Reasonable'. *Philosophical Review* 62(October): 554-60.
Smith, M. (1994). *The Moral Problem.* Oxford, Basil Blackwell.

Strawson, P. (1962). 'Freedom and Resentment'. In *Free Will* eds. and Gary Watson. Oxford, Oxford University Press. 51-80.
Taurek, J. (1977). 'Should the Numbers Count?'. *Philosophy and Public Affairs* 6: 293-316.
Thomson, J. J. (1990). *The Realm of Rights*. Cambridge, Harvard University Press.
Waldron, J. (1993). 'Can communal goods be communal rights?'. In *Liberal Rights*. Cambridge, Cambridge University Press. 339-369.
Warnock, G. J. (1971). *The Object of Morality*. London, Methuen and Co.
Williams, B. (1982). 'Persons, Character and Morality'. In *Moral Luck*. Cambridge, Cambridge University Press. 1-19.
Williams, B. (1985). *Ethics and the Limits of Philosophy*. Cambridge MA, Harvard University Press.

Subject Index

A
abstraction, method of in moral argument, *see* method of abstraction
acts, as opposed to rules, 22–23
aggregate value of outcomes
    as a consequentialist strategy (generally), 5
    in utilitarianism, 9, 26,137,141
    rejection of, 2, 98, 120, 126–127, fn. 26, 137, 141, 146–148
aggregation, 4, 26–27, 45, 68, 116–121, 125–130
alternative social worlds approach, 103–105, 108, fn. 15, 126
altruist, 68
animals, moral treatment of, 19–20, 33
authorizing v. requiring, 105
autonomy, 105, 108

B
balance of undefeated reasons procedure, 137–141, 143–146
beliefs, false, 24
beneficence approach (see also, self-oriented approach), 30, 33–34
bindingness, 20, 39

blame, 17, 36
burden(s), 68–69, 72–75

C
case implication critique, 6
claim(s), 130–134
coin toss, 126, 129–130, 135–136
common language, 64
complaint model, fn. 42, 73, 97–100, 104, 109, 111, 134
consensualism
    account of motivation, 29–30, 34
    and the weighing of reasons, 147–148
    and Kantian Rationalism, fn.14, 105, 150–152
    as a version of contractualism, 2–3
    as arbitrator between self-oriented and beneficence approaches, 33–37
    definition of, 2, 41
    difference between contractualism and, 3, 64
    normative content in, objection of, 151–152
    reasonableness in, 149–152
    reasonableness v. rationality,

149–152
  role of *method of abstraction* in, 56–62, fn. 13, 123
  rules in, 36–39, 90–96
consensus, 25, 36, 50–51, 55, 57, 61–62, 64, 79
consensus, hypothetical, *see, hypothetical consensus*
consequentialism
  act-, *see, act utilitarianism*
  as utilitarianism, fn. 6, 8
  definition of, 1
  impartiality, conception of, 87
  in *self-oriented approach* (Nagel's), 30
  indirect, 84, 94–95
  response to aggregation (general), 4
contractarian, 39, fn.1, 43
contractualism
  as alternative to consequentialism, 2
constraint(s), 112–16
constraint(s), formal on the admissibility of reasons, 150

D
deliberative priority, 87–89
dignity, 35
distributive, 26

E
egoistic, 33–34
equal chance, 130–132
exclusionary reason(s), 90, 92, 93–95
extremist, 79

F
fairness, 26
fair arbitrator, 129
favoritism, 139
functionings, 75

G
goods, collective, 125
guilt, 17, 91

H
hypothetical consensus
  role of motivation in, 11, fn.37, 28

I
impartiality
  consenualist account of, *see, consequentialism*
  formal, 5
  in justification, 27
  its reliance on rational will, 14, 150
  Rawls's interpretation of, fn. 3, 7
  role of, in moral deliberation, 6
  utilitarian account of, *see, utilitarianism*
impersonal value, 32–33
individualism, 122
inescapability, 39
interests, 45–46
intersection approach, 62–63
intuitive plausibility, 6
intuitionism, ethical, 43, 45

J, K, L
justified principle, 26
Kingdom of Ends, 38
lotteries, 130–36

M
mentally underdeveloped, 19
meta-level considerations, 121–122
method of abstraction, 56–59, 61–62, fn. 13, 121
moral justification, 55
mutual aid principles
  rough mutual aid principle, 104

Subject Index

mutual aid principle #2, 105–109
restricted mutual aid principle, 109

N

neutrality requirement, 52–53
no options argument, 79–81
non-consequentialism
    differences between consensualism and, 79
    general principles of, 77, fn. 5, 79
normative
    conception of the person, fn. 2, 6
normative ideal of the person, 3, 15, fn. 6, 81
normative self–conception, 31, 33
normative situation, 35, 62–63, 86, 91–93

O

options, 96–109

P, Q

personal reasons, 121–122
personal reasons restriction, 121, 122
principle(s)
    as basis for interpersonal accountability, 36
    as concerned with resulting *capability set*, 78–79
procedural solution, 128–129
prudence, 150–151
publicity, 37–38

R

rational choice theory, fn. 1, 43, 43–44
rational will, 14, 19–20
reasonableness, *see, Consensualism: Reasonableness in*
reactive attitude(s), 82
rejectability, *see, non-rejectability*
relationships, personal, 61

relativistic, 66
relevance requirement, 53–54
restricted desire theory standard, see, subjective standard
rights, 45, 152
Rough Mutual Aid Principle, see, Mutual Aid Principles
rule(s), 85, 117–119

S

second-order reason(s), 92–93
Self-oriented approach (see, beneficence approach), 30–34
self-worth, 40
shame, 17
social world(s), 99
status
    definition of, fn. 16, 14
subjective standard, 52–54, 55
substantive basic preconditions standard, 54–57
sub-rational, 21
suffering, minimization of, 46
supererogatory acts, 105
symmetry condition, 28, 68, 103, 126, 132

T

teleology
    criticism of, 1
    its relation to consequentialism, 1

U

unanimity, 8, 27–29, fn. 37,27
union of persons, 38
unmotivated desire, 30
utilitarianism
    direct v. *act*, fn. 6, 8, 78, fn. 11, 85
    rule, 9–11, fn. 11, 85, fn. 13, 86, 95–96

V
value, intrinsic, 122–125
value pluralism, 47–48, 50–51
veil of ignorance, 79

W, X, Y, Z
well-being restriction, 67–71

Name Index

A
Ackrill, J.L., 47
Amscombe, E., 120, 125-127
Aristotle, 47

B
Brandt, R.B., 22
Brink, D., 3, 6, 16, 121, 127
Broome, J., 130-134, 136, 139

C
Carruthers, P., 19
Cohen, G.A., 55

D, E
Daniels, N., 13
Dunant, S., 71
Dworkin, R., 45, 48, 50-51, 103, 123

F
Foot, P., 2, 12, 39, 57, 113, 122, 147
Freeman, S., 36
Frey, R.G.: 16
Fried, C., 126

G
Gauthier, D., 44, 152

H, I
Hacker, I., 92
Hampton, J., 43
Hare, R.M., 38, 104
Hart, H.L.A., 17-18, 39
Hill, T., 41
Harasanyi, 79
Hooker, B., 22
Hurka, T., 47, 62, 66, 118

J
Johnson, C., 94

K
Kagan, S., 70, 79-81
Kamm, F.M., 38, 113, 119, 134, 137
Kant, I., 16, 38, 67
Kornhauser, L., 130
Korsgaard, C., 16, 85, 120
Kymlicka, W., 8, 45

L
Lyons, 10, 22

M
McKerlie, D., 28
Mill, J.S., 10, 17, 22

Miller, F.D., 70
Morris, C., 16
Mulgan, T., 110

N
Nagel, T., 3, 12-13, 16, 30-33, 46, 51, 56, 85, 98, 114, 128, 141, 143

O
O'neill, O., 152

P
Parfit, D., 60, 97, 118
Pettit,P., 15

Q
Quinn, W., 38-39, 113

R
Railton, P., 94-95
Raz, J., 39, 51, 58, 92, 95
Rawls, J., 1, 7, 39, 45, 56, 65, 79, 102, 103, 149, 150
Rorty, A.O., 47

S
Sager, L., 130
Scanlon, T., 2-3, 7-8, 11-12, 14, 16, 18-19, 27, 36, 39, 43, 45, 46, 54, 55, 62-65, 67-68, 72-73, 74, 82, 86, 90, 93, 96, 98, 101, 121-122, 127, 149, 152
Scheffler, S., 13, 34, 44, 94, 101
Sen, A., 8, 38, 62, 75
Sibley, W.M., 149-150
Smith, M., 50
Strawson, P., 7, 82
Sumner, W., 67

T,U,V
Taurek, J., 120

Thomson, J., 101, 147, 149

W, X, Y, Z
Waldron, J., 123
Warnock, C.J., 92
Watson, G., 7
Williams, B., 20, 38, 93-95

For Product Safety Concerns and Information please contact our EU
representative GPSR@taylorandfrancis.com
Taylor & Francis Verlag GmbH, Kaufingerstraße 24, 80331 München, Germany

www.ingramcontent.com/pod-product-compliance
Lightning Source LLC
Chambersburg PA
CBHW070616300426
44113CB00010B/1551